To Rockwell D. Hunt —
   With deep appreciation
for your guidance down
through the years along
trails that lead to
understanding and
spiritual beauty.
      Warmest regards,
         Randall Henderson

ON DESERT TRAILS

. . . *Today and Yesterday*

"*Remember that the yield of a hard country is a love deeper than a fat and easy land inspires; that throughout the arid West the Americans have found a secret treasure....*"

—Bernard DeVoto in
The Year of Decision: 1846

ON DESERT

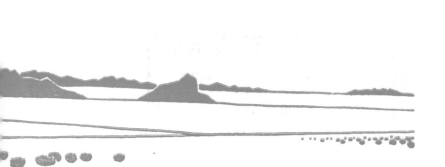

TRAILS
TODAY AND YESTERDAY

by
RANDALL HENDERSON

Designs by DON LOUIS PERCEVAL
Desert Maps by NORTON ALLEN

WESTERNLORE PRESS
LOS ANGELES 41 . . . CALIFORNIA

COPYRIGHT 1961
BY RANDALL HENDERSON

Library of Congress Catalog No. 61-18735

PRINTED IN THE UNITED STATES OF AMERICA BY WESTERNLORE PRESS

TO

Wilson McKenney, Arles Adams, Bill Sherrill, Malcolm Huey, Paul Cook, Luther Fisher, Arthur Woodward and all those other companions of the trail with whom I have shared flapjacks around remote desert campfires.

APPRECIATION

Much of the factual material in this book was published in *Desert Magazine* during the 21 years when I was its editor. I am deeply grateful to Charles E. Shelton, the present publisher, for his permission to revise and make use of this material. My appreciation also to the many contributing associates whose research and loyalty down through the years not only gave accuracy and prestige to the magazine, but also added immeasurably to my own knowledge of this land of far horizons.

RANDALL HENDERSON.

TABLE OF CONTENTS

xi

TABLE OF ILLUSTRATIONS

MAP ILLUSTRATIONS

PAGE

PREFACE

URING MY cub reporter days on the staff of the *Los Angeles Times* it was my privilege to serve under Harry Carr, who for an interval in 1910-11 was the sports editor. Carr was a triple-threat journalist. He was a columnist, feature writer and the star member of the reportorial staff, whose stories always carried his by-line.

A contemporary writer once suggested the secret of Carr's success as a newspaperman. He wrote: "The difference between Carr and an ordinary reporter is that in any situation Harry sees the people while another reporter sees only the facts."

Yet despite his high standing in his profession, Harry had a yearning which I suspect is shared by many other brilliant men in metropolitan journalism. He rather envied the independence, the freedom and the opportunities of a small town newspaper publisher.

Often in the late evening when the last copy for the morning edition had gone down the chute to the composing room, we would relax and talk shop. During those periods Harry said to me more than once: "If I were a young fellow like you I would go out and get a country newspaper of my own, even if it was so small I would have to set the type myself and then go out and deliver the papers."

Eventually I followed Harry's advice. I bought a one-way ticket to Arizona and took the first job offered—as a printing apprentice on the weekly *Parker Post*, one of the smallest newspapers in the state. With the exception of service in two world wars the desert has remained my home for nearly half a century.

During the years of my newspaper training I was taught that a reporter should always be objective. I found it difficult at times. How can one be objective in describing the gorgeous panorama of a desert sunset, the tranquillity of an evening beside a remote desert campfire, the song of a canyon wren, the majesty of stately wild palms beside a cool spring in an arid land, or the lift of an evening of meditation in a desert wilderness?

These are subjective experiences. They spark an emotional response no reporter can rationalize. And so it was that in the early 1930s when I was pondering the editorial formula for a magazine of the desert which I planned to publish, I discarded the idea of purely objective reporting. The *Desert Magazine* was to be a journal of both fact and interpretation. That was the beginning of my adventure in interpretive reporting—and that is to be the pattern of this book. I could not write it in any other way, for the charm of the desert is largely a matter of personal response.

A mature lifetime of close association with the things of the desert, and particularly the natural environment of this arid land, has had a profound impact on my habits, education, religion and my response to life in general. If I have gained some understanding of, and sense of community with the primitive tribesmen of the desert land, it is because over a much longer period of time they had been cast in the same environmental mold.

While it may appear that the many subjects covered by the chapters in this book are unrelated, they have a common denominator—the American desert. The drama of these pages all has its setting in the geography, art, history, literature, religion, wildlife and human aspirations of this arid land of far horizons, sand-blown dunes and precipitous rimrocks—the American land of little rainfall.

I have not forgotten the lesson taught me by Harry Carr—that people, perhaps because they are so baffling, are infinitely more interesting than things. I have left it to the men of science, and their research is recorded in many books, the task of delving into the miracles of adaptation and evolution which made possible the survival of myriad forms of life in this harsh land. My interest primarily has been in the people, the strong ones who accepted the challenge of burning heat and meager water, and who by their hardihood, have in large measure effaced the white man's traditional concept that the desert is a fit place only for reptiles, thorned plants and aborigines.

And so I invite the reader to share with me some of the highlights of my experience as a desert reporter, and to accept with tolerance any views—or interpretations—which seem to be in conflict with the conventional patterns of life and conduct in this great land which is North America.

RANDALL HENDERSON.

Palm Desert, California,
August, 1961

THERE ARE TWO DESERTS   I

A BAREFOOT PADRE wearing the gray robe of the Franciscan order arrived one day in May, 1539, at the summit of a hill overlooking a valley in what is now western New Mexico. In the distance he could see the stone and adobe village of Indian tribesmen rumored to be fabulously rich in gold and turquoise.

The friar, with the help of his little band of Indian neophytes from the west coast of Mexico, erected a cairn of stones on which he placed a small cross. Then, in the name of the king of Spain and the viceroy of New Spain, he laid claim to all the vast territory to the east, north and west. This simple ceremony completed, he and his companions returned along the foot-trail to Culiacan, Mexico, from whence they had started their 600-mile trek into the desert wilderness two months previously.

There was good reason why Friar Marcos de Niza turned back without making himself known to the Indians in the distant pueblo. Only a few days previously, a black Moorish slave known as Estaban, who had served as guide and herald for the expedition, was taken prisoner and killed by the Indian villagers.

Marcos de Niza and Estaban are the first known explorers from the Old World to have penetrated that vast arid region known today as the Great American Desert.

They had been sent out by Antonio de Mendoza, viceroy of New Spain, with administrative offices in Mexico City, to scout the land and its people. Rumors had been drifting into the Spanish colony which occupied Mexico following the conquest of Fernando Cortez, that many days' travel to the north were Indian tribesmen having such great wealth that the men wore girdles of gold and the women many necklaces of silver and turquoise. These savages in the north were said to dwell in houses of stone and mud, two and three stories high. The villages, according to legend, were known as the Seven Cities of Cibola.

Although he had departed in haste following the death of his guide, and had seen only one of the pueblos of Cibola from a distant hilltop, Fray Marcos returned from his mission with glowing reports. It was true, he said that the tribesmen dwelt in houses that shone like silver in the sunlight. They had wealth which might even rival the treasures of Montezuma.

With this information, Viceroy Mendoza hastened the preparations already being made to send an army of conquest into the north country. To head the expedition he had named Francisco Vasquez Coronado, then governor of the province of New Galacia.

Nine months later, on February 23, 1540, Coronado departed at the head of a cavalcade that included 225 caballeros in armor of mail or buckskin, 60 foot soldiers, and more than a thousand

servants and Indians in charge of the pack trains and the herds of
sheep and cattle which would provide food for the expedition.
They were equipped for three years of exploration and conquest.
Fray Marcos had laid claim to the country in behalf of the king
and viceroy. Now they would take possession, and while the
soldiers were collecting the gold of the tribesmen, the friars who
accompanied the expedition would be striving to save their
heathen souls.

The advance guard of the Coronado force reached Hawikuh,
the first of the Cibola villages, in July. The tribesmen—ancestors
of the Zuni Indians of today—attempted to defend their homes,
but their arrows and spears were impotent against horsemen in
armor with lances and sabres. After many of them had been
killed, the old men of the tribe asked for peace. Within a few
weeks all the Zuni villages had been captured, most of them
without resistance.

It was a disillusioning conquest for Coronado. The Zunis had
a few ornaments of turquoise, but no gold. Fray Marcos' story
was pure fabrication. But there were corn and squash in the
Indian granaries, and for the underfed soldiers and servants in
the expedition these perhaps were more welcome just then than
golden treasure.

The Indians in the Zuni pueblos told about other tribesmen
to the north and west, and perhaps to be rid of their invaders, suggested that these might have much gold. To verify these stories
Coronado sent out detachments while he led the main expedition
eastward across the plains as far as Quivira in what is now Kansas.
Pedro de Tovar led a troop to the Hopi Mesas, where he got a
cool reception and no loot. Then he continued west and is
credited with being the first white man to view the great chasm
which is Grand Canyon. Garcia Lopez de Cardenas, with 17
horsemen, was sent west to the Rio Colorado, to follow its course
downstream to its outlet in the sea. Melchor Diaz was sent to
the headwaters of the Gulf of California to try to make contact
with vessels under the command of Hernando de Alarcon. The

Spaniards had no maps, and only a vague concept of the geography of North America, and Alarcon had been dispatched from the west coast of Mexico to sail to the head of the Gulf and seek an open waterway, rumored to exist, to the Pacific or Atlantic oceans. In any event he was to make contact and deliver supplies to Coronado's army.

It was September 1542 when Coronado, with less than 100 of his trail-weary troopers, straggled back to Mexico. They brought no plunder. The net gain of their nearly three years of hardship and desultory fighting with the Indians, insofar as the Spanish crown was concerned, was the opening of New Mexico to settlement and Christianization.

Coronado was the last of the conquistadores, and in the judgment of many historians, although his mission had failed in its main purpose, he was the most stalwart leader among them. His was the first extended exploration of the American desert, and the chroniclers of his expedition have left invaluable records of the region and the primitive people of that period.

After this brief reference to the entrada of Coronado, less than 50 years after Columbus came to America, my story of the conquest and settlement of the desert Southwest continues in greater detail.

✺   ✺   ✺   ✺   ✺

Geographically, the desert about which I am writing includes all the states of Arizona, Nevada, New Mexico and Utah, and the desert sector of California lying east of the Sierra Nevada. Actually, the Great American Desert has no well-defined boundaries. It includes approximately that part of the United States and northwestern Mexico having an average annual rainfall of less than ten inches. This region of aridity extends into western Texas and Colorado, Southern Wyoming and Idaho, and eastern Oregon and Washington.

Within all these states are mountain ranges, the upper levels of which perennially receive rainfall much in excess of ten inches, and where the slopes above the 5000-foot level often are covered with fine stands of coniferous trees and luxurious gardens of shrub foliage and wildflowers. But where these mountain massifs are surrounded by arid plains of sparse vegetation, blow sand and intense summer heat, they may be regarded only as high altitude oases in a vast terrain of aridity.

It is these mountains, which appear on the distant horizon of every desert locale, that make the desert habitable for mankind. Without them the American desert would be as inhospitable to the pursuits of the human species as are the Sahara and Kalahari deserts of Africa, or the Nullarbor desert of Australia. It is the extra quota of rainfall or snow which these mountaintops receive by reason of their elevation, that provides water for domestic use of the townsmen and the cultivation of farms in the valleys below. Some of it is captured by dams and diversion channels as it courses from the rocky slopes; some of it seeps into underground fractures and reservoirs and finds its way to the springs and water tables of the surrounding plains. Without water there can be no life on the desert. Even those reptiles, rodents and insects which seem to thrive without ever going near a waterhole, derive moisture from other species of the biota which are their food.

Over four million human beings have now established more or less permanent homes on this desert. At least another million spend a portion of the year as sojourners in this land of winter sunshine. The number who have gained some acquaintance with the desert as motorists passing through, or as vacationists or weekenders seeking escape from the chill and smog of the coastal cities, is inestimable.

The United States acquired its desert domain in two parcels. Under the Treaty of Guadalupe Hidalgo, which ended the Mexican War in 1848, the areas now known as California, Nevada, Arizona and Utah, and New Mexico and Colorado west of the Rio Grande and the Rocky Mountains, were ceded to Uncle Sam. But the treaty did not clearly define the southern extent of the

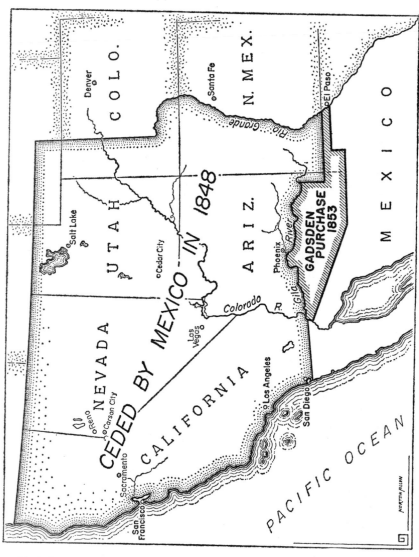

Map showing the dates and the area acquired by Uncle Sam from Mexico over a hundred years ago. With the exception of the coastal region in California, this is the region commonly known as the Great American Desert.

ceded territory, and boundary disputes soon began to plague the administration in Washington.

One of the pledges of Franklin Pierce when he was elected president in 1852 was that he would settle the boundary argument. The issue had become important because eastern financiers wanted to build a southern transcontinental railroad to the Pacific at Los Angeles, and surveys indicated the most feasible route would be south of the Gila River, over territory claimed by Mexico.

Soon after his inauguration, President Pierce appointed James Gadsden, a railroad executive from South Carolina, as a special envoy to Mexico to seek an agreement with Santa Anna, then head of the Mexican government, which would make it possible to construct the railroad on Uncle Sam's terrain.

Gadsden was successful in his negotiations. In December 1853 Santa Anna signed a treaty which involved the sale of approximately 45,000 square miles of territory south of the Gila, and extending from the Colorado River at Yuma on the west to the Rio Grande at El Paso on the east. The price was $10,000,000.

The treaty had to be ratified by the U. S. Senate, and a bitter controversy ensued. Americans of that period took a dim view of a proposal that the United States should pay 35 cents an acre for 30 million acres of desert which, according to Kit Carson, was so barren "a wolf could not make a living on it." Editorial writers referred to it as "Uncle Sam's cactus garden," or "rattlesnake heaven." The *Philadelphia Public Ledger* suggested "The treaty might as well be called a purchase of a right-of-way for a railroad to the Pacific as by any other name."

Abolition politics entered into the Senatorial fray. Northern Senators were afraid the added territory would align with the Confederacy and result in the spread of slavery to the Pacific. Senators from the South perhaps had the same idea, for they favored the purchase.

Gadsden originally had included territory which would make possible an American tidewater seaport on the Gulf of California.

But when the treaty finally was ratified the boundaries had been contracted to the territory which became the Gadsden Purchase, establishing the international boundary as it appears on the maps today.

To the Americans of that period the desert was a God-forsaken land, a region of desolation to be feared and scorned. This appraisal was supported by reports reaching the East from wagon-train emigrants who were suffering bitter hardship in their westward trek across the waterless intermountain region to the gold-fields of California.

During the century which has elapsed since the Treaty of Guadalupe Hidalgo was signed, there have been four epochal movements in the westward trend of migratory Americans. Two of them took place simultaneously. But before giving definition to these social mutations in the evolution of the nation, I want to pay tribute briefly to two courageous bands of men who preceded them in the exploration of the desert wilderness.

The native tribesmen of course were the original known dwellers in this arid land. They played an unwitting role in the caravan of civilization, for it was to save their pagan souls that missionaries of the Catholic faith blazed the first trails across the dunes and mountains of New Mexico, Arizona and California in the late 17th and through the 18th centuries—more than a hundred years after Marcos de Niza had scouted the Seven Cities of Cibola for Coronado. These padres were the indomitable priests of the Jesuit, Franciscan, and for a short period, Dominican orders. The names of many of them are well known—Fathers Eusebio Francisco Kino, Junipero Serra, Francisco Garces, Juan Maria Salvatierra, Juan de Ugarte, and there were scores of others who came into this land with little more than the robes they wore and the crucifix symbolic of their faith. Inspired by the leadership or driven by the discipline of these dedicated churchmen, the wild tribesmen of this region built imposing mission cathedrals and began learning the rudiments of a civilized way of life based on faith in one supreme God. Following the arbitrary expulsion of the Jesuits by the edict of Charles III of Spain in 1767, the new world theocracy which the Catholic padres had envisioned began to disintegrate in the late 18th century.

In the early years of the 19th century another type of trail-blazer began penetrating the vast unknown region west of the Rocky Mountains. They were worldly men, dressed in fringed buckskins and their pack animals carried traps and muzzle-loading weapons. They were the Mountain Men, a new generation of Daniel Boones whose quest was not the salvation of pagan tribesmen, but for the hides of fur-bearing animals. They followed the courses of western rivers, fought the Indians when necessary, served on occasion as guides or scouts for the military. These were tough, adventurous men, to whom hardship merely was a challenge. While the trapping and sale of furs was the immediate source of their livelihood, they could have found less hazardous ways of earning a living than snaring beavers in a land of hostile Indians. They were impelled to come into this western wilderness by that deeper challenge which down through the ages has inspired men to explore the unknown, to scale the highest peaks and to probe the mysteries of the universe. The names of some of these Mountain Men often recur in the lore of western America. Jedediah Smith, Ol' Bill Williams, James O. Pattie, Antoine Leroux, Joseph Walker, "Uncle Dick" Wooten and Pauline (Powell) Weaver were among them.

The Padres and the Mountain Men were the pathfinders in the white man's colonization of the desert Southwest. But the epochal westward movement of Americans did not begin until 1848, the year placer nuggets were found at Sutter's mill in California. The gold rush which brought thousands of men and their families overland across the continent or around Cape Horn was but the prelude to a century of fervid mining activity that extended over the virgin mountains and desert west of the Rockies. In 1859 the great Comstock Lode was discovered at Virginia City in Nevada. From Cripple Creek to Tonopah and from Tombstone to Anaconda, jackass prospectors were plodding the hills and sampling the ores in search of the precious minerals for which an industrial age was providing a ready market.

By the end of World War I the land had been so thoroughly prospected that the grizzled desert rat and his burro virtually had passed from the scene. Then following World War II a new generation of prospectors took the field. They rode in motor vehicles, and their main tools were a Geiger counter and a jeep. They were combing the same hills again, for another kind of mineral—uranium ores. With surface prospects rather thoroughly explored, their numbers have thinned in the last decade, but they have discovered for Uncle Sam, a great reserve of potential nuclear energy.

Today the Southwest is dotted with the ghost camps of mining men who made their strikes, sometimes fabulously rich, more often mere pockets that soon petered out, but nearly all of them finally abandoned when the earth had been stripped of its treasure. But the heritage of this mining epoch cannot be measured by its deserted towns and empty tunnels. Mining stimulated the construction of roads and communication facilities that have made more accessible the agricultural and horticultural resources of the Southwest. It contributed to the building of permanent cities and the advancement of territories to statehood. It brought people, who found other sources of livelihood when the mines had been worked out.

Simultaneously with the initial impetus given to western settlement by the discovery of gold in California, there took place another epochal migration of Americans to the desert West. This movement, like the coming of the Catholic padres, had its roots in religious faith. In 1847, persecuted to the point where life on their midwestern farms had become intolerable, 15,000 disciples of the Mormon Church made a great trek westward to establish homes in a wilderness where they would be free to worship God according to their own creed.

Under the leadership of Brigham Young, one of the great stalwarts of American history, they moved for the most part in horse and ox-drawn wagons across Iowa, Nebraska, Wyoming, and through a pass in the Wasatch Mountains glimpsed the great plain of central Utah. "This is the place," their leader told them, and here, with a Beehive as their symbol of industry, they set about creating a new homeland for themselves with the zeal that only a dedicated religious faith can impel. They brought water from the mountains, erected sawmills, and built homes, leveled the land for irrigation, and within a short span of years had provided all the essential services and goods of a self-contained community.

Sturdy people and diligent missionaries, these Mormon people. Even before they had fully established their initial settlement on the lands adjacent to the Great Salt Lake, their elders were dispatching colonization missions far and wide over the great inter-mountain plateau and into the neighboring territories of Nevada and Arizona. In the river valleys and mountain meadows, wherever there was water and fertile soil, they founded new settlements. And as they set about building homes and planting seeds, their central project was always the erection of a modest tabernacle not only for worship, but as a social center for the community. Theirs is a dynamic religious faith, and it is doubtful that history has ever recorded a more harmonious welding of the spiritual, social and economic interests of a group of people than the bond of union among those whose Bible is the *Book of Mormon.*

The third epochal migration to and settlement of the arid and semi-arid lands of the United States began with the passage by Congress of the Reclamation Act of 1902. Theodore Roosevelt, who assumed the presidency following the assassination of William McKinley in 1901, is credited with having contributed more to this westward movement of population than any other one American. It was under his direction that the Bureau of Reclamation was organized, and the first major dam, storing water for a million acres in the Salt River Valley of Arizona, was named in his honor.

Roosevelt dam was started in 1906 and dedicated in 1911. Yuma Valley project followed in 1912 and Elephant Butte dam in the Rio Grande in 1916. The half-million acre below-sea-level project in Imperial Valley, California, engineered by Charles R. Rockwood, had begun diverting water from the Colorado River in 1902, but this was financed by private capital until 1935 when, following the completion of Hoover dam, the Reclamation Bureau installed a new diversion dam and main canal arteries. In the meantime, and continuing to the present day, Congress has authorized many projects, large and small, distributing water to an estimated 9,000,000 acres of land in the desert Southwest which otherwise would be wholly unproductive insofar as the national economy is concerned.

Irrigated lands are highly productive, especially in the Southwestern border states, where crops are harvested every month of the year. The migration of farmers to these newly reclaimed lands was accompanied by an even greater influx of merchants, professional people, tradesmen and commodity and service industries. Cactus and creosote were cleared to make way for towns and towns became cities where desert dwellers could have the cultural no less than the economic advantages of the good life Americans already had created for themselves in older communities of more abundant rainfall.

Briefly reviewing the cavalcade of Southwestern colonization, there came first the Spanish padres, whose mission was salvation of savage souls. They were followed by those picturesque adventurers in the buckskins—the Mountain Men. Next came the gold-seekers in covered wagons, and prospectors with burros, and following the westward trails in the same period, the trek of a great caravan of God-fearing men and women seeking for themselves freedom from the bigotry of a different religious faith. They were followed by engineers and construction men, whose mission was to harness the streams in preparation for a new generation of farmers depending on the headgates rather than the clouds overhead for their water supply.

Now we come to the final epoch in the conquest and colonization of arid-America—a movement that began to take definition soon after the first World War, and is continuing with accelerated momentum today. The contemporary migration of Americans to the desert does not spring from such specific motivation as the quest for gold, for religious freedom, or farming opportunities. Rather, it stems from a combination of factors inherent in industrial progress: motor transportation and good highways; the perfection and availability of air-conditioning equipment; and perhaps more than anything else, from an affluent national economy and the leisure which has been made possible by a highly efficient technology.

There have been other and more specific factors contributing to the migration of Americans to a land their ancestors feared and shunned. Paradoxically, the nation's defense administration has been both an impelling and a repelling agency insofar as colonization of the desert is concerned, but it has brought a thousand new sojourners to this arid land for every one who has been driven away by the closure of great parcels of desert land. And many of those who came as service men or civilian employees of defense installations in Tucson, Phoenix, Los Alamos, China Lake, Yuma, Las Vegas and a score of other military, aircraft and Atomic Energy bases, have remained as permanent residents.

During World War II over seven million acres of desert terrain in Nevada, California, Utah, Arizona and New Mexico were taken over by the Army, Navy and Air Force as bombing, gunnery and testing ranges. In the war emergency, a general or admiral found it possible to acquire another million acres of desert domain by the simple process of sending a memorandum of request to the federal Bureau of Land Management. Desert people accepted this encroachment on their mineral and grazing ranges during the war as a matter of patriotic duty. But when, following the war, the men in the Pentagon continued to close off large areas with "No Trespass" signs there was increasing resentment among the civilian population. To curb this invasion of desert lands, Congressman (now Senator) Clair Engle of California sponsored, and the 85th Congress approved, a measure forbidding further transfer of public lands in parcels exceeding 5000 acres for military installations without legislative and executive consent.

Another measure which has brought great numbers of homebuilders to the desert wastelands, especially in Southern California, was the Small Tract Act passed by Congress in 1938. This legislation opened the public domain, much of which is desert land, to a new generation of homesteaders. The Act provided that "The Secretary of Interior is authorized to sell or lease . . . a tract not exceeding five acres of any vacant unreserved, surveyed public land . . . which the Secretary may classify as chiefly for home, cabin, camp, health, convalescent, recreational or business site in reasonable compact form under such rules and regulations as he may prescribe."

The regulations originally drafted by the Secretary provided that an applicant could secure a five-acre lease for $5.00 a year. To acquire patent to the tract the lessee must erect a habitable cabin acceptable to Bureau inspectors before the expiration of the lease. In recent years revised regulations have made it possible to buy the land outright, generally at a public auction.

In the late 1940s the rush to acquire small tracts on the Southern California desert became almost a stampede, and the Los Angeles Land Office was swamped with applications. The lands available had little value for agriculture or grazing, the good homesteading land in the West having been taken up long ago. But they had a great appeal for metropolitan dwellers who lived within a few hours' motoring distance, and the cabins of "jackrabbit homesteaders" began to dot the Mojave desert in all directions.

Nolan Keil, assistant supervisor for the U. S. Bureau of Land Management in California and manager of the Los Angeles office, told me in January 1961, that during the 23 years since the Small Tract Act became law, his office had received 81,000 applications for parcels of public land, most of them on the desert. Over 16,000 of these applicants already had received patents to their land.

Some of the five-acre homesteaders, with pride in their desert "estates," erected substantial dwellings, landscaped them with native rocks and shrubbery, and through cooperative financing developed water for domestic purposes. But in many instances they built only to meet the minimum requirements of the federal inspectors, and after a few desert sandstorms had blasted the new paint, their cabins became mere shacks on the landscape, unkept and seldom visited by the owners.

County authorities, under obligation to provide roads, police protection and school facilities for owners whose property had little value on the tax rolls, protested against the inequity of this situation. In 1957 Southern California lands were withdrawn from entry, and pending applications placed in abeyance until new regulations could be formulated in cooperation with county governments.

More recently, in February 1961, Secretary of the Interior Stewart Udall, newly appointed by President Kennedy, announced an 18-month moratorium on applications for the purchase of federal lands. This moratorium, it was explained, was to enable the Bureau of Land Management to process a big backlog of pending applications, and to allow time for the Department to draft new legislation designed to close loopholes in existing land laws which have permitted widespread racketeering by unscrupulous land locators.

But jackrabbit homesteaders and defense workers on desert installations are small minority groups. The major influx of Americans since World War II is attributed to a mild winter climate, air-conditioning in homes and shops, and the lure of far horizons and recreational opportunities. During the last two decades the populations of Santa Fe and Albuquerque in New Mexico, Las Vegas and Reno in Nevada, Phoenix and Tucson in

Arizona, the Palm Springs-Palm Desert area in California, and scores of smaller towns, have mushroomed beyond the wildest dreams of the old-timers. The newcomers are families seeking a more healthful climate, or who can afford the luxury of two homes. Many of them are retired business and professional men lured by the opportunity to play golf under sunny winter skies or swim in temperature-controlled pools. In the Coachella Valley of California there are twelve golf courses within a radius of 12 miles of Palm Desert.

The coming of great numbers of higher-than-average income families has been a boon to the construction industry and the real estate men. Fortunes have been made in land speculation. In Coachella Valley, where General Patton cleared a patch of creosote bushes to set up a motor pool for his training maneuvers in 1941, business lots recently sold as high as $25,000. In Tucson, 71 square miles of incorporated area, which was part of the Gadsden Purchase at 35 cents an acre, now has an appraised value of $683,000,000. Phoenix and Las Vegas can cite similar examples of real estate inflation. Luxury hotels and country clubs have multiplied. And of course this influx of well-to-do sojourners or permanent residents has brought opportunity for great numbers of professional people, merchants and tradesmen, and especially for the service industries. The extreme summer heat has ceased to be a fearsome thing where every home and office has temperature control, and even the auto mechanics work in air-cooled shops.

Unquestionably, the climate, fast, easy transportation, and the artificial appeal of a sophisticated environment have been the key factors in the migration of men and capital to a land their forebears shunned. But there are others—perhaps only a small minority—who come for another reason. For there are two deserts:

One is a grim, desolate wasteland. It is the home of venomous reptiles and stinging insects, of vicious thorn-covered plants and trees and unbearable heat. This is the desert seen by the stranger speeding along the highway, impatient to be out of the "damnable country." It is the desert visualized by those children of luxury to whom any environment is intolerable which does not provide all the comforts and luxuries of a pampering civilization. It is the concept fostered by fiction writers who dramatize the tragedies of the desert because there is a market for such manuscripts.

But the stranger and the uninitiated see only the mask. The other desert—the real desert—is not for the eyes of the superficial observer or the fearful soul of a cynic. It is a land which reveals its true character only to those who come with courage, tolerance and understanding. For these, the desert holds rare gifts: a health-giving sunshine; a sky that after the sun goes down is studded with diamonds; a breeze that bears no poison; a landscape of pastel colors such as no artist can reproduce; thorn-covered plants which during countless ages have clung tenaciously to life through heat, drouth, wind and the depredations of thirsty animals, and each season send forth blossoms of exquisite coloring as symbols of courage that triumphed over appalling obstacles.

To those who come to the desert with tolerance it gives friendliness; to those who come with courage it gives new strength of character. Those seeking relaxation find in its far horizons and secluded canyons release from the world of man-made tensions. For those seeking beauty the desert offers nature's rarest artistry. This is the desert that has a deep and lasting fascination for men and women with a bit of poetry in their souls.

This is the desert I have undertaken to reveal in the pages which follow—the desert which lies beyond the golf courses, the cocktail bars and the heated swimming pools—beyond the forbidding mask of aridity. It has been my privilege as a newspaper and magazine reporter to tramp and camp upon this desert for half a century—and to acquire a substantial library relating to its conquest and settlement, its miracles of adaptation and evolution. It is hoped the reader will be intrigued by the remote desert trails, as I have been.

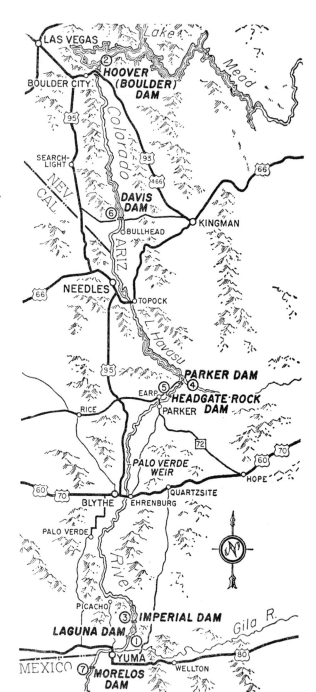

Seven dams and a weir constructed in the lower Colorado River since 1910.

WATER FOR A THIRSTY LAND — II

How is it possible to maintain an agricultural and winter resort economy supporting over four million Americans in a region where the most favorable weather conditions yield less than ten inches of rainfall annually, and where much of the terrain receives less than six inches?

The answer is the snowpack which accumulates on Southwestern mountain peaks and ranges during the winter months, and two great river systems which gather water at the higher elevations and distribute it, with the help of man-made reservoirs, canals and headgates, to the plains and valleys below.

The arid Southwest is rimmed by mountain ranges having elevations above 10,000 feet. On the east in Colorado, Wyoming and New Mexico, is the great Continental Divide. On the north in Utah are the Wasatch and Uintah ranges, and to the west are the Sierra Nevada and White Mountains of California. Dotted over intervening plain and plateau, like island oases in an ocean of sand, are numberless individual peaks and massifs which by reason of their altitude gather an extra quota of moisture from passing clouds. There are the Sangre de Cristo range in New Mexico, the White Mountains and San Francisco Peaks in Arizona, Charleston and Boundary Peaks in Nevada, the Henry Mountains in Utah, the Panamints and Santa Rosas in California, and many more.

From October through April much of the precipitation at these higher elevations accumulates in the form of great snowbanks. Thus the mountaintops serve as natural reservoirs where life-giving moisture is stored for gradual release when warm days come. Without this storage, millions of acres of highly-productive land on the floor of the desert would remain economically valueless.

The two great river systems, including hundreds of tributaries which channelize the precipitation on the mountain watersheds and distribute it to the lands below are the Colorado and Rio Grande. The Rio Grande, with headwaters in Colorado, is 1885 miles long and has an annual stream flow averaging 4,846,000 acre-feet. Prehistoric Indians living in pueblos along the Rio Grande probably developed the most stable communal organization and the finest skill in manual arts of any tribesmen in what is now the continental United States. They were growing maize and squash in irrigated fields long before Europeans came to the New World. Today the descendants of the original pueblo dwellers are still there, frugal farmers, skilled craftsmen and stable members of the American community. Beginning with the Elephant Butte project in 1915, large areas of once arid land in

New Mexico and Texas are now being served by irrigation water from the Rio Grande and its tributaries.

Of much greater importance to the Southwest and to the economy of the nation, is the 1450-mile Colorado River with its major tributaries, the Green and San Juan, and such secondary streams as the Fremont, Escalante, Little Colorado, Paria, Virgin, Bill Williams and Gila. Rising in Wyoming and Colorado, the Colorado River system spreads over the arid lands of five states like the branches of a great tree having a very crooked trunk. Its average annual stream flow, estimated at 16,000,000 acre-feet, provides domestic water for millions of westerners and irrigation water for lands in New Mexico, Utah, Arizona, Nevada, California and Mexico.

The Colorado is literally the life-stream of the major part of the Great American Desert. When the melon growers in California's Imperial, Palo Verde and Coachella Valleys, the cotton growers in Baja California, the alfalfa growers in the Salt River Valley and the citrus orchardists in the Yuma Valley of Arizona, open their headgates, a major portion of the water which flows through them was once snow on the western slopes of the Rocky Mountains or the White Mountains of eastern Arizona.

The wealth created and the benefits derived from precipitation on the mountains that rim the desert valleys is not limited alone to desert dwellers. From millions of faucets in the Southern California coastal metropolitan areas of Los Angeles and San Diego flows water which once tumbled over the cascades in the Grand Canyon of the Colorado. And the distribution of domestic and industrial power from the turbines at Hoover Dam is even more widespread than the water which flows in the desert streams.

Early in April each year the U.S. Weather Bureau office in Denver issues a report on the seasonal rainfall at the headwaters of the Colorado's main tributaries, and a forecast of the runoff during the spring and summer months based on the depth and water content of the snowpack. To farmers with fields to irrigate and engineers who regulate and are in some measure responsible for the distribution of the water supply, these reports are of critical interest. At Hoover Dam, for instance, where the lower basin water supply is regulated, the operating engineers know well in advance what storage capacity will be required to contain the annual peak runoff in June and July. Depending on the anticipated flood discharge, they may release only the daily minimum of water required for their power turbines and the irrigation of crops in the lands of the lower basin, or they may increase the outflow to insure adequate storage capacity when the flood discharge arrives.

The weather gods of the desert, as all around the world, are capricious deities. Rain and snowfall are subject to wide fluctuation. There is always a drastic variation in the seasonal flow of the Colorado. The peak discharge generally comes in June each year, following the melting of the snowpack in the Rockies. In June 1928, the year Congress authorized the construction of Hoover Dam in Black Canyon, the flood discharge at Lee's Ferry below Grand Canyon reached a peak of 110,000 cubic feet per second. Four months later the volume dropped to less than 8,000 second feet.

Prior to the completion of Hoover Dam in 1936, farmers in the rich bottom lands along the lower Colorado worked always under the double menace of flood and drouth. There was the threat that an abnormal peak flood in June would top the levees which protected their crops. And since this region has a twelve-month growing season, there lurked the danger that when the seasonal flood had passed, the fall discharge would not provide sufficient water for winter peas, lettuce and alfalfa.

It was a series of unseasonal winter storm floods in 1905 which, combined with a chain of other freak circumstances, resulted in the costly break which threatened the inundation of California's Imperial Valley and created the present below-sea-level Salton Sea. For nearly three years, through two peak runoffs, the stream abandoned its channel to the Gulf of California and discharged its entire volume into the Salton basin, slashing deep earthen canyons through the fertile farming area. It was only the money of the Southern Pacific Railroad, the faith of its president, E. H. Harriman, and the herculean efforts of a corps of engineers of whom Epes Randolph, H. T. Cory, C. R. Rockwood and C. K. Clarke are the best known, that finally closed the breach and saved the Imperial Valley from complete inundation.

Seventy-five miles upstream in the Palo Verde Valley where A. L. Hobson, Frank Murphy and a colony of homesteaders were trying to reclaim 75,000 acres of rich bottom land, the Colorado on flood rampage broke through an inadequate levee system three times between 1912 and 1922 and submerged thousands of acres of productive farm land.

It was during these years that I had the opportunity to witness both the extreme penalties—flood and drought—which the erratic stream might impose on those who sought to utilize its waters. I recall the late afternoon in 1916 when the alarm spread through Blythe in the Palo Verde Valley where I was editing a weekly newspaper, that the levee had broken. A gopher hole was believed to have started a trickle of water through the dike, and before it was discovered water was surging through a 10-foot breach in the dirt embankment. Every available man in the community rushed to the scene of the disaster. All through the night we worked filling burlap bags with dirt and piling them on the crumbling bank in an effort to prevent it from widening. We had no tools with which to attempt a closure, and our efforts were of little avail. Fortunately the flood level dropped within a few hours, but not until many hundreds of acres of cropland had been inundated.

In 1934, just a few months before the storage of flood water was begun in the Lake Mead reservoir above Hoover Dam, the river dropped to a low discharge of 3000 second feet. Every drop of water that came down the stream in September was being diverted through the headgates for farmers in Yuma and Imperial Valleys. Below the diversion dam I walked across the dry bed of a river which only four months previously had carried 30,000 second feet of water. For two months no water reached the Gulf of California. The estimated crop damage due to water shortage that year was $10,000,000.

Water-users in the lower Colorado basin had dreamed for years of an up-stream flood-control dam which would regulate the discharge of water and remove for all time the hazards of peak floods and drouth. One summer I accompanied a delegation of Palo Verde Irrigation District directors to Imperial Valley to inspect the levee system Imperial engineers had installed. After the disastrous flood in 1905 Imperial Valley had obtained federal aid to finance the construction of railroad tracks on top of its levees, and had brought in great quantities of rock for revetment. The Palo Verde engineers were considering the same procedure, and the trip to the neighboring valley was to secure cost estimates and appraise the effectiveness of rock reinforcing.

One of the members of our party was Chester Allison, then engineer for both the Palo Verde Irrigation District, and for a 700,000-acre delta ranch owned by Publisher Harry Chandler of the *Los Angeles Times*, and associates. Allison led us to a high point where we could look out across the mesquite-covered delta which extended to the far horizon.

"We have to keep strengthening our levees," Allison said. "If we don't, the high water will drown us out. But that is not the ultimate answer. Dirt and rock dikes are fragile things at best. Somehow, the congressmen in Washington must be persuaded that this great fertile basin of the lower Colorado will never be secure until a flood-control dam is built in one of the upstream canyons. Then the Colorado will become nothing more nor less than a great irrigation canal with a push-button headgate to regulate the stream flow."

Allison's dream became a reality twenty years later. In 1922, Senator Hiram W. Johnson and Congressman Phil D. Swing, both of California, introduced a bill for the construction of a flood control dam at or near Boulder Canyon and an All-American canal to replace Imperial Valley's main lateral which originally had been routed for economic reasons through Mexico. For six years the Swing-Johnson bill was the subject of debate at every session of Congress. Finally it was passed in December 1928, and President Calvin Coolidge signed it as one of his last acts as chief executive. Black Canyon, rather than Boulder Canyon further upstream, was selected as the site for the dam. Work was started in 1931 during the administration of Herbert Hoover, and a Republican congress gave it the name Hoover Dam. When the Democrats came into power in 1932 they changed the name to Boulder Dam. Under the Eisenhower administration it again became Hoover Dam. The millions of beneficiaries of its water storage and power production are quite indifferent to petty political bickering over the name.

In 1916 when Allison was visualizing plans for harnessing the unruly Colorado, there was but one small dam across the lower stream. This was a concrete weir known as Laguna Dam, constructed in 1910 by the Bureau of Reclamation to divert water to the Yuma irrigation system.

Since that time three major dams and four diversion barriers have been installed in the Colorado River below Grand Canyon. The most turbulent and erratic major stream in North America has become, as the engineer suggested, just a big irrigation canal with its stream flow regulated by push-button headgates. These dams, in the sequence of their construction, are as follows:

Hoover Dam. Construction started in 1931, completed in 1936. Height 726.4 feet, length of crest 1244 feet. Length of Lake Mead behind the dam 115 miles. Storage capacity 32,359 acre-feet of water. Power plant capacity 1,835,000 horsepower. Built for storage, flood control, irrigation and power generation.

Imperial Dam. Started in 1936, completed in 1938. This is a diversion dam for the canal system serving lands in Imperial and Coachella Valleys in California and Yuma and Gila Valleys in Arizona.

Parker Dam. Started in 1934 and completed in 1938. Height 320 feet, crest 856 feet. Length of Lake Havasu behind the dam

45 miles. Storage capacity 716,600 acre-feet. Built for storage, power and as a diversion dam for the Los Angeles Metropolitan aqueduct.

Headgate Rock Dam. Construction started in 1938, completed in 1941. This is a diversion dam to serve as headgate for the irrigation of 80,000 acres in the Colorado River Indian Reservation below Parker, Arizona.

Palo Verde Weir. Following the completion of Hoover Dam the Colorado River—no longer carrying silt in solution—began scouring its channel below the dam. Palo Verde Irrigation District put in this rock weir just below its intake to insure continued flow of water into its canals.

Davis Dam. Started in 1946 and completed in 1950. Height is 200 feet and crest is 1600 feet. Length of Lake Mojave behind the dam is 65 miles. Storage capacity is 1,820,000 acre-feet, power plant capacity 311,000 horsepower. Built for regulation of stream flow and for power.

Morelos Dam. Started in 1948, completed in 1951. This is a diversion dam built by Mexican engineers with Mexican capital to feed the canal system in the Mexican delta area south of the International border.

The foregoing projects are all in the lower Colorado River, and the beneficiaries of their water control and power facilities are almost entirely within the states of Arizona, California, Nevada and Mexican Sonora and Baja California.

Four other states—New Mexico, Colorado, Wyoming and Utah—also have a stake in the asset-value of the 1450-mile stream and its tributaries. And since they are located in the upstream drainage basin where most of the water originates, they have at least a geographical advantage.

Obviously, it was of critical importance to all seven states that before any major development program be undertaken, there should be some manner of agreement as to the allocation of water and power to each of them. At least such an agreement would forestall endless litigation as to the priority of rights. It was assumed the federal government would provide the major part of the financing for any development, and in the absence of agreement among the states involved, the way would be open for political jockeying at Washington in which a more populous state would have a definite advantage.

It was to forestall confusion as to the rights of and allocations to the various states that the Governor of Utah called a conference of representatives of the seven states in Salt Lake City in January 1919. The outcome of this and subsequent meetings was the appointment of a delegate from each state who would serve with a federal representative on a commission authorized to draft a Colorado River Compact. President Harding named Herbert Hoover, then Secretary of Commerce, to serve on the commission and at the first meeting in January 1922, he was elected chairman.

Agreement was reached at a meeting in Santa Fe, New Mexico, November 24, 1922, and the Compact, which became known as the Santa Fe Pact, was signed by the commissioners of all seven states. However, the decision of the commissioners had to be ratified by each of the state legislatures and the federal government. In Arizona, Governor Hunt opposed ratification on the ground that the Compact did not specifically guarantee adequate water to his state, nor an equitable share of the revenues to be derived from power dams. Ratification became a bitter political issue in Arizona, and when Governor Hunt was reelected to office the legislature construed his victory as a mandate from the people to refuse approval of the agreement.

The Compact created two divisions: An upper basin consisting of Colorado, Wyoming, Utah and New Mexico, and a lower basin which included Arizona, California and Nevada. Lee's Ferry in northern Arizona was to be the dividing line.

Each basin was allotted 7,500,000 acre-feet of the stream's estimated annual discharge. In addition, the lower basin was given the right to an additional 1,000,000 acre-feet out of any surplus above the 15,000,000 primary allotment. The Compact also recognized the right of Mexico to water for its lands in the delta of the river. Mexico was to be granted any surplus above 16,000,000 acre-feet. If there was a deficiency in the fulfillment of the international obligation, then the two basins should share equally in making up the shortage.

Allocation of water and power revenues within each of the basins was left to the states to settle among themselves. And therein the stage was set for a prolonged legal battle between Arizona and California. Nevada had very little land adaptable for irrigation. California already had established rights, by reason of beneficial use, to more than a half million acres. Arizona was irrigating less than 100,000 acres from the Colorado at that time, but the state contained millions of acres of undeveloped desert which it was hoped eventually would be watered from the river.

In 1925, when hope for Arizona's ratification had faded, the remaining six states embarked on plans for a Six-State Compact, which with minor revisions, would be identical with the seven-state agreement. Despite Arizona's objections, the Six-State Compact was ratified by Congress in 1928 in connection with the passage of the Boulder Canyon Project Act which had been sponsored by Senator Johnson and Congressman Swing.

The dispute between Arizona and California has never been settled, and as this is written early in 1961, the case is in the hands of the U. S. Supreme Court. In the meantime, in California the Imperial Valley's canal system has been extended to serve nearly 100,000 acres in the Coachella Valley, and the Metropolitan Water District, with a filing on 1,000,000 acre-feet of Colorado River water, has invested over $300,000,000 in the construction of a storage and diversion dam at Parker, Arizona, and a distribution system to serve not only Los Angeles but a score of other municipalities in the Southern California coastal area.

While California and Arizona continue to feud over the division of water allocated to the lower basin, the upper basin states have taken steps to protect their rights to the 7,500,000 acre-feet allocated to them. In 1956 Congress passed the Colorado Development and Storage Act which authorized river conservation in five states, including three major dams by the Bureau of Reclamation. These are the Glen Canyon Dam in northern Arizona, the Flaming Gorge Dam in the Green River in northern Utah and Navajo Dam in the San Juan River in northeastern New Mexico. All three dams are now under construction.

Major unit in the $760,000,000 Colorado River storage project is the Glen Canyon Dam, scheduled for completion in 1963. Located 13 miles downstream from the Utah state line, it will rise 700 feet above bedrock and will be the fourth highest dam in the world. Its primary purpose is stream regulation and the generation of power. Situated in precipitous terrain, no irrigation is contemplated. It will have a storage capacity of 26,000,000 acre-feet and an electrical output of 900,000 kilowatts.

The Glen Canyon reservoir—Lake Powell, named in honor of Major John Wesley Powell, first American to navigate the Colorado's rapids in 1879—will extend into Cataract Canyon 187 miles upstream. Its 1500 miles of shoreline, mostly in Utah, is to be administered by the National Park Service as a public recreational area. As the water rises in Lake Powell, penetrating innumerable recesses in southern Utah's redrock canyon country, it will create fiords, bays and coves of exquisite loveliness. Those familiar with this highly eroded virgin wilderness are predicting it will become one of the nation's most popular recreational areas.

Flaming Gorge Dam in the Green River, largest tributary of the Colorado, also is scheduled for completion in 1963. Located in the Uintah Mountains of Utah five miles south of the Wyoming state line, it will rise to 500 feet above bedrock, and will have a storage capacity of 3,930,000 acre-feet of water. This project is planned for river regulation and hydro-electric power generation only. Three generating units will have an output of 108,000 kilowatts. Its reservoir will back up through colorful Flaming Gorge a distance of 91 miles.

Navajo Dam in the San Juan tributary is in New Mexico 14 miles south of the Colorado state line. This is primarily a storage and diversion dam for the benefit of the Navajo tribesmen. It will rise 388 feet above the streambed and will have an estimated capacity of 2,000,000 acre-feet. Irrigation water is to be provided for 110,630 acres of land south and west of Farmington, New Mexico. Farming units of 100 acres are to be allotted to Indian farmers selected by the Navajo Tribal Council. A 1200-acre training farm near Shiprock has been in operation since 1959 where tribesmen are being taught the techniques of irrigation farming. It is estimated this project will provide an adequate living standard for 18,000 Navajos who are now eking out a bare subsistence as sheep raisers on their arid reservation lands.

In addition to the major dams in the upper and lower Colorado basins, there are scores of smaller projects, some of them constructed by the Bureau of Reclamation, others by state funds, and many by private owners and corporations.

It would be inaccurate to suggest that the desert Southwest is dependent entirely on storage and diversion dams and irrigation headgates. There are areas on the great intermountain plateau of western Colorado, Utah and northern Arizona where a rainfall of 10 to 15 inches not only creates good grazing range but enables growers to carry on dry farming with varying degrees of success. For many generations, the Hopi Indians in northern Arizona have subsisted on patiently nurtured patches of corn, squash and melons, grown in soil so arid it would be scorned by an Anglo-American farmer.

Even on the low desert, defined as areas below the 2000-foot level, it is possible to grow both forage and field crops on occasional river-bottom lands where the water table is fairly close to the surface.

In zones of abundant rainfall, human beings are inclined to take their water supply for granted. The rain clouds may not always come when moisture is needed and there are seasons of over-supply and months of drouth, but water is regarded as something beyond man's control. Generally the faucets in homes and industrial plants are reliable sources of water, and farmers know that sooner or later showers will refresh their wilting foliage. But this is not true on the desert.

Paradoxically, mountains are both the cause and the remedy for the aridity of the intermountain region in the western United States. The Sierra Nevadas and the Cascades paralleling the west coast act as barriers to the moisture-laden clouds which prevailing winds blow in from the Pacific. The terrain east of these ranges lies in what Dr. Gayle Pickwell in his book *Deserts* terms the rain shadows.

Fortunately for the American economy, the same cold air which at high altitudes drains the moisture from the clouds, also congeals it in a form which makes it available months later for distribution to the lands that have been cheated of their rainfall quota.

This is the reason why dams are built, and why, since the coming of skilled engineers financed by Uncle Sam, more than four million Americans have migrated to the desert Southwest where they have found profitable employment and healthful recreation in the Great American Desert.

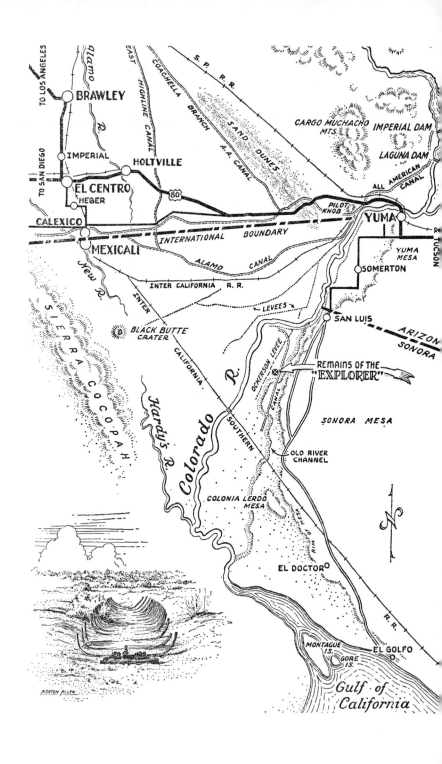

OLD IRON BOAT ON THE COLORADO **III**

"WE WERE shooting past the entrance to Black Canyon," wrote Lieutenant Joseph C. Ives in his mariner's log book on March 8, 1858, "when the *Explorer,* with a stunning crash, brought up abruptly and instantaneously against a sunken rock.

"For a second the impression was that the canyon had fallen in. The concussion was so violent that the men near the bow were thrown overboard; the doctor, Mr. Mollhausen, and myself, having been seated in front of the upper deck, were precipitated

MAP ON OPPOSITE PAGE—*Skeleton of Ives' steamboat, the "Explorer," was found in the mesquite-covered delta of the Colorado River nearly ninety years after the boat had completed its mission, and broken away from its mooring at Yuma during a heavy flood.*

head foremost into the bottom of the boat; the fireman pitching a log into the fire, went halfway in with it; the boiler was thrown out of place; the steam pipe doubled up; the wheel-house torn away, and it was expected the boat would fill and sink instantly by all. Finding after a few moments had passed that she still floated, Captain Robinson had a line taken into the skiff, and the steamer was towed alongside a gravelly spit a little below . . ."

Thus ended, after three and one-half months of arduous labor, the initial cruise of the *Explorer,* the iron steamboat commissioned by the U. S. War Department in 1857 to determine whether or not the Colorado River was a navigable stream.

The *Explorer* was built in Philadelphia. It was a 50-foot stern-wheeler. After a brief trial run on the Delaware River it was knocked down in eight sections, shipped by boat to the Isthmus of Panama, hauled overland to the Pacific, thence by boat to San Francisco, and finally to the mud flats where the silt-laden discharge of the Colorado enters the Gulf of California. Here it was to be re-assembled for the trip up the river—as far as it would go.

The hull was of cast and sheet-iron, with a 3-ton boiler mounted in the center of the deck. Since it was to be stoked with firewood gathered along the shore as the boat progressed upstream, the boiler was over-sized and proved to be so heavy when mounted as to warp the frame of the boat. To correct this weakness, four wooden scantlings were bolted to the bottom outside the hull. This clumsy makeshift later caused no end of trouble in navigating the shallow water over countless shoals in the channel of the lower Colorado.

The crew of 12 included A. J. Carroll of Philadelphia as steam engineer, Dr. J. S. Newberry as physician and director of natural history observations, F. W. Eglofstein, topographer, and P. H. Taylor and C. K. Booker, astronomical and meteorological assistants. H. B. Mollhausen accompanied the expedition as artist and naturalist. D. A. Robinson, a veteran river pilot on the Colorado and the proprietor of Robinson's Landing at the head of the Gulf, was recruited as captain and pilot.

Lieutenant Tipton of the Third Artillery and 25 soldiers from the garrison at Fort Yuma were to serve as a military escort. Due to the limited capacity of the boat the escort with a pack-train carrying food and supplies was to follow the old Indian trails upstream and contact the river party whenever possible. It was an escort in name only, for the troopers did not leave Fort Yuma until several days after the *Explorer* had steamed away, and did not catch up with the river party until Ives reached the Mojave Valley nearly 200 miles upstream on his return voyage.

Lieut. Ives completed his reconnaissance without serious mishap aside from the collision with a submerged rock at the entrance to Black Canyon, and on the basis of his report to the Secretary of War, John B. Floyd, the Colorado in 1860 was declared a navigable stream.

A few months after the return of the *Explorer* to Fort Yuma it was sold to rivermen, who planned to use it for freighting between Yuma and Robinson's landing, where ocean-going ships deposited supplies for Yuma and other army garrisons in the Southwest. There was no trans-continental railroad at that time. According to old Arizona records quoted by Godfrey Sykes in his book *The Colorado Delta*, after a few trips hauling wood, the steamer broke away from its mooring at Pilot Knob on the California side of the river opposite Yuma, floated downstream and disappeared from sight.

Thus ended the first chapter in the saga of the good ship *Explorer*.

Seventy years passed. The men who piloted the *Explorer* and stoked mesquite wood in its huge boiler remained as living names only to students of history who had read the graphic report left by Lieut. Ives.

Then in 1929 word came out of the mesquite, willow and arrowweed jungle which covers the million-acre delta of the Colorado River that an aged Cocopah Indian named Calabasa had reported seeing the rusting hull of an old *barca* partly buried in the silt in one of the many channels which the river had abandoned during the countless years of its fickle meandering across the great delta.

Much of the Baja California delta was owned at that time by Harry Chandler, publisher of the *Los Angeles Times,* and a group of associates, under a grant from former President Diaz of the Republic of Mexico. Engineers, making surveys for the Chandler ranch, talked with the old Cocopah. He told them about the old boat and gave directions which enabled them to locate it, on the Sonora side of the Colorado.

I was publishing the *Daily Chronicle* at Calexico, on the California-Mexican border, at that time, and learned from Gus Seligman, one of the surveyors, about the discovery of the old iron boat. Gus showed me a picture of the hull and when I checked this with Ives' description of the boat, and Artist Mullhausen's sketch as published in the Lieutenant's report, little doubt remained that this was the remains of the *Explorer.*

Herbert M. Rouse, chief engineer for the 800,000-acre Chandler ranch, offered to guide me to the spot. I was eager to make the trip, for the picture indicated that the old boat might be recovered and restored. I envisioned it as an historical relic which would become the stellar exhibit in Arizona's first state prison at Yuma, long abandoned and now being restored by the City of Yuma as an historical museum.

Rouse and I followed the road south from Yuma to San Luis, port-of-entry on the Arizona-Sonora border. As our visit to Mexico would require but a few hours no passports were necessary. The only formality was the registering of my foreign-made camera at the American customs house so it could be returned to the United States without duty.

There were no improved roads in the delta sector of Sonora—only a crazy-quilt of winding dusty ruts through the mesquite forest. Mexican farmers had been clearing little fields for raising cotton, corn and beans; crops which they irrigated with water discharged at the border from the Yuma irrigation system.

The bottomland silt of the delta grows fine crops—one farmer boasted of two bales of cotton to the acre—but as road material this silt, eroded from the great watershed of the Colorado River in the United States and ground to the fineness of flour during its precipitous plunge through the Grand Canyon of Arizona, is a total loss. Sometimes we edged along in low gear, with the wheels running hub deep in dust. If we stopped the car for an instant, with the wind at our backs, we were enveloped in a fog of dust so dense we could not see beyond the windshield. Sometimes there were crude bridges across the irrigation ditches and sometimes—well, we just had to backtrack and look for another route.

Finally we came to an adobe ranch house where the *ranchero* took us to a little rise and pointed far across the tops of the mesquite trees to a cottonwood tree, a conspicuous landmark on the horizons. *La barca* was near the tree, he said.

How would we get there in our *carro*? He did not know. He had gone there only on his pony. There was no bridge over the canal just ahead of us. But Frank Pacheco, an acquaintance who had accompanied us from San Luis, solved our dilemma. He revealed an uncanny accuracy in taking a left turn at this junction and right turn at the next—with the cottonwood always as his marker.

Eventually we came to the *Rancho del Chavez,* and Baulio Chavez, with the graciousness so characteristic of the uncorrupted peon, offered to lead us through the arrowweed thickets to *la barca*—in an uncleared corner of the tract of land on which he had filed under the rather simple homestead procedure in Mexico.

I must confess a surge of disappointment when I first glimpsed the remains of the *Explorer*. My vision of a riverboat mounted as the central exhibit within the turreted walls of the old Arizona state prison—or in some other museum—evaporated into thin air. This was what remained of the *Explorer* without doubt, but it was a sorry looking skeleton. There was nothing left but the ribs, some of them still in place, but held together by such a fragile foundation of rusted iron and adobe earth as to make their removal wholly impracticable. The sheet iron sides had all been removed. Soon after its excavation from its silt grave, the Mexicans in the vicinity had found a practical use for its sheets of iron. They made excellent griddles on which to cook tortillas.

And so the old *Explorer* was still serving a useful role—and perhaps it is better that way than that it should have turned to rust and been lost forever in the silt of the river bottom.

When first discovered, only a narrow rim of iron outlining the hull was visible above the surface of the ground. However, curious visitors had excavated the earth from the inside and around the shell, and the skeleton was resting in a three-foot pit.

As I sat on the edge of the pit I recalled some of the passages from Ives' report. It was a thrilling adventure, that voyage up the Colorado in the winter of 1857-58, through a country inhabited by savages who, except on ceremonial occasions, still wore G-strings and regarded all white men with distrust, if not enmity.

Ives' difficulties started on the mud flats, where the Colorado empties into the Gulf of California. The eight sections of the *Explorer* had been transported from San Francisco in the *Monterey*, a 120-ton schooner piloted by Captain Walsh. As there were no docking facilities at the mouth of the river, the captain with great reluctance chose the only alternative. He ran the ship up on a sandbar at the mouth of the river during high tide at full moon —hoping the next flood tide would float him free again. As soon as the tide receded his own crew and the men of the Ives party unloaded the parts of the *Explorer* on the mud banks.

It was necessary then to improvise ways from the driftwood found on the bars, and assemble the boat before the returning flood tide crest would submerge the bar. It was a laborious task dragging in driftwood logs, often through knee-deep mud, to erect the ways and later to secure fuel for the boiler.

As the work proceeded, Cocopah Indians, who occupied the delta region and regarded it as their tribal domain, often visited the camp. Their interest mainly was in the food passed out by the cook. They came in increasing numbers, and when supplies began to run low the Lieutenant instructed the cook to give them no more handouts. "As bedtime approached they looked blue with disappointment," Ives wrote in his log book. "I thought that by morning they would have disappeared; but the latter part of the night was dark, and the sentinel I suppose not very wakeful after a hard day's labor, for this morning I found them seated around the fire, shining with repletion, and in a high state of glee. This evening the preparations to guard the provisions were so elaborate they gave up in despair and started home in a very unamiable frame of mind."

When the Lieutenant sought to employ two of the Indians to carry a message to Fort Yuma they refused, making known by signs that they probably would get their heads chopped off by their enemies up the river.

Later Ives had another revealing experience with the tribesmen. "It became necessary to provide a stock of firewood before starting," he wrote, and "I told two or three of the Cocopahs that if they would go after drift logs, and drag them to camp before dark, they should have plenty to eat and a large piece of cotton cloth. They were strong athletic fellows, and after an hour of solemn deliberation, and the further offer of some beads and a fancy tippet, they agreed to do it. Having once made the bargain it is but just to them to say they performed their part faithfully, though they became heartily sick of the business long before the day was over. Each one, after bringing in a log, would lie on his back and rest, making horrible grimaces and rubbing his astonished arms and legs. When night came I paid them half again as much as had been promised—thinking that this, and the virtuous consciousness of having for once in their lives done an honest day's work, might induce them to try it again; but I believe that nothing in camp would have prevailed upon them to repeat the experiment."

The work of assembling the boat was started December 5, 1857, and on December 31 the *Explorer* was completed and the engineer had steam up ready to start when the tide would lift the craft off its ways. That night the tide came in, and the *Explorer* was off on its great adventure. Mesquite and willow were used for fuel, and when the supply ran low the skipper brought his boat to the bank and all hands went overboard to cut more wood.

The steamer reached Fort Yuma January 9, and remained there two days while final preparations were made for the voyage up the river. The shore was lined with Indians as the stern-wheeler started on its way. Lieut. Ives described the departure in his report: "The men grinned, the women and children shouted with laughter, which was responded to by a scream of the boat's whistle. In the midst of the uproar the line was cast off, the engine put in motion, and, gliding away from the wharf we soon passed through the gorge abreast the fort and emerged in the open valley above."

Describing the Yuma Indians of that time, Ives wrote: "Many of them, if left to their natural state, would be fine looking, but for everything that resembles clothing they have a passion, and a tall warrior clad like an Apollo, will strut along in a dilapidated hat and a ragged jacket or pair of trousers made for a man two or three sizes smaller, and think he is amazingly beautiful by his toilet. A knot of them gathered together exhibits a ludicrous variety of tawdry colors and dirty finery."

The winter flow of the Colorado was abnormally low at the time of the Ives expedition, and the shallow water and frequent sandbars proved to be a never-ending source of enforced toil and delay. When the steamer would go aground the crew would bale out and push and tow until a deeper channel was reached. The Yuma Indians, who then lived along the river as far north as the present sites of Blythe and Ehrenberg, gave unwitting assistance to the navigators. The Lieutenant reported:

"The Yumas have been constantly encountered since we have been in this valley (Palo Verde Valley). They collect in knots upon the banks to watch us pass, and their appearance is invariably the precursor of trouble. Whether their villages are near the places where the river is most easily forded, or whether they select for points of view where they know we will meet detention, we cannot tell; but the coincidence between their presence and a bad bar is so unfailing that Mr. Carroll considers it sufficient reason to slow down the engine when he sees them collecting on the bank."

Continuing upstream the expedition encountered Indians of a different character. "The Yumas are no longer seen," wrote the Lieutenant. "Our sharp-eyed friends, the Chemehuevis, seem to have exclusive possession of the upper end of the valley (Parker Valley). Not having the same experience in steamers as the former tribe, for they seldom go to Fort Yuma, they have doubtless watched with great curiosity for the long-expected boat. If we had anticipated inspiring them with any admiration or awe, we should have been sadly disappointed, for I am sure they regard our method of ascending the river with unaffected contempt. They have been demonstrating to Mariano and Capitan (Indian interpreters with the Ives party)—who are disposed to espouse our cause and yet are a little ashamed of being in such ridiculous company—how vastly inferior our mode of locomotion is to theirs. They can foot it on shore, or pole along a raft upon the river without interruption; and that we should spend days in doing what they can accomplish in half as many hours strikes them as unaccountably stupid. The gleeful consciousness of superiority at all events keeps them in an excellent humor."

"When we approached the Sand Island shoals, as usual, they were awaiting the approach of the steamer at points opposite the bars. At first our trouble gave them unqualified delight. They watched the boat with breathless eagerness as we tried in vain to get through one place after another, and every time we ran aground a peal of laughter would ring from the bank; but after a while our mishaps appeared to move their compassion, and one of them would run ahead and point out to Captain Robinson the part of the bar that had greatest depth upon it, which their frequent fording of the stream enabled them to know.

An old woman, among others, endeavored to help the captain along, but as we approached the place she indicated, his knowledge of the river showed him it would not do, and he sheered off without making the trial. The benevolence of the old hag was at once converted into rage, and with clenched fists and flaming eyes she followed along the bank, screaming at the captain as long as he was in hearing, a volley of maledictions."

The Chemehuevis, like the Hopi today, have a reputation among the desert tribesmen for being shrewd traders. But they learned something new from Lieut. Ives. Describing his experiences in the Chemehuevi Valley—now covered by the waters of the Los Angeles Metropolitan reservoir and named Lake Havasu—he wrote: "Our camp is at the headquarters of the Chemehuevi nation, and great numbers of all ages and both sexes visited us today. They have been perfectly friendly, and considering their knavish character and restless inquisitive disposition, have behaved very well and give little trouble. The amount of cultivable land in their valley is so inconsiderable, and themselves so inclined to vagrancy, that I could not expect to find them with much provisions to spare, but last evening about two dozen brought baskets and earthen bowls of corn and beans.

"I saw that they had come prepared for long haggling, and I made them place their burdens in a row on some boards that we laid out for the purpose. Asking each in turn whether he preferred beads or *Manta* (cotton cloth), I placed what I thought a fair amount of the desired article opposite the proper heaps of provisions. The whole tribe had crowded around to look on, and their amusement during the performance was extreme. Every sharp face expanded into a grin as I weighed the different piles in succession in my hand, and gravely estimated their contents; and when the apportionment being over I directed two of my men to bag the corn and beans, and coolly walked away, the delight of the bystanders at the summary method of completing the bargain, reached a climax and they fairly screamed with laughter. A few of the traders seemed not to comprehend why they should have had so little to say in the matter, but having been really well compensated, according to their idea of things, the tariff of prices was established, and this morning when fresh supplies were brought in, they received the same rate of pay without question or demur."

Entering the Mojave Valley at Needles, Lieut. Ives was impressed by the superiority of the Mojave tribesmen. "All day the Indians have followed us," he wrote, "examining the boat and its occupants with eager curiosity. They, on their side, have been subjected to critical inspection, which they can stand better than the tribes which live below. The men as a general rule have noble figures, and the stature of some is gigantic. Having no clothing but a strip of cotton, their fine proportions are displayed to the greatest advantage. Most of them have intelligent faces and an agreeable expression.

"The women, over the age of 18 or 20, are almost invariably short and stout, with fat good-natured faces. Their only article of dress is a short petticoat made of strips of bark sticking out about eight inches behind. Some of the younger girls are very pretty and have slender graceful figures. The children wear the apparel in which they were born, and have a precocious impish look. Their delight today has been to mimic the man who stands at the bow and takes soundings, every call being echoed from the bank with amusing fidelity to tone and accent."

Communication with the Indians was not easy. Of the two interpreters on the expedition, Mariano was a Diegueño and Capitan a Yuma. Neither of them was a versatile linguist. Describing a pow-wow with one of the Mojave chiefs, Ives wrote: "Oral communication under existing circumstances is a complicated process. I have to deliver my message to Mr. Bielawaki who puts it into indifferent Spanish for the benefit of Mariano, whose knowledge of the language is slight. When Mariano has caught the idea he imparts it in the Yuma tongue, with which he is not altogether conversant, to Capitan, who in turn puts it into Mojave vernacular. What changes my remarks have undergone during these different stages I shall never know, but I observe that they were received sometimes with an astonishment and bewilderment that the original sense does not altogether warrant."

It was March 8, 68 days after the *Explorer* left the ways at the mouth of the Colorado, that the expedition entered the narrow gorge of Black Canyon—and there the boat hit a submerged rock which brought the upstream journey to an end.

While repairs were being made on the steamer, Lieut. Ives and Captain Robinson continued through Black Canyon in a skiff and spent four days exploring the river above, going as far as the mouth of the Virgin River. The commander decided it was not feasible to take the *Explorer* beyond the point where it met near-disaster, and so the river reconnaissance ended at Black Canyon, not far from the present site of Hoover Dam.

The steamer returned downstream to Mojave Valley, and there, near the ford where Lieut. Beale had crossed the river on a previous overland reconnaissance, near the present site of Needles, the party was divided. Captain Robinson with his boatmen were to return downstream to Fort Yuma, while Lieut. Ives, Dr. Newberry and Messrs. Egloffstein and Mollhausen, with 20 soldiers as escort, planned to continue overland following the course of the upper Colorado as far as was feasible.

They hoped to meander the South Rim of Grand Canyon, which Ives referred to as the "Great Canyon." But the labyrinth of precipitous tributary gorges which slash through the Colorado Plateau of northern Arizona made it impossible for them to gain more than an occasional glimpse of the great river coursing the depths of the main canyon a mile below them.

They passed through the tribal lands of the Hualpai and Yampai Indians, skirted the base of the San Francisco peaks near the present site of Flagstaff, Arizona, crossed the Flax River (Little Colorado) at a point above the Great Falls, and thence northeasterly to the Moqui (Hopi) Pueblos. The Hopis received them hospitably, and furnished guides for the remainder of the trek through Navajo country to Fort Defiance, where the reconnaissance ended. Lieut. Ives returned by stage to Fort Yuma to dispose of the *Explorer,* and the other members of the party continued eastward to Fort Leavenworth.

By river and on foot the expedition had spent four months and eleven days in a desert wilderness inhabited only by the primitive tribesmen of virgin America. The overland journey had been especially difficult, more arduous even for the pack mules than for the men, due to the lack of forage along the way.

Historians have accorded Lieut. Joseph C. Ives a place of honor among the dauntless leaders who a hundred years ago were blazing the first trails across western United States. The record he left—the daily log which was incorporated in his report to the Secretary of War—was a masterpiece of human interest reporting.

He was a better reporter than prophet. During the days when he and his companions were tracking and backtracking through the bewildering maze of gorges which gash the Colorado Plateau of northern Arizona, he wrote in his diary: "Our reconnaissance parties have now been out in all directions, and everywhere have been headed off by impassable obstacles. The positions of the main water courses have been determined with considerable accuracy. The region last explored is, of course, valueless. It can be approached only from the south, and after entering it there is nothing to do but leave. Ours has been the first, and will doubtless be the last to visit this profitless locality. It seems intended by nature that the Colorado River, along the greater part of its lonely and majestic way, shall be forever unvisited and undisturbed."

Today, rangers in the Grand Canyon National Park, located in the heart of the region to which Lieut. Ives was referring, are registering more than a million visitors every year.

To me—and I am sure this is true of all those who are inclined to be sentimental about the historical relics of man's conquest of the desert Southwest—it was a matter of disappointment and regret that the old iron stern-wheeler, the *Explorer,* could not have been salvaged and restored as a memento of one of the most courageous episodes in the history of this region. But thanks to the painstaking work of Lieut. Ives and his companions, the record of this wilderness trek is still available to us. And after all, it is the work that worthy men do—and not the tools of their achievement—that is important.

GOLD, MEN AND BURROS IV

ONE OF my most colorful friends in 1912 and the following
years during which I edited a little weekly newspaper at Blythe
on the California bank of the Colorado River, was Gus Lederer,
a prospector whose cabin was at Corn Springs in the Chuckawalla Mountains.

Gus came to town once a month in an old jalopy for his groceries. He was a typical hard rock miner during that period of
transition when motor cars gradually were replacing burros as
the transportation of gold-seekers who roamed the western hills.

Lederer still had his burros. Six or seven of them came to his cabin door every morning and their braying was a reminder that it was time for their daily ration of flapjacks.

But the 90-mile round trip from Corn Springs to Blythe would have taken a week with the burros, whereas he could make it in his wheezy old Ford in a day.

Gus always came to the newpaper office for a chat, and his never-failing optimism made him a welcome visitor. He was sure that somewhere out in the Chuckawallas was a rich ledge of gold awaiting his pick. He sometimes brought ore samples for me to mail to an assay office in Los Angeles. On every trip to my office he renewed a long-standing invitation to visit his cabin. I knew the 45-mile road was a nightmare for automobiles, but when he finally told me he had staked a claim "with a lot o' color in the rock" in my name, that was bait I could not resist.

Finally, in 1920, four of us loaded our bedrolls in a car and headed for the Chuckawallas for a weekend with our prospector friend. Much of the trail across the Chuckawalla Valley—now spanned by paved U. S. Highway 60—was low gear travel and several times three of us had to get out and push the wooden-wheeled car through the sand, but we reached the camp late in the afternoon.

As we rounded the last bend we came suddenly in view of the lush green fronds of a stately group of native palm trees silhouetted against such a colorful sunset as may be seen only on the desert. Gus had heard our car chugging up the wash, and was coming down the road to greet us.

He had lived in an unpainted one-room shack among these palm trees for years, his door unlatched to all who came this way. He was the self-appointed guardian of Corn Springs. He kept the waterhole clean. He fed the quail and burros which came to his cabin. He had built a crude fence around two fig trees which an unknown hand once had planted among the palms.

To his friends, Gus was the mayor of Corn Springs. He was a prospector who had staked many claims, but never found pay ore in any of them. During the annual melon harvest in California's Imperial Valley he would wrangle his car through passes in the Chuckawalla and Chocolate Mountains and work as a fruit tramp near Brawley. In six weeks he would make a grubstake sufficient to keep him in flour and bacon and beans the other 46 weeks of the year.

Between prospecting trips Gus spent his idle hours with paint brush and canvas. His was the untutored art that knows no rules except to create on canvas as faithfully as possible the beauty and color of the desert landscape. And considering the fact that he had never attended an art class he did amazingly well. I doubt if he ever sold a picture, or even tried to. He just painted for the happiness that comes with creative work—and then gave the pictures to friends who admired them.

Indians had once lived at this oasis. The rocks around the spring were covered with petroglyphs, that strange Indian art work which is seen so often in the remote canyons of the desert Southwest, and yet which no white man or living Indian has ever been able to decipher. Perhaps the Indians had grown squash or maize along the little trickle of water that flowed from the springs—just as Gus Lederer was growing radishes and lettuce there during his sojourn in the cabin.

Gus became ill in 1932, and was taken to the county hospital at Riverside by his closest neighbor, Desert Steve Ragsdale of Desert Center, 17 miles away. A nurse wrote me a note telling of Lederer's illness. When I went to see him he wanted to write me a check for the few dollars he had in the bank. "You'll need it for my funeral expenses," he said. I thought his melancholy was just a passing mood, due perhaps to his never before having been in a hospital bed. I told him to keep his money, he would need it for grub when he returned to the Springs. A few days later I got the message he was dead.

In accordance with his wish, he was buried beneath a mound of stones at Aztec Well, three miles up the canyon from Corn Springs. There are two mounds on the little mesa above Aztec

Well. The other marks the resting place of Tommy Jones, another prospector of the Chuckawalla desert, who had passed away some years before. Tommy and Gus had once lived in the Corn Springs cabin together. But it did not work out. They were always arguing about politics or rocks or art. They disagreed on every subject under the sun, and Tommy finally moved to Aztec. But beneath the sharp words they often spoke to each other there was a deep attachment. Life could become very dull in a place so isolated, but it was never boresome when these two prospectors were together. Gus wanted to be buried beside his old side-kick, and Tommy probably would have made the same request.

Although he had never spent much time as a prospector, Desert Steve Ragsdale is one of the last survivors of that fraternity of hardy frontiersmen who somehow eked out a living on the Colorado Desert of Southern California a half century ago. Steve had started life as an itinerant preacher in Arkansas, and then had come West looking for homestead land. He filed on 160 acres along the Colorado River in the Palo Verde Valley, but with no water immediately available for irrigation he opened a real estate office in Blythe to provide a living for his large family.

But the land boom in the Palo Verde which followed the opening of the valley to settlement in 1910 began to lapse about the time World War I was started, and Steve acquired an abandoned homestead in the Chuckawalla Valley. There, at a time when the average daily motor travel across the 90 miles of uninhabited desert between Blythe and Indio was less than six cars, he opened a service station and lunch counter. Somehow Steve stuck it out, and eventually the State of California, with federal aid, paved Highway 60, and Ragsdale's service station became a thriving business concern. The doctors gave Steve up years ago, but the medical profession has not yet learned to appraise the vitality of the human spirit. The old desert rat still hobbles around with a cane, enforcing his pet prohibition—that no alcoholic beverage will ever be sold on his premises.

One of the prospectors of that early period was Justus Smith, who lived in a weathered tent at Chuckawalla Spring, where he had staked out some placer claims. Justus was losing his eyesight, and the time finally came when it seemed inhuman to leave him there alone. Despite his protests, Desert Steve brought him to Desert Center and provided a cabin for him. But the old prospector was unhappy. He was sure the sands at Chuckawalla Spring held a fortune for him.

One morning he was missing. Ragsdale found the old man's tracks leading across the desert in the direction of his Chuckawalla camp, and caught up with him several miles east of Desert Center. Obviously, it was futile to try to keep the aged prospector cooped up in idleness. Steve solved the problem by returning his friend to his camp, and taking a box of groceries out to him every week.

I had known Justus for many years, and when Steve told me the circumstances I drove out to the spring. Justus recognized my voice and asked me to come into his tent. The table top was cluttered with a miscellaneous assortment of canned food. "Steve had these cans all sorted out," he explained, "but they've gotten all mixed up. Please arrange them so I will know which is which." I realized then that Ol' Justus could not read the labels on the cans. When mealtime came he was never sure whether the can he opened would be chile beans, sauerkraut or stewed prunes.

Another of the jackass prospectors on the Colorado Desert a half century ago was Frank Coffey who for many years lived in a cabin at Dos Palmas, near the western tip of Salton Sea. Soon after his graduation from mining school in the 1880s, Frank had been sent by an eastern syndicate to report on a gold-silver property in the Chocolate Mountains. The report was adverse, but Frank had acquired a string of burros and he resigned his job to remain a single blanket prospector in the Southern California desert mountains until his death in 1936.

He lived and followed the trails alone much of the time, but he was not a recluse. He loved to talk, and his tales would go on endlessly if the listener could take it. Dr. Edmund C. Jaeger, scientist, who has written several books on the deserts of the Southwest and has spent much of his time for 40 years studying the plant and wildlife of this region, often stopped at Coffey's cabin. Dr. Jaeger related this experience:

"Frank had a rich voice and a gifted vocabulary, and his narratives would go on for hours. His longest tale that I recall was started at ten o'clock one morning soon after I arrived at his camp. At midnight he was still talking. When I protested that I must get some sleep, he suggested that he finish the story the next morning. Sure enough, he had me out of bed at daybreak, and the story was resumed. I never heard the finish, for in desperation I packed my burro and pulled out at noon. He followed me a half mile talking all the while, and then reluctantly turned back."

Once a year, Coffey who proclaimed himself the mayor of Dos Palmas, and Gus Lederer, mayor of Corn Springs, would exchange official visits, each making the 40-mile trek with his string of burros. And when Gus went on his annual grubstake mission to the Imperial Valley melon harvest he always left his "reptiles," as he called his donkeys, with Frank. Also he shared his fruit tramp grubstake generously with his neighbor, for in late years Frank had little income.

Coffey had worked for the Southern Pacific railroad in 1905-6-7 when the Colorado River broke through its levees below Yuma and began filling the below-sea-level basin which is now Salton Sea. As the sea level rose, the railroad company had to keep moving its tracks to higher ground to avoid inundation. Frank and his burros were members of the emergency construction crew.

The paradox of Frank Coffey was that so friendly and talkative a character should choose for himself the lonely trails of the sparsely inhabited desert. More than once I have come upon little inscriptions written in his fine pen-artist script, posted on palo verde or mesquite trees, with some such message as this:

"Gone to Mecca for grub. Back in the morning.
Make your camp here and we'll cook a stew
with all the trimmings when I return. Frank
Coffey, mayor of Dos Palmas."

Nearby would be the blackened stones of an old campfire,
and a little pile of wood. Frank never left a camp without gathering wood for those who might come that way later.

I stopped many times for a chat with the old prospector when
he was living at Dos Palmas. The main regret on such occasions
was that invariably I would have to leave in the middle of one
of his tales. But he did not seem to mind. Generally he would
invite me into his cabin. I accepted the invitation the first time I
visited him. After that I would suggest a compromise—that he
have a snack with me on the running board of my big-tired
jalopy. As a housekeeper—well, he just couldn't be bothered. The
four-legged stand which was his dining and general utility table
was a clutter of cans, bottles, socks and ore specimens, disarrayed
on a greasy newspaper. Evidently he put on a new "tablecloth"
occasionally by adding a fresh newspaper to the accumulation of
old ones.

In the 1870s Dos Palmas had been a watering place on the old
Bradshaw freight and stage road over which passengers and supplies were hauled from San Bernardino, California, to La Paz
on the Arizona side of the Colorado River, where rich placer
gravel had been discovered. The gold had been worked out within a few years and the freight road abandoned, but the ruts could
still be followed across the desert.

One day a family of wagon tramps arrived at Dos Palmas
Spring on their way to Los Angeles. During the night, a baby
in the family died. The next morning its parents buried it in a
grave near the palm trees, leaving no marker except a mound of
rocks. Frank always took visitors out to show them the grave and
tell the story of "Poor Baby White." To provide the grave with a
proper marker he made a trek with a couple of his burros to the
Cockscomb Mountains, forty miles to the north. There he chiseled

out a slab of soapstone, inscribed it with the date and the family name, and during the years he remained at Dos Palmas never failed—when the wildflowers were in blossom—to place a bouquet of flowers on the mound.

Frank Coffey liked people, and he had only good words for most of those he had known during his years on the desert. But there was one exception. Twenty miles away at the southern base of the Chuckawalla Mountains was the ruin of a long-abandoned mining camp—the Red Cloud. Frank had worked there in the early days and had helped build a small smelter. The Red Cloud was one of his favorite stories.

"They didn't need a smelter," he would exclaim. "There wasn't enough gold in that whole mountain to supply a one-armed dentist. All they had was a hole in the ground, a lot o' them fancy stock certificates, and one o' them fast-talkin' city galoots to sell 'em to the suckers." The subsequent history of the Red Cloud in a large measure bore out Coffey's appraisal.

Frank Coffey and Desert Steve Ragsdale were hospitable old desert rats—but they shared a common vice. The coffee they made for their guests was a vile potion. Frank's formula was to add a tablespoon of fresh coffee grounds and some water to the blackened old pot each morning. The water was a brackish liquid from a spring in alkali-impregnated soil, and he never dumped out the old grounds until the pot became so congested there wasn't room for the day's supply of beverage. Steve Ragsdale's formula was one cup of ground coffee for each two cups of water.

In the 1930's Coffey became too feeble to take care of himself, and friends took him to the county hospital at Riverside. But the confinement was like putting a wild animal in a cage. He was so crushed and unhappy he finally was transferred to a nursing home, where he died in 1936.

Tommy Jones, Gus Lederer and Frank Coffey were the names best known among the prospectors who tramped the Southern California desert a half century ago, but the Mojave Desert to the north also had its colorful personalities. Among those whose names have become legends in the California desert were Death Valley Scotty, Dad Fairbanks, Shorty Harris, Pete Aguereberry, Jim Dayton, John LeMoigne and Charlie Walker. The bizarre career of Death Valley Scotty is told in another chapter of this book. Pete Aguereberry probably was the only one of the six who actually mined and mucked ore.

Dad (Ralph Jacobus) Fairbanks was a tough, versatile frontiersman who came into the Death Valley region in the late years of the last century and with an equally courageous wife provided food and service for the men who were prospecting the hills and working the mines. Dad and Ma Fairbanks opened the first restaurant at Beatty, Nevada, grew hay in Ash Meadows for the town of Shoshone on the edge of the Amargosa desert and later established a caravansary at Baker, California.

Fairbanks was a trader at a time and in a region where men wore six-shooters. He was reputed to be a fine marksman and a shrewd poker player. He grubstaked prospectors who more often than not failed to find gold of paying assays. For more than any other reason, his name is remembered for his rescue missions. He is said to have brought more lost and thirst-crazed wanderers out of the Death Valley region than any other frontiersman of that period. Dad Fairbanks was a humanitarian in a hard cruel land.

Shorty (Frank) Harris was the prospector who discovered the gold which started a stampede to Bullfrog, Nevada, followed by the finding of rich ore in nearby Rhyolite—both of them now ghost camps. The strike in the Panamint Mountains at Harrisburg was named in his honor, although it is not certain that he actually found the first gold-streaked ore there.

According to the story told by Pete Aguereberry, he and Shorty were prodding their burros over the Panamints, sampling ore as they went. Pete broke off a chunk of rock which appeared to have some color. He called to Shorty, who was carrying the magnifying glass. Shorty took one look and began to dance a jig. It was rich in free gold. They staked out adjoining claims, and

Harris was to continue exploring the area while Pete went to Ballarat for supplies.

Pete was delayed a couple of weeks at Ballarat awaiting the arrival of mail with some money. When he returned, the hillside where their claims had been staked was swarming with prospectors. Shorty had talked too much.

A mining syndicate offered Harris $150,000 for his claim, payable in stock. He made the deal with them. But before any dividends were declared an assessment was levied on the stock. Shorty could not raise the money to pay the assessment—and he left the camp as broke as when he had arrived there. To Shorty Harris the quest for gold was everything—the gold itself meaningless. It is said he sold his rich Bullfrog claim for $1000, and spent the money within a week. Pete Aguereberry once said he doubted if Shorty Harris or Death Valley Scotty had ever done a hard day's work with a mining pick or a mucking shovel in their lives. But for all his faults, Harris was a likable companion, generous, honest and like most of the others who followed the burros in quest of gold, a perennial optimist. He was buried beside the grave of his old friend Jim Dayton on the floor of Death Valley. On the cairn of native rock built by friends to mark the two graves was this inscription:

> "Bury me beside Jim Dayton in the Valley we
> loved. Write: 'Here lies Shorty Harris, a single
> blanket jackass prospector'" Epitaph requested
> by Shorty (Frank) Harris, beloved gold hunter.
> 1856-1934.

> Here Jas. Dayton, pioneer, Perished 1898.

Jimmy Dayton of Death Valley was the friend of every prospector who came his way, but he never followed the elusive trail of gold himself. In 1882 he was a swamper on one of the 20-mule team borax wagons which freighted Death Valley's mineral wealth to the railroad at Mojave and later to Daggett. Then he became foreman of the Greenland Ranch, as the Furnace Creek Ranch was known before 1907. It was then owned by the Harmony Borax Works at the base of the Funeral Mountains a few miles north.

Here Jimmy raised alfalfa for the mule teams and pasturage for the cattle and hogs which supplied the mess hall for the borax miners. The mining operation generally closed down during the summer months when Death Valley temperatures often exceed 120 degrees. At this season Dayton would employ Shoshone Indians to guard the mine property and irrigate the ranch for a few weeks while he was in Los Angeles spending his year's accumulation of wages.

He was a quiet, soft-spoken worker, who seemed entirely content to live alone in this scorched land of sand blizzards. At least that is the way it was for many years. Then on one of his trips to Los Angeles he fell in love, and a few days later returned to the Ranch with his red-headed bride. But she could not take the lonely life in a land where the only night lights were the stars overhead and a coal-oil lamp.

Life was never quite the same after she left. Then the Borax Works closed down. The miners and mule-skinners departed, and only an occasional prospector came that way. "If we are to live together," his wife had told him, "you will have to go where there is life." For the first time in his life he felt lonely. His caretaker's job at the Works left him much time to brood. He had been in Death Valley twenty years. Why spend the rest of his days in this inferno?

Dayton wrote a letter of resignation to Superintendent Wash Cahill, at Daggett, the nearest office of the Borax company. He would be leaving within a week he said, and would be transporting his personal belongings in a wagon with a four-horse team. He arranged with Indians to guard the mine property, and employed one of them to carry his letter over the Panamints to Ballarat, the nearest postoffice.

The letter was delayed, and Jimmy's arrival at Daggett was long overdue when Cahill received the message. After waiting another day or two he became alarmed. Jim Dayton had always been punctilious in his appointments. Two members of Cahill's crew volunteered to return over the wagon road to Death Valley, to see if Dayton was in trouble.

Nineteen miles before reaching the Ranch they came upon the wagon—the four horses dead in their harness. The heat-crazed animals had tried to struggle free. But the brakes on the wagon had been set, and only the churned sand bore evidence of their efforts. The rescuers heard the whine of a dog in a nearby thicket. There they found the body of Jim Dayton. Evidently he had suffered a heart attack or a heat stroke. The dog was the only survivor.

Ol' John LeMoigne, like Pete Aguereberry, was a Frenchman. As a young man he came to the United States as a sailor in the early 1870s, and loafing around the bars of San Francisco's Barbary Coast, heard talk of the fortunes to be made in the mines of California and Nevada. He left the ship and through an employment agency got a job in the mines at Darwin, California.

There he improved his English, gained a little knowledge of mineralogy, and as soon as his savings would permit, invested in a pack outfit with burros. With a sizable grubstake in his wallet he quit his job and headed over the Panamints toward Death Valley.

It was current gossip among the miners that the Shoshone Indians knew the location of a rich lead deposit. It was even said they shaped bullets for their muzzle-loading guns with the metal obtained there. LeMoigne followed an old Indian trail down Cottonwood Canyon, which drains into Death Valley. There were springs and an abundant supply of good water in Cottonwood. Petroglyphs on the sidewalls today bear evidence it was occupied by tribesmen even in prehistoric periods. LeMoigne found several Indian families camped by the springs, and remained with them for several months, making this his base camp for prospecting trips into the surrounding mountains. He was a big man, fine

looking and of good character according to such meager refer-
ences as are available today.

Through his friendly dealings with the Shoshones LeMoigne
learned the source of their lead—in the next canyon south of Cottonwood. It is known today as LeMoigne Canyon, and its portal
may be seen seven miles north of the Park Service checking station at the Towne's Pass road into the Monument.

LeMoigne filed on the lead claims in 1882 and for years did
exploratory mining, much of the time working alone. He lacked
the capital to develop the property and finally offered it for sale.
It is said he once was offered $35,000 for his rights. The buyers
wanted to give him a cashier's check, but to John LeMoigne
that was just a piece of paper. He wanted real money, and the
deal was never consummated. He planned to return to France
as soon as he could sell the mine. But the fates decided otherwise.

In June 1918, he left the mine to go to Furnace Creek Springs.
He was 82, had been in ill health, and thought some baths at the
springs might be beneficial.

Several days later, Death Valley Scotty, riding his mule down
the valley from Grapevine Canyon, saw buzzards circling a
thicket some distance from the road. When he went to investigate
he found the body of LeMoigne lying on his bedroll. He had
tied the burros to a scrub mesquite, unpacked them and laid
down in the shade. He was buried on the spot, and it was never
known whether he was the victim of a heart attack or heat prostration.

LeMoigne had never patented his claims, and since there were
no known heirs to acquire them, other prospectors moved in and
took possession. In subsequent years the ownership changed
many times.

I visited LeMoigne Canyon with George Palmer Putnam in
1949. George had retired from the publishing business which
bears his family name, and with his second wife, Peg, had purchased and was operating the Stovepipe Wells Hotel in Death
Valley. We rode horseback up Cottonwood Canyon to its head-

waters and then down LeMoigne Canyon. Mining operation had practically ceased at that time, but there was evidence of much activity in previous years. We saw many tunnels in the sidewalls of the lower canyon, with some equipment still in place. Every niche and cove where a cabin could be built above the flood channel of the arroyo was cluttered with the ruins of makeshift dwellings which evidently had once housed a considerable mining camp.

During this ride, Putnam told me about Charlie Walker, who for many years had been a surveyor and draftsman at Beatty. Charlie was said to be a wizard at finding section corners in a land where few corner stakes had ever been installed, and where, due to drifting sand and an occasional cloudburst flood, the mortality rate was very high among those corner posts which had once been established. Walker's idea of a vacation was to take off in a mongrel old car which he called his Mixture, because it was an assembly of parts from so many other junked vehicles, and spend a couple of weeks or months prospecting the Nevada and Death Valley canyons.

Little Charlie, as he was known, was a sparkling personality on a stage where only rugged individualists survived. His was the poise and the wit of a humorist who could look down the barrel of a six-shooter and wise-crack the man who held the gun out of pulling the trigger. In his book *Death Valley And Its Country*, Putnam quoted Walker's suggestion that Death Valley be publicized as a fishing resort: Said Charlie: "What you're after when you go fishing is to have a rest and be away from worries. The Valley's perfect for that. Your fly won't get caught in the willows. Your feet won't get wet, nor tuckered out chasing along a danged stream to find a better pool. And there'll be no fish to clean."

Jim Dayton and John LeMoigne were not the first, nor the last to succumb to the burning intensity of the sun in the Death Valley sink. But the years which have elapsed since these men trekked from waterhole to waterhole have brought many changes. The winter climate there is delightful. Death Valley is now a National

Monument, accessible by three paved highways. Park rangers now patrol the area, and excellent accommodations are provided by the Fred Harvey Company at Furnace Creek Inn and Ranch, at Stovepipe Wells Hotel by Peg Putnam, and at Scotty's Castle by the Gospel Foundation team in charge.

In November 1960 more than 18,000 visitors, thousands of them in motor trailers, came to participate in the 11th annual Encampment of the Death Valley '49ers, an historical society organized to conserve the scenic, scientific and recreational values of the Monument and to perpetuate the tradition of courage and heroism of the first Americans to face the challenge of this desert wilderness.

I did not personally know all the characters in the cast of this chapter, but I have lived in their country for half a century, and my acquaintance with the associates of those with whom I did not have the privilege of personal contact, has given me an intimate knowledge of their contribution to the taming of arid America.

The prospector and his burro virtually have passed from the stage of American history. But they left something worthwhile for the generations to follow them. They left a tradition of courage, integrity, generosity, stamina and spiritual freedom—which after all is a more lasting legacy than men can dig from the ground with pick and drill and dynamite.

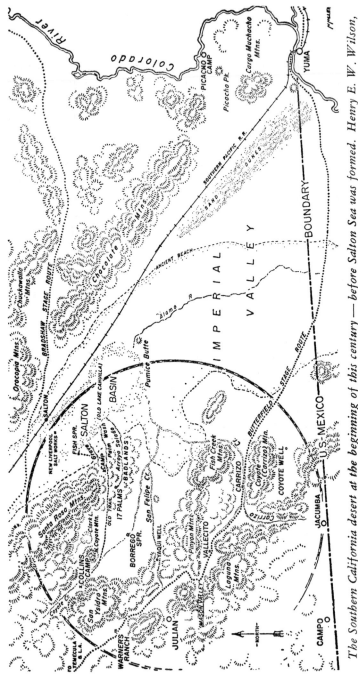

The Southern California desert at the beginning of this century — before Salton Sea was formed. Henry E. W. Wilson, who searched for the Lost Pegleg gold off and on since 1900, believes it will still be found within area marked by circle.

PHANTOM TREASURE IN THE DESERT   V

ONE DAY in the early 1870s a German prospector, Jacob Walzer, came out of Arizona's Superstition Mountains, his mules loaded with rich gold ore. Walzer died in 1891 without revealing the source of his wealth. Although many have searched, and some have lost their lives in the quest, no one has re-discovered the fabulous mine.

But the legend of the Lost Dutchman persists. The Dons Club of Phoenix each year in March conducts a ceremonial lost mine hunt to keep alive a tradition which has some elements of historical authenticity, and much mystery. It was my privilege to accompany the Dons on one of their pilgrimages as the guest of Tom Lesure, Arizona writer and member of the organization.

I had known about this Lost Dutchman trek for many years, and somehow had gained a wrong impression of it. I thought it was a swanky affair staged for the entertainment of rich dudes who flocked to Phoenix every winter season. Actually it was a glorified family picnic, open to mother and dad and all the youngsters. We had a glorious field day in a lovely setting of saguaro cactus and palo verde trees at the base of the Superstition massif.

Over 600 Arizonans and their guests motored the fifty miles from Phoenix to take part in the festivities. The Dons, conspicuous in their caballero costumes, provided a busy day's program. Over half the visitors took the nine-mile hike up into the Superstitions on a mock hunt for the legendary mine. Divided into groups of fifty, with one of the hosts as guide for each party, the hikers ascended steep winding trails, and during the frequent rest periods were told the story of the mysterious Dutchman and the futile quest for the re-location of his mine extending over nearly a century.

For those who felt the trail would be too strenuous, a lively day of entertainment was provided at the base camp. A Mexican band and a cowboy orchestra took turns serenading the crowd. A quartet of Papago Indian women spent hours cooking and serving their native bread to a waiting line of patrons who wanted to sample this primitive staff of life. The Powder Horn Clan, a group of fire-arms hobbyists, held target practice with their muzzle-loading weapons, and the Phoenix police did some crack target and trick shooting.

Dr. Herbert Stahnke, one of the Southwest's leading authorities on venomous reptiles and insects, had an under-glass exhibit of some of the poisonous denizens of the desert. Later, on the stage of a little amphitheatre he handled scorpions, a Gila monster, a coral snake, a sidewinder and a rattler as if they were old friends. He even brought some of the children up on the platform to pass a desert tarantula among them, as evidence this hairy spider is quite harmless.

The climax of the day's program came in the evening when, following Mexican and Indian dances, a brilliant display of fireworks from the rim of a 3000-foot cliff above was the prelude to a gorgeous firefall which rivals the famous Yosemite National Park firefall in California.

The legend of the Lost Dutchman mine goes back to the original discovery in the 1840s of a rich gold ledge in the Superstitions by Pedro Peralta, son of a wealthy family of mine-owners in Chihuahua, Mexico. Peralta is said to have found rich gold-bearing ore at several locations in these mountains, and to have brought a crew of Mexican miners to take out the high-grade and transport it by muleback to arrastres on the floor of the desert below.

But this was Apache country, and the Indians resented the intrusion of white men in their traditional hunting grounds. Before any of the gold ever was taken back to Mexico, the Indians attacked in large numbers, dispersed and killed some of the men working at the arrastre, and massacred the crew at the mine, including Don Pedro. The supplies were stolen and the mules killed or scattered. The Indians are believed to have tossed the mining tools into the shafts and tunnels, which were either filled with rock or camouflaged so well with boulders and vegetation their location remains a mystery to this day. This version of the fate of the Peralta mining expedition was pieced together later by members of the family who came from Chihuahua to search for the missing Pedro.

Jacob Walzer, often erroneously spelled Walz or Waltz, was a German miner who, in the 1860s, came to the Salt River Valley —which lies at the base of the Superstitions. The story of the Peralta tragedy was common knowledge in that area, and Walzer confided to friends that he was going to get an outfit together and search for the old Spanish diggings.

His first discovery in 1869 was placer sand with a high content of gold. He induced a German relative to join him in his mining venture, and the two of them later discovered the rich ledge from which the placer gold was eroding. Whether or not this ledge was one of the original Peralta discoveries was never confirmed. Over a period of ten years Walzer would arrive periodically in Florence, Mesa or Superior, his burros loaded with high grade ore, including nuggets from his placer workings.

He is said to have made his last trip to the mine in 1878. He was an old man then, and had accumulated enough wealth for his remaining years. Before leaving, he concealed the location and evidence of his mining operations so thoroughly that many hundreds of searchers who have since gone into the area seeking the Lost Dutchman mine have returned empty-handed, or remained in this wild mountain terrain the victims of heat and thirst.

Walzer built a little cabin in the Salt River Valley. In 1891 a flood torrent carried away the cabin. He escaped, but the exertion and exposure of his struggle with the flood water brought on the pneumonia which caused his death a few weeks later.

There are many versions of the Peralta and Lost Dutchman legends, and old maps purporting to show the location of the workings have appeared from time to time. Most of them place Walzer's claims in the vicinity of a conspicuous landmark known as Weaver's Needle. Barry Storm, one of the most persistent of the phantom gold seekers, believes the more probable location is the mineralized country around Iron Mountain in the vicinity of Pinto Creek. But the mystery remains unsolved.

If Jacob Walzer, with his Lost Dutchman, is to be classified as the most widely known among the phantom treasure legends of the desert Southwest, the second place honor unquestionably will go to Pegleg Smith and his black nuggets from a little hilltop somewhere in the Southern California wastelands.

During my fifty-year sojourn on the Arizona and California deserts I have known intimately many of the men who tramped this region in search of Pegleg's gold. Perhaps the most diligent among them has been Henry E. W. Wilson who, since 1901, has followed the phantom trails for intermittent periods which would add up to many years.

Wilson's search centered in a wild, highly-eroded region known as the Borrego Badlands, much of it now in California's Anza-Borrego Desert State Park. I have camped with Wilson, and many times have sat by his evening campfire listening to the oft-repeated story of Pegleg Smith and the nuggets which from long exposure to the desert sun had acquired an almost black coating of desert varnish.

Today one hears many versions of the Pegleg discovery, but the story which first aroused Henry Wilson's interest in the legendary treasure appeared in the *Los Angeles Express* July 13, 1900, and with some added details in *Munsey Magazine* in December, 1901. Briefly, the story is this:

Thomas L. Smith, a native of Kentucky—although some chroniclers give his birthplace as New Hampshire—left home while still in his teens to follow the westward trails. Eventually he reached Santa Fe, New Mexico, where the Mountain Men of that period were finding a ready market for the beaver furs they trapped on western rivers. Smith joined one of the trapping expeditions. Some time later, in a skirmish with hostile Indians, his left ankle was shattered by an arrow. With only whiskey as an anesthetic and skinning knives for instruments, his companions amputated his foot. The squaws in a friendly Indian camp provided herbs which healed the wound. Smith whittled out a crude pegleg for himself and thereby acquired the nickname he carried through life. As soon as he was able to travel he returned to his trapping.

With a companion he was snaring beavers along the lower Colorado River in 1852 and reached Yuma. They decided to make the overland trek to Los Angeles to dispose of their furs. West of Yuma in the great sand drifts known today as the Algodones Dunes they became lost. Their water supply ran low and Smith climbed one of three low hills to scan the horizon for vegetation which might mark the location of a spring. They were somewhere in the great Salton Sink which 53 years later was partly submerged with flood water from the Colorado River and became known as Salton Sea.

Smith noted the hilltop was covered with waterworn black pebbles. They were heavy, and believing they might be copper, he put a few of them in his pocket. Some weeks later the men reached Los Angeles, disposed of their furs, and during the spree which followed, Smith showed some of his rocks to a mining man he met in a bar. His acquaintance scraped away the varnish surface and declared they were pure gold.

The news spread quickly and Smith was deluged with offers from men who wanted to grubstake a return expedition to the desert and re-locate the hill strewn with nuggets. Pegleg finally selected a few companions, and they started from San Bernardino, well equipped with pack animals and supplies.

But Smith, on his trek from Yuma, had been more concerned about water supply than gold, and had failed to make careful note of the landmarks. He became confused, and his companions lost confidence in their guide. With supplies running low there was dissension in the party and finally the search was abandoned.

Pegleg is said to have returned as the guide for another searching party many years later, but with no more success than on the previous attempt. In the meantime, many treasure-hunters have traversed the region in fruitless search for the black gold, with only the three low hills as an identifying landmark for their search. Many years later, after Salton Sea had been formed, some of the prospectors in this region came to the conclusion the hills had been submerged by the flood water which filled the basin.

One report is that Pegleg died in 1866 in a county hospital in the San Francisco Bay area. He was penniless and discredited. Another version is that he became a squaw man in Utah and died in the camp of his Indian wives.

But interest in the Pegleg gold was never dimmed. Down through the years as the tale was retold in barrooms and mining camps, many deviations in the original legend appeared. Among today's prospectors no two will agree as to the details of the story. The search has been extended into Baja California to the south, and north into the Mojave Desert. When the legendary life of Pegleg Smith became too complicated to be encompassed within the career of one man, another Pegleg Smith was created to explain the discrepancies. I even met one old prospector who insisted there were three Pegleg Smiths.

Nearly all informants agree Pegleg was a heavy drinker and sometimes made a nuisance of himself in the saloons. There are some who discredit the story of his gold discovery in its entirety. They will tell you he was a hijacker who held up and stole his gold from packtrains transporting the precious metal from mines, in the days before there were railroads or highways.

James A. Jasper, San Diego County Supervisor, who sign-posted some of the first trails across the Southern California desert more than half a century ago, and whose acquaintance included men who had known Pegleg personally, once described Smith as a horse thief, a cattle rustler, and a polygamist with five Indian wives.

While Jacob Walzer and Pegleg Smith have been accorded leading roles in the folklore of lost mines and buried treasure in the Southwest, there are many other tales of phantom wealth that lies buried in western hills and arroyos, awaiting the skill or the luck of another generation of treasure-seekers.

On the Mojave Desert of California, after a century of failure, men are still seeking two missing silver claims, the Lost Breyfogle and Lost Gunsight. Farther south, the Lost Dutch Oven, the Lost Arch of the Turtle Mountains, and the Lost Ledge of Sheep-hole Mountains are waiting to be rediscovered.

In Arizona, perhaps more than any other state in the Southwest, the treasure hunter's map is thickly dotted with legendary deposits of wealth, among them the Lost Mine of the Iron Door, the Lost Apache, the Lost Adams Diggings, the Lost Pick, the Organ Grinder's Lost Ledge, Squaw Hollow Gold, the Lost Pesh-la-Chi and the Black Maverick.

In Nevada, Tim Cody's Lost Ledge is the legendary mine most frequently mentioned. In Utah it is the Pothole Placer and in New Mexico the Lost Guadalupe. These are but a few of literally hundreds of legendary treasure troves which lure men—all kinds of men, from the cities no less than from the mining camps—into remote mountains and precipitous canyons. There is scarcely a community in the Southwest which does not have its tradition of hidden wealth somewhere in its back country. In the Grand Canyon region there is the story of a lost ledge behind a waterfall, and in Death Valley the Cave of the Golden Sands.

Nor is this mythical wealth confined to the elemental deposits of geological evolution. In southern Arizona, and extending south into the Mexican states of Chihuahua, Sonora and Baja California, there are numerous tales of gold and silver mined by neophytes and horded by the padres who established missions in this region nearly two centuries ago, or buried jewels and gold and silver plate and altar accessories from missions which for one reason or another had to be abandoned. Many of these stories are associated with the expulsion of the Jesuit missionaries from the New World in 1767 by order of Charles III of Spain. Before their hasty departure the Jesuit priests are said to have cached their valuables in caves and underground vaults where they might be recovered if and when the expulsion order was rescinded, as they confidently expected. The legend of the Lost Treasure of del Bac near Tucson, Arizona, is in this category, and the Hidden Treasure of the San Pedro Martyr Mission in Baja California another.

Then there is the story of a tunnel in the Tascos Mountains of southern Arizona where the altar fixtures from both Altar and Tumacacori Missions were buried during an Indian uprising in which several of the padres were killed.

In the chain of circumstances relating to every tale of lost gold or buried treasure, there is always a missing link: The original discoverer met with violent death before he could return to recover his fortune; the map showing the exact location was lost; the Indian guide deserted during the night; a cloudburst torrent or rock avalanche covered the area with debris; the landmarks, as in the case of Pegleg's gold, could not be recognized; the location cairns had been destroyed; the tale had become so garbled in its transmission from person to person it is impossible to know which version is correct—always there is a plausible reason why the searchers have been foiled in their efforts to go directly to the original location.

During the 21 years of my association with the *Desert Magazine* we published scores of lost gold and treasure tales. Invariably, the mail would bring inquiries—requests for more specific information as to some obscure detail. I could only answer these queries by explaining that we had published all the information available to us—that if all the answers were known there would be no lost mines.

With one exception, I never accepted a lost treasure manuscript which I did not believe to have some basis of fact in its origin. The one tale which I knew to be geographically impossible was the oft-repeated story of the Lost Pearl Ship of the Southern California desert.

This is the legend: In the early 17th century a Spanish sailing vessel was cruising the coastal waters of the Gulf of California, its crew doing some trading with the Indians, but primarily engaged in pearl fishing in the vicinity of La Paz near the southern tip of the peninsula of Baja California. When many chests had been filled with pearls, the captain decided to return to Spain by way of a deep channel said to connect the headwater of the Gulf with the Atlantic Ocean. Such a route would be preferred to the long stormy voyage around Cape Horn.

Reaching the head of the Gulf he found a channel extending inland between two ranges of mountains. The vessel passed through the channel without difficulty and the captain found himself on an inland sea so vast he could not see the distant shoreline. Continuing his journey across the sea he could find no passage beyond. Several weeks were spent in seeking an outlet, and in hunting and fishing to replenish the ship's food supply.

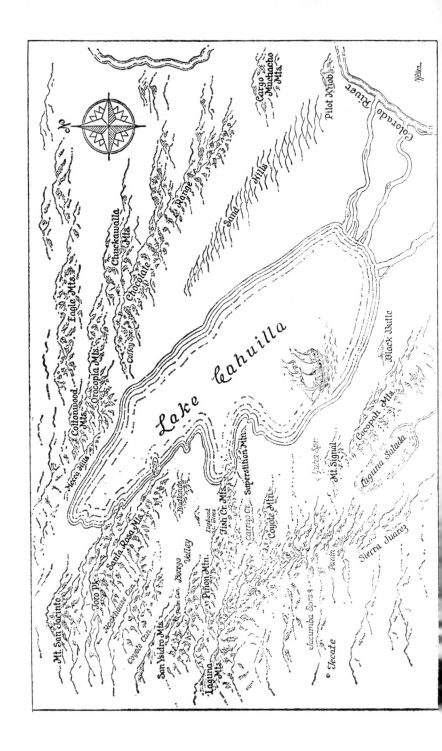

Then the ship turned back, but when it reached the channel through which it had entered the sea the way was blocked by debris which had been carried down from the mountains in a storm. Shoals barred the way in every direction. The captain and his men were trapped in a landlocked sea. Finally they had to abandon the ship, and their fate is unrecorded.

A sequel to this version of the pearl ship tale, is the story related 150 years later by a young muleteer who accompanied the expedition in which Captain Juan Bautista de Anza brought California's first white settlers overland from Tubac in Mexico to Monterey in 1775-76. A few days after the de Anza caravan crossed the Colorado River at Yuma the mule driver was sent to scout the desert for water. He came one evening to the decaying hulk of an ancient sailing vessel partly buried in the sand. The deck had rotted away and partly concealed in the sand which had drifted into the hold he saw what appeared to be iron-bound chests. When he climbed down and broke into one of them it was filled with pearls. He filled his pockets with them and said nothing to his companions in the expedition. Eventually when the de Anza colony reached a mission settlement near Los Angeles, he left his mule train, and induced some of the soldiers stationed at the mission to return with him to the desert to recover the pearls. They were never able to re-locate the ancient ship.

Obviously, this story is fiction. The inland sea could only have been a body of water in the great Cahuilla Basin, now known as the Imperial and Coachella Valleys and growing mil-

MAP ON OPPOSITE PAGE—*Indian legend goes back to the time when the basin now known as Imperial and Coachella valleys, in California, was filled with a great clear water lake—Lake Cahuilla —into which the Colorado River poured its flood waters at periodic intervals. An outflow channel probably carried excess waters south to the gulf when the lake reached a level high enough to overflow the silt dike on the south. The accompanying sketch by Norton Allen suggests the approximate shoreline of the ancient sea, with present day place names given for the surrounding mountain ranges.*

lions of dollars worth of farm and garden crops under irrigation annually. The Salton Sea occupies the lowest levels of this basin.

It is true this basin was once an inland sea. Its shoreline may be traced today by fossil deposits on the rocks, and by the recovered artifacts of Indian tribesmen who dwelt on its perimeter. But it was a clear water lake—the fossils confirm this—fed by the Colorado River and having no outlet to the Gulf of California. This lake is estimated to have evaporated between 600 and 700 years ago, long before Columbus discovered America. The Lost Pearl Ship was only a fable.

However, the drifting sand of the Cahuilla Basin is the burial place of an old boat. This is an historical fact revealed by the research of Arthur Woodward, former Curator of History in the Los Angeles County Museum. Woodward has verified that in the early 1860s, soon after Pauline Weaver had discovered placer gold along the Colorado River at La Paz in western Arizona, a 21-foot skiff, rigged with a mast, was built in Los Angeles for use on the Colorado at La Paz. The boat was put on wheels and was to be pulled to its destination by four-horse teams. Crossing the Colorado Desert in the heat of early summer, the teams gave out, and the men were forced to abandon the craft.

The accidental discovery of the decaying hulk of this boat partly buried in the sand, many years later, led to rumors that the legendary pearl ship from the Gulf of California had been found. There is also the story told by a Mexican from Tecate on the California-Mexico border that he had seen the dismantled skeleton of a large vessel in a canyon bordering the Cahuilla Basin.

But anyone familiar with the geological history of the lower Colorado River will know at once that the tale of a sea-going vessel stranded in the sands of this desert region could be accepted only as mythology.

My introduction to the fraternity of lost mine hunters came in 1911 when as a teen-age schoolboy I spent most of a summer earning vacation money as a fruit tramp in the Imperial Valley melon harvest. Toward the end of the season one of the older men in the packing house suggested that I join him on a trip to the nearby Chocolate Mountains to look for the lost Pegleg gold. He was a prospector who was working in the melons merely for a grubstake. He had a couple of burros in pasture, and proposed that we pool our earnings at the end of the harvest and head for "a place where the gold is lying on top of the ground." He had spent years looking for Pegleg's black nuggets, and was sure he had a clue which would solve the mystery. I had no doubt he would be an agreeable companion, but I had other plans and I passed up the opportunity.

I must confess that now, a half century later, I have become a skeptic insofar as lost mines are concerned. I have known many of the men who followed the trails in quest of phantom treasure, but not once in these fifty years have I been able to confirm an actual re-discovery of a missing ledge of gold or silver, or of any lost treasure. Periodically the newspapers have carried reports of the finding of a lost mine or cache of gold. Within the last month I have clipped from an Albuquerque newspaper the claim of a New Mexico man that he is positive he has found the Lost Adams Diggings. He has not brought out any of the gold yet, but he is sure it is there. I do not think the man is untruthful. I suspect he is a dreamer whose hope has become reality—in his own imagination.

While much of the hearsay of lost mine legendry must be regarded as pure myth, there is much in the vocation or avocation of treasure hunting in the open spaces of the wilderness country to be commended. Human beings need goals. They must have a faith to live by. The alternative is a cynicism that is devastating to the soul. And I can think of a thousand less worthy goals than tramping the hills in quest of the mythical pot of gold at the end of the rainbow. It is a healthful, invigorating pastime that builds physical stamina and self-reliance. These men are living close to the good earth, and I can think of nothing more important to our civilized world today than a formula which will somehow close the gap between close-to-the-earth living and the artificialities of the sophisticate life.

SCOTTY BUILDS A CASTLE   VI

Dᴜʀɪɴɢ the heyday of its operation in 1910 when the old National mine at Winnemucca, Nevada, was producing ore of fabulous assays, word spread through the saloons that Death Valley Scotty, the former mule-skinner from California who had become the mystery man of the western mining camps, had made a strike. It had been known for several weeks that he was out prospecting in Humboldt Canyon and the adjacent hills.

It was only natural then, when Scotty rode into town on his mule a few days later, with a flour sack of rock tied to his saddle, that loungers along the main street should gravitate toward the bar in front of which he was tying his animal.

"Whatta ya got in the bag?" one of them called out. "Let's take a look?"

Scotty ignored the questions. He was not talking, but he had an air of self-assurance that seemed to lend credence to the rumors of a new bonanza. That was Scotty's way—"keep 'em guessing."

The crowd followed him into the saloon, where he tossed the sack on the bar. "Order your drinks," he said to the men around him. "Jest take some of the rocks fer your pay," he addressed the bartender.

The drinks were served, and then the barkeeper slowly untied the string and looked in the sack. "Holy mackerel!" he exclaimed, and backed away, dropping the open end of the bag on the counter. Scotty grinned, then tied the string again without permitting anyone to get a glimpse of the contents.

The crowd grew bigger as Scotty made his way to the next saloon. The drinks were served again, and the barkeeper started to reach into the sack—then drew back as if in fright. "Jest keep your rocks," he muttered to Scotty.

The suspense increased as the man from Death Valley, with his following, continued along the street from bar to bar. Everywhere the act was much the same. The reaction of the bartenders ranged from surprise to horror—but not one of them took a rock from the sack.

When they had made the rounds Scotty tossed the bag on a table and slouched into a chair. One of the bystanders, emboldened by the liquor he had consumed, reached for the bag.

"Hands off!" warned Scotty. "I know you fellers is all itchin' to know what's in that ol' flour sack, an' I'm gonna show you." He untied the string and dumped the contents on the table. The pile consisted of several pieces of ordinary country rock and a coiled dead rattlesnake.

This story may be true—or it may be just another wisp in the halo of fiction that crowns the memory of one of the most colorful men in western mining camps during the hectic period around the turn of the century when the West was described as "wild and woolly."

Scotty lived in a world of fancy, and with the rare art of a natural showman, he created and cultivated the mythology that surrounded his strange career. The facts of his life, aside from the fabulous Castle in Death Valley which bears his name, are not well known. Scotty—his name was Walter Perry Scott—would never answer direct questions about the prosaic details of his roving career.

Two years before his death in 1954 I was sitting in the little bedroom just off the patio at the Castle, which was Scotty's place of retreat from the "emigrants"—as he termed them—who drove long distances to take the guided tours through the fabulous manor, and if possible to see the man whose name it bore. Scotty was in an amiable mood despite the fact that he was convalescing after a rather critical confinement in a Las Vegas, Nevada, hospital. He liked reporters, although he was never patronizing toward them. This was a good time, I thought, to clear up some questions regarding his early life.

According to hearsay, Scotty had come to Death Valley when he was a teen-age boy as a roustabout for a crew of surveyors. I wanted to learn about his youth, his experience as a swamper on one of the 20-mule team borax freight wagons, as a cowhand and later as a trick rider with Buffalo Bill Cody's Wild West Show. But I did not get far with my questions.

"We don't talk about them things," Scotty cut me short, and he said it in a way that closed the door to any further discussion of his personal life.

He liked to talk, but he wanted to choose his own subjects. One of his favorite topics was an episode which brought him nation-wide notoriety. This was the much-publicized trip from Los Angeles to Chicago in 1905 when he paid the Santa Fe

Railroad $5500 for a chartered train—the Coyote Special—to establish a new speed record between the two cities. The run was made in 44 hours and 54 minutes, with Scotty in the engineer's cab much of the time.

The source of the wealth which enabled him to shower lavish tips during his occasional visits to Los Angeles, and to finance the excursion to Chicago, was said to be a secret gold mine somewhere in the hills of Nevada or California. In the early days of his extravagant spending he sometimes referred not only to one but several rich caches hidden away somewhere on the desert. But the legend of his mysterious bonanza more often was cultivated by innuendo than by direct assertion. For instance, he liked to narrate experiences in foiling real or mythical sleuths who sought to learn the secret of his hidden caches by following him when he was out on the desert.

For 35 years he maintained the fiction that the gold which financed his widely-publicized extravagance came from a hole in the ground. But in 1941, when he had to go on the witness stand to defend himself against the claims of a former associate, he admitted that his sole source of wealth was the eccentric Albert M. Johnson who had made a fortune in insurance. Nevertheless, the legend of his inexhaustible ledge of gold persisted until the day of his death.

Scotty was a master showman, and that talent, plus the friendship—and the wealth—of Albert M. Johnson, were the factors which lifted a sun-bronzed desert rat to a lasting niche in the hall of famous western characters.

The partnership of Scotty and Johnson was a strange paradox. One was a cultured and highly successful business executive who was reported to have made $60 million in the insurance business. The other was an uncombed denizen of the land of sun, sand and sage who had never finished the eighth grade of school and who often spent his last dollar buying drinks for the boys in the bar rooms.

Scotty traveled widely in both the United States and Europe during his twelve years with the Wild West Show. He is said to have met Johnson in Chicago when he went there looking for a grubstake after he lost his job during an argument with Col. Bill Cody. Johnson was in ill health, and had been told by his doctor that his best tonic would be a few months in a dry, warm climate. He looked at the bronzed face and clear blue eyes of the visitor in the slouch hat, and began asking questions.

Before the interview was ended, Johnson handed Scotty a big roll of bills, and made a date to meet him some time later at a railroad stop in Nevada.

These men rode the desert together on mules or in a buckboard. Scotty was endowed with a natural sense of drama, and he proved an entertaining companion. Out of his varied experiences on the California and Nevada deserts as camp roustabout, mule-skinnner, 20-mule team swamper, cowboy, trick rider—and more recently as a prospector—he had a vast store of tales which he related in a jargon that was always amusing.

Johnson had made his stake—more than he would ever need for himself. Making money had ceased to be a challenge to him. His need now was for health, and for the attainment of such intangible goals as an imaginative man dreams for himself. He was a generous man, with a deep sense of religious obligation. His philanthropies were many. Once he had been told about a small destitute tribe of Indians—the Seris—whose home was the Island of Tiburon in the Gulf of California and on the Mexican mainland shore nearby, and he had outfitted Clifford L. Burdick to go down there, live with the tribesmen for a few weeks, and report to him what might be done to improve their living conditions.

The change from the plush environment of a luxurious office and home in Chicago to a life of rigorous activity in a land of pure air and distant horizons proved good tonic for Albert Johnson. More than that, he had found the companionship of a man whose utter disregard for the niceties of a pampering civilization was in stark contrast to the make-believe of the sophistic society in which he had always lived. He liked it. These men were opposites in almost every respect except in their mutual quest for freedom of the human spirit. They camped together along the desert trails for days at a time, and eventually Scotty brought Johnson to the little one-room shack in Grapevine Canyon, which he regarded as his home base. There was a good spring of water, and three miles downstream—it was a dry creek most of the time—the canyon opened up and revealed the vast panorama of salt-encrusted Death Valley.

Perhaps the palatial home later erected at this place was Scotty's idea, possibly it was Johnson's. Neither of the partners would ever give a direct answer to this question. It is enough to say they planned and built it together, with Scotty's name and Johnson's money.

The story of the Castle's construction was told to me by Matt Roy Thompson, the construction engineer in charge. For six years, from 1925 to 1931, Thompson lived at the site and directed the work in accordance with the instructions of the owners.

While the building of the Castle was started in 1925, the story of its architectural design and the selection of Thompson as the builder goes back much earlier than that. It began on the campus of Stanford University in the 1890s.

Thompson was one of the first students to register at Stanford when it opened its doors as an institution of higher learning in 1891. Having had a year's engineering study at Rose Polytechnic in Terre Haute, Indiana, he entered Stanford as a sophomore at the age of 17.

In the social life of the school he met a pretty blonde freshman, Bessie Morris Penniman. "Bessie and I attended the first football game between Stanford and the University of California, at Haight Street Park in San Francisco," he recalls. "Stanford, playing under the management of an under-graduate student named Herbert Hoover, won the game 10 to 7."

In the financial panic of 1893 Matt's father, in the real estate business in Tacoma, Washington, met with financial reverses and young Thompson had to leave school. A year later Bessie Penniman transferred to Cornell. At first they corresponded regularly. Then she met a rich young engineering student named Albert M. Johnson, and letters became less frequent. A year later, Thompson and his bride, Patience O'Hara Thompson, received the announcement of Bessie's marriage to Johnson.

During the following thirty years Matt Roy kept contact with the Johnsons and saw them occasionally. In the meantime Thompson had made notable advances in his own career as a construction engineer. He was a member of the Interstate Commerce Commission's board of appraisal, with an office in Washington, D. C. in 1925 when, unexpectedly, he received a telegram from Albert Johnson in Chicago, asking him to take charge of a building project in Death Valley, California.

"At that time Johnson was reputedly a very wealthy man," Thompson related. "He was the principal stockholder in the National Life Insurance Company. His back had been broken in a railroad accident in which his father had been killed some years previously. The permanent effects of this injury plus the pressure of operating a big business had affected his health and his doctor advised him to go West for recuperation." Matt Roy continued:

"It was about this time that he met Walter Scott who, following a dispute with Col. William Cody that cost him his job, was in Chicago looking for someone who would grubstake his search for a rich gold deposit somewhere in the desert. Johnson took a liking to Scott, and arranged to meet him in Nevada a few days later.

"Just when the idea of a palatial home on the desert was born I do not know, but when I arrived in Death Valley with the Johnsons some improvements already had been made on the Grapevine Canyon site. These consisted of a large two-story box-like building about 50 x 150 feet which was used as a hide-away camp and storage house for Johnson and Scotty. Also, there was

Scotty's Castle, in the northern end of the Death Valley National Monument, may be reached by paved road either from

an L-shaped garage about 250 feet long near the other building.

"I was assigned office space and comfortable living quarters in the front end of the garage, and with the exception of a few weeks' vacation each summer, I lived there alone for six years."

Stories have been current that Johnson originally had plans drawn for his desert retreat by Frank Lloyd Wright, the noted architect, but Thompson stated that he never saw such plans nor were they ever mentioned.

Actually, the architectural motif of the Castle was suggested by the buildings on the campus at Stanford. Matt Roy Thompson recalled the words of President David Starr Jordan on the occasion of his inaugural address at Stanford October 1, 1891: "These long corridors with their stately arches . . . will occupy a warm place in every student's heart . . . never to be rubbed out in the wear of life."

It was a prophecy which had made a deep impression on the new sophomore at Stanford. Matt Roy could envision the ugly box-like structure in Grapevine Canyon completely transformed by the addition of a series of Stanfordesque arches and crowned with red tile as at the Palo Alto school.

"I made a pencil sketch showing the lines of the transformed mansion as I proposed to build it," recalls Thompson. "Johnson protested, saying that he preferred straight lines and rectangular type of architecture because it symbolized that everything he did was on the square. But Bessie had a warm place in her heart for Stanford and liked my sketches. In the end she had her way, and with some compromises, the structure was planned as it appears today.

"We undermined the old building with a full concrete-lined basement from which tunnels radiated to the other structures in the group. The walls were trebled in thickness by adding a hollow-tile veneer and insulating them against desert heat by filling them with insulex, a powder which with the addition of water expanded to 12 times the original volume. It dries into a porous stone-like substance.

"Water was piped from the springs a mile up the canyon—enough to supply the domestic needs of 1000 persons, provide hydro-electric power, and fill the planned swimming pool. An immense solar heater was designed and built to supply hot water for the half dozen kitchens and the dozen gorgeously-tiled bathrooms.

"The ties of the abandoned Tonopah & Tidewater railroad track, from Beatty to Tonopah, Nevada, were purchased—120,000 of them. They were bought for $1500 and it cost $25,000 to gather them up and haul them to our building site over almost impassable roads and stack them in a little tributary gorge known as Tie Canyon. It was estimated they would provide fuel for the 18 fireplaces in the Castle for 150 years. Long tiers of them remain today where they were stacked 33 years ago.

"A huge pipe organ was installed, with the largest set of chimes west of Chicago at that time. According to Scotty, the cost of the organ was $160,000 and he paid cash for it with $1000 and $500 bills. No expense was spared either in the construction of the Castle or in its furnishings. Johnson said he wanted a home that would last a hundred years.

"Costs were high due to the remoteness of the site. Probably no one will ever know the amount of the total investment, but it was in excess of a million dollars, and may have added up to double that estimate."

Workers on the project were recruited from two sources: the Shoshone Indian camps in Death Valley, and the employment offices in Los Angeles. The Shoshones did much of the manual labor and as many as 70 of them were employed at one time. In Los Angeles they found the Austrian wood-carvers who did the beautiful and intricate designs on the overhead beams and interior woodwork. The detail sketches for the beams were created by Martin Devy de Dubovey, a Los Angeles architect. The actual carving was done at the Castle under the supervision of H. Brewster Brown, of Inglewood, California. Dewey R. Kruckeberg of Glendale, California, was brought in to landscape the grounds.

Albert Johnson was essentially a business man, and neither he nor Scotty contributed much to the creative detail of the Castle's construction. However, Bessie Johnson took a keen interest in the structural artistry that went into the Castle, and she shares with Matt Roy Thompson the credit for the beauty of the Castle, both as to general design and interior decoration and furnishings.

Some of the furnishings were purchased personally by the Johnsons on trips abroad. C. Alexander McNeilledge also contributed to the interior planning, making several trips to Europe to select rare furnishings. He also acted as purchasing agent until he and Johnson had a serious disagreement.

As the Castle was nearing completion in 1931 the owners found themselves in a critical dilemma. They had been negligent in confirming title to the land, and had built on real estate they did not own. This information came to light in Washington when the establishing of a National Monument in Death Valley was under consideration.

In 1930 Herbert Hoover had withdrawn nearly two million acres in the Death Valley region from public entry, preparatory to the issuing of a presidential decree creating the Monument. The Castle site was just within the northern boundary of this withdrawn area.

It would be a simple matter to delete the Castle site from the proposed Monument, but this would restore the land to the public domain and any war veteran with a preference right to public land could have filed claim to it.

Johnson rushed to Washington to see what could be done about it. Horace M. Albright, then director of the National Park Service, solved the problem. Albright had spent much of his life on the California desert, and he knew the Death Valley region intimately. He told Johnson to have the Castle site surveyed, and promised to ask Congress for legislation enabling the owners of the Castle to buy the land on which it was located. Albright made good his promise, although further difficulties were encountered.

Congress passed the bill in 1933, but President Franklin D. Roosevelt vetoed it on the recommendation of Secretary of Interior Harold Ickes. Ickes felt that the measure as proposed did not give adequate protection to the Monument. Another bill was passed and signed, providing that if Johnson and Scotty offered the Castle for sale the Federal government would have first option to purchase it. The bill also contained stipulations which would forever bar it from degenerating into a honky-tonk retreat.

One of the many details assigned to Thompson was the casting of reinforced concrete posts to enclose with wire fence the 1270 acres which Johnson and Scotty acquired under federal patent. Die imprinted on each post were two circles, one containing the letter S and the other with the letter J. Johnson, who thought nothing of handing Scotty a huge roll of paper money with which to go to Los Angeles and toss out extravagant tips which would gain headlines in the newspapers, complained to the construction engineer that Scotty's initial had been placed above his own on too many of the posts. If it was a 50-50 partnership, perhaps Johnson had a just complaint, for visitors to the Castle today will note that Scotty's Circle-S appears above his partner's on nearly all the posts visible from the paved road up Grapevine Canyon.

Until the Tonopah & Tidewater Railroad discontinued its service, materials for the Castle were shipped over this line to the Bonnie Clare mine, near the head of Grapevine Canyon. The Bonnie Clare at that time was a boom gold camp with a post-office and store. Later materials were trucked in from Beatty and Las Vegas, Nevada, from Los Angeles and other points.

Until the insurance company met with financial troubles in 1933, the Johnsons spent much of their time in Chicago, making only occasional trips to Death Valley. Thompson was in complete charge in their absence. However, all plans were submitted to Albert and Bessie, either by mail or in person.

At the beginning of the project Johnson arranged for Scotty to counter-sign the checks issued for labor and materials. But after three months Scotty threw up his hands. He did not want to be bothered with clerical work. After that, checks were honored on Thompson's signature only.

Scotty always referred to the new mansion as "the Castle," and this name gradually was adopted. During the construction days an ever-increasing number of visitors swarmed over the place. As the building was not yet occupied as a home, Johnson gave instructions that visitors were to be treated hospitably. Matt Thompson estimates that more than 5000 of them were "fed and bedded down" as Scotty expressed it, during the construction period. In some instances their cars were repaired and they were given gas without charge.

"When the Castle was nearing completion," continued Thompson, and the owners were ready to move in and enjoy the seclusion for which a fortune had been invested, the visitors kept coming. Finally a sign was posted at the entrance gate: "THE CASTLE IS CLOSED. POSITIVELY NO ADMITTANCE."

"The white sign soon resembled a bulletin board, covered with hundreds of protesting epithets penciled by tourists who in many instances had traveled long distances to see the Castle. These protests eventually became so vociferous that the Castle was thrown open for guided tours at $1.00 a person."

Today the guided tours are still available at the same rate, and during the winter tourist season in Death Valley thousands of motorists follow the lonely macadam road to Grapevine Canyon to see for themselves, and wonder what strange quirk of human nature would prompt sane men to invest in such luxury and beauty in this far-off corner of the Great American Desert.

When work on the Castle was stopped, in the fall of 1931, there were several unfinished details, including an 85 x 185 foot swimming pool in front of the main building. The concrete walls of the pool were poured, and the beautifully glazed tile for finishing it had been trucked in and stored in the maze of tunnels when the work was discontinued. The tile remain there in storage today.

Johnson intended to complete the construction some day when the nation's economy had become more stable. In 1947 he wrote to Thompson, asking if he could resume the work. The letter was forwarded to Matt Roy on Okinawa Island, where he was associated with the construction of a military installation. When he returned to the States, Thompson discussed the resumption of work with Johnson, who was then confined to his Hollywood home with illness. He passed away in January 1948, without having recovered sufficiently to get the work started.

Bessie had met with a tragic death in 1941, when the car in which the Johnsons were riding skidded and overturned on the Death Valley road near Panamint Springs. Johnson suffered only minor injuries. They had no children.

Following his death in 1948 it was disclosed that Johnson had bequeathed the Castle and other holdings to a non-profit organization, the Gospel Foundation of California. The will provided that Walter Scott was to be provided with a home there as long as he lived, and that all the profits from tourist admissions to the Castle were to be used for charitable purposes. The Foundation is administered by Mary Liddecoat, president. Miss Liddecoat previously had devoted her time to social work in association with her father, Tom Liddecoat, who founded and for many years conducted the Midnight Mission in Los Angeles. Walter Webb, associated with Albert Johnson corporations for forty years, is the manager of the Foundation properties, including the Castle.

A beautiful room in the Castle had been provided for Scotty, but it is said he never slept in it. When the "damned emigrants" who came to Grapevine Canyon became more and more numerous, Scotty moved to a little cabin over the hill, a mile and a half away, where he and his dog "Windy" could have the seclusion they preferred. In 1951 a crippled foot made it necessary for him to go to Las Vegas for hospitalization. After leaving the hospital he returned to the Castle, where he occupied a back room facing the patio, and only on rare occasions would he appear to satisfy the curiosity of tourists who always wanted to see the character for whom the Castle was named.

Late in 1953 it was necessary again for Scotty to go to the Las Vegas hospital, and there his colorful career ended, January 6, 1954.

In accordance with a request expressed before his death, Scotty was buried on the top of a little hill overlooking the Castle. The directors of the Gospel Foundation, who had now taken over the operation of the palatial home, in cooperation with the Death Valley '49ers, another non-profit California corporation, erected a cairn of native stone beside the grave. Here, November 12, 1954, a memorial service was held, at which State Senator Charles Brown of Shoshone, California, paid a final tribute to his old friend and neighbor. John Hilton, artist and musician, strummed his guitar and sang *The Last Bonanza*, his own composition which was one of Scotty's favorites.

On the cairn was mounted a bronze plaque crowned with a sculptured portrait of Scotty, the work of Cyria Allen Henderson, noted western sculptress. Beneath the bronze face of one of the desert's most colorful characters was an inscription taken from Eleanor Jordan Houston's book *Death Valley Scotty Told Me*, a quotation embodying much of Walter Scott's philosophy, as he had said it:

> "I got four things to live by: Don't say nothing that will hurt anybody. Don't give advice, nobody will take it anyway. Don't complain. Don't explain."

A few days after the news came over the wires that Death Valley Scotty was dead, an editorial writer on the staff of the *San Francisco Chronicle* wrote this eulogy:

"Somewhere out in the wastelands of Death Valley, according to legend, Scotty had struck gold—a fabulous bottomless mine of it—enough to do all those foolish things that a thousand other grizzled prospectors had dreamed of doing, if they ever struck it rich.

"Scotty tipped bellboys with halves of $50 bills—then bought back the halves with $20 gold pieces. He hired a train to carry him to Chicago, and sitting in the cab exhorted the engineer to such headlong speed that he set a record which stood for a quarter of a century. He built a storybook castle in the midst of the desert and sallied forth from his stronghold like some grizzled knight to perform lavish feats that awed the whole nation.

"We have always been a little sorry that the humdrum world of fact finally encroached upon Scotty's incomparably more interesting world of fancy—that the 'gold mine' turned out to be a Chicago financier, indulging in a fancy for the bizarre ...

"On the other hand we are immensely grateful to Scotty for his long and faithful stewardship of the legend. He wrote a warm and amiable chapter in the story of the West, and more than that, he brought sparkle and romance into a world which has a surfeit of reality. Some say he was a fraud; we disagree. He was a purveyor of wonderful nonsense, whose medium was not the pen or a brush, but life itself."

ADVENTURE IN CRATER ELEGANTE   VII

O N A January day in 1910, Carl Lumholtz, explorer and writer employed to make an economic survey of the region around the headwaters of the Gulf of California in the State of Sonora, Mexico, stood on the rim of a great crater which he had spotted previously from a nearby peak. He was so impressed with the beauty of this volcanic cavity he gave it the name Crater Elegante.

In his book about this region, *New Trails in Mexico*, published in 1912 by Charles Scribner's Sons and now out of print, Lumholtz wrote: "I do not know how deep it is, for I had no opportunity to make the descent, which is said to be feasible though difficult, and it looks difficult too, for the walls have crumbled less than in the other craters I saw later in the vicinity."

Forty-one years later I learned the answer to the question in Lumholtz' mind—the depth of the crater. I stood on the rim where my altimeter showed an elevation of 975 feet. Four hours later, after a hand and toe descent of the precipitous wall that led to the floor of the mammoth cavity, the instrument registered 365 feet. The depth was 610 feet.

Measuring the depth of the ancient volcanic landmark was a challenging adventure, but it was by no means the principal lure which took me to this remote corner of northwestern Sonora. From Lumholtz' book, and from a previous volume, *Campfires on Desert and Lava*, written by W. T. Hornaday in 1908, I learned that the arid region of dune and lava immediately south of the Arizona-Sonora boundary, and eastward from the delta of the Colorado River, was an expansive museum of interest not only to the student of natural history but of anthropology as well. For here, in the period immediately preceding the migration of Americans to the western territory acquired in the Louisiana Purchase, tribesmen of the Papago nation had sought refuge from the scourge of raiding Apaches. Eventually, American troops had brought the Apaches under control. Then the Papagos gradually had returned to the more fruitful lands of southern Arizona. But they left behind in many places the artifacts and shrines of their occupancy, and because of the inhospitable character of this land, these remain virtually intact today.

Elegante Crater merely is one of many natural landmarks in this vast area which is known as the Pinacate region. It was named for its principle range of mountains, the Sierra Pinacate. This name is the Mexican word for a black beetle often seen in the United States and commonly called a tumble bug. When disturbed it sticks its head in the ground and rears its hind end like a clown standing on his head. No doubt it was the coloring of the lava-strewn landscape which gave rise to the naming of this mountain range, rather than the presence of an excessive number of beetles. For this region at some prehistoric time was a spouting inferno of volcanic action. The Papago Indians call it Tjuktoak, meaning black mountain.

Lumholtz and his party explored the area with wagon and saddle horses. Three companions and I went there in two jeeps. Other members of our party were Wilson McKenney, editor of the *California Teachers' Association Journal;* Arles Adams, the best jeep wrangler I have known and my pal on many previous desert trips, and William (Bill) Sherrill of the U. S. Immigration Border Patrol.

Leaving California we crossed the Colorado River at Yuma, Arizona, and then left U. S. Highway 80 to follow the old *Camino del Diablo*—The Devil's Highway—which parallels the Mexican border on the Arizona side. It is a highway in name only. Its sandy ruts winding across a desert of fierce desolation were first traveled by prospectors from Mexico attracted by the California gold rush of 1849.

Our route took us past the old Fortuna mine, once a rich gold producer. But the ore had pinched out, then the caretaker departed, the machinery and buildings were sold or pilfered, and today the site is marked only by rotting and rusting debris.

We crossed the Gila River through Surveyor's Pass and came to the first of the scant waterholes along the *Camino—Tinajas Altas,* or High Tanks. Here a series of erosion cavities stepped one above the other in a precipitous granite trough caught and held storm water even through long periods of drouth. The lowest tank, the only one accessible to livestock, was generally dry. The slick-rock ascent to the upper tanks was so difficult that weary travelers coming in over the sun-scorched trail sometimes died of thirst because they had not the strength to climb to the upper tanks. When I first visited the Tinajas many years ago there was a little cemetery of unmarked grave mounds which seemed to confirm the tragic reports. In 1950, when the foot and mouth disease was epidemic in Mexico and a daily border patrol was maintained to enforce a quarantine against Mexican livestock crossing the border, a sheet-iron shack was erected for patrolmen, and the cemetery disappeared beneath the blades of grading machines. Nothing is sacred to a bulldozer.

Seven miles along the trail east of Tinajas Altas is a gigantic ironwood tree, a landmark conspicuous for miles across the desert plain. I had once photographed the tree for comparison with a picture Lumholtz had taken many years previously. It had changed but little, for the ironwood is the aged patriarch of the desert tree family. *Olneya tesota,* or *palo fierro* as the Mexicans call it, is the most useful of the seven species of trees native to this desert region according to Lumholtz. He wrote: "Although there was considerable galleta grass growing here and there, all the mules, donkeys and horses gathered around a lone but very large *palo fierro* to eat its bark and green juicy leaves, which they preferred . . . Usually some of its branches are dry, and they furnish the very best campfire, especially for cooking purposes."

Lechuguilla desert, through which we were now passing, was named by the Mexicans for an edible lettuce-like plant which grows here. This is the desert famed for the stone that floats and the wood that sinks. For ironwood has a higher specific gravity than water, and the pumice stone which we would encounter in the volcanic formations a little further along the trail will float.

Three miles beyond the giant ironwood we came to a circle of rocks by the roadside, perhaps 25 feet in diameter. According to the late Tom Childs, who spent a long lifetime in this part of the desert, the circle marks one of the tragedies of the Devil's Highway. Nearly 100 years ago, on the spot, Papago Indians killed a party of Mexican prospectors enroute to the California gold fields. Some of the Indians told Tom about it several years later. They said they killed for loot.

Tragedy was commonplace along the *Camino del Diablo*. We passed many unidentified mounds of rocks, marking the graves of travelers, some of whom had been killed by the Indians, but more often they were victims of dehydrating heat, bottomless sand and lack of water. Waterholes are far apart in this region.

We camped overnight at Tule well. This is in a game refuge and we were awakened at daybreak by the calls of quail in the thickets surrounding our bedrolls.

Fifteen miles beyond Tule well we came to the first tongue of the great lava field which covers the area south of the border here. Thirty or forty miles to the south we could see clearly the dark massif of the Pinacate Range, in the heart of the volcanic area. Godfrey Sykes, a scientist formerly with the Carnegie Desert Laboratory at Tucson, Arizona, estimated there were 500 extinct craters within a radius of 50 miles of Pinacate Mountain. Lava flows extend over the landscape in all directions, making much of the area impenetrable except on foot or with burros. While the principal eruptions probably were at Pinacate and Carnegie peaks which are the high points in the range, so great was the gas pressure beneath the surface that smaller vents opened up all over the region, many of them being of the type known as blow-outs from which no liquid rock flowed.

Late in the afternoon we arrived at Quitovaquita, an old waterhole camp, the name of which is the Mexican translation of an Indian word meaning "little springs." Here an American patrolman and his wife were living in a tenthouse surrounded by cottonwood and mesquite trees. The Sonoyta River channel is on the Mexican side of the border at this point and while the river often is dry, there is a good underground water table. Here we were in the Organ Pipe National Monument, the monument having been established for the preservation of a fine stand of a picturesque tubular species of cactus, the American habitat of which is limited to southern Arizona. The remaining 15 miles of the road to the port of entry at Sonoyta was a well-graded boulevard compared with the ancient wagon trail we had been following.

Carrying border permits issued by the Mexican immigration service at Mexicali, we were given a speedy clearance by the officers at the international gate and our dusty jeeps passed through the village and headed for the Pinacate Range. The or-

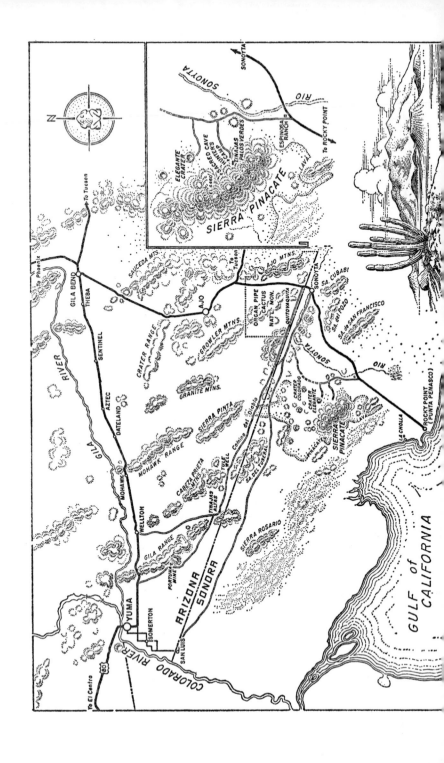

iginal Sonoyta—old town—is three miles from the border and we
stopped at the office of Alfredo Barillo, chief of police and wildlife commissioner, and were given detailed directions for reaching
Crater Elegante. He told us there were an estimated 500 bighorn
sheep in the Pinacate area. We assured him we carried no fire-
arms, and our quest was for information and adventure, not for
trophies.

On the next 33 miles we enjoyed the luxury of paved highway.
Four years previously the State of Arizona and the Sonora highway department had cooperated in the construction of a macadam
road from U. S. Highway 80 at Gila Bend, through Sonoyta to
Punta Penasco on the Gulf of California. This immediately became a popular route for American sportsmen, for the Gulf is
happy fishing water for deep sea anglers.

Some miles down the road we crossed the Sonoyta River,
which according to all maps, empties into the Gulf. The maps
are incorrect—because the cartographers who make them cannot
conceive of a river which has no outlet. They do not know about
a desert land where sizable rivers evaporate into thin air, or disappear in the sand. The Mojave River in California is like that,
and so is the Sonoyta. Its terminus is a normally dry playa out
somewhere among the dunes which extend along the eastern
shore of the Gulf. In flood time, the Sonoyta flows quite a stream,
but it never reaches the Sea of Cortez—as the Gulf of California
was known in the days when Spanish padres first charted this
region.

We left the highway at the *rancherita* where Rudolfo Espinosa irrigates a few acres and gives friendly information to all who
inquire. A former Californian, he speaks excellent English. He said
there were many tracks made by woodcutters in the area where

MAP ON OPPOSITE PAGE—*The Pinacate region in Sonora, Mexico,
south of the Arizona border, is a wild lava-strewn desert accessible
only to sturdy cars. A paved road extends from Sonoyta on the
border to the fishing village of Punta Penasco. Elegante Crater is
the largest of several extinct craters which dot the area.*

we were going, and drew a sketch in the sand to guide us to Elegante. There were no well-defined roads through the black lava beds ahead, just tracks, and so many of these it was quite confusing. When darkness came we unrolled our sleeping bags in a sandy arroyo. It was a warm desert night, with neither cloud nor haze to dim the sparkle of a billion stars overhead.

Sr. Espinosa had told us the rim of the crater would appear as a low mesa or plateau in the distance. At daybreak McKenney was up and scanning the horizon for that low mesa. With hills on the skyline all around us, and little buttes sticking their black heads above the plain in every direction, we were uncertain. As we continued along the trail we stopped frequently to climb a hillock for observation. Finally we headed for what appeared to be a low plateau and when we came to its base the jeeps were blocked by a deep arroyo, with vertical banks.

We climbed the slope, perhaps to an elevation of a hundred feet above where the jeeps were parked. And when we reached the summit, there in front and below us spread the panorama of a vast pit that could be none other than Crater Elegante.

From the rim there was a gentle slope downward from 100 to 150 feet to the ledge of a ragged escarpment, and at the base of this 50-foot precipice was a long talus slope which ended in the white sand of the dry basin in the bottom of the great cavity. We had brought climbing ropes, and it would have been easy to rappel down the face of the escarpment. But how would we return to the top again? Obviously the route into the crater at this point, without pitons and the skills of the expert mountain climber, was not feasible. We searched the rim in both directions, hoping to find a crevice or chimney that would provide a feasible route for return to the top.

We were exploring the south rim. A mile across the chasm on the northwest side appeared to be a streak of deep red talus which extended from the floor to within a few feet of the top of the escarpment. We followed a dim trail around the rim to the opposite side of the chasm, perhaps a mile and a half. From there it was easy to descend the slope to the top of the escarpment. We came to a rock ledge and made a traverse along the top of the cliff to our landmark, the red talus.

There we found the route to the bottom. The talus was of pea gravel, and at every step we started a rock slide. Most of the way we slid with the loose gravel. It was easy going downhill. We knew the return in that kind of rock would be tough, but it could be done.

Wilson McKenney was leading. I have been on many exploring trips with Wilson. When the going gets rough he is always out ahead, breaking trail. Arles Adams had been given explicit instructions by his doctor not to do any mountain climbing on this trip. He remained at the top, and it was a fortunate circumstance for the rest of us that he did not make the descent.

We reached the bottom at one p.m. We had been away from our cars four hours and our canteens were empty. It was hot down there. The weather gods had gotten their dates mixed. They were giving us August temperatures in October. This crater had been dead so many years I am sure none of the heat was radiating from beneath the surface. It came direct from the sun overhead and the reflected rays from the rocky walls which surrounded us.

The two things we wanted most were water and shade. There were a few scrubby palo verde trees, but the palo verde is poor shade, even at best. Finally we located a cluster of three saguaro cacti growing through the branches of a tree—and the four of them gave us some relief from the sun. My thermometer registered 110 degrees in the shade. I put it out in the sun and it went up to 132 degrees.

The prospect of making our way up the steep sliding talus pitch in 132-degree temperature was not a cheerful thought. Then McKenney opened his knapsack and took out three apples. Apples never have tasted so delicious. I sliced mine thin and kept a piece in my mouth as long as it lasted.

We found no evidence of previous descents into the crater, although I am sure we were not the first to scale the walls of this monstrous pit. Lumholtz suggested that the Indians may have hunted bighorn down there. We erected a little cairn of loose rocks at the base of a healthy senita cactus and left a record of our visit in a plastic container.

Elegante differs from many of the other craters in the Pinacate region in that it shows no evidence of volcanic action. There was no lava around its rim, and no cinders in the sidewalls or on the floor. Geologists with whom I have discussed these phenomena have suggested that the crater may have been caused by a great subterranean gas explosion—a blow-out rather than a vent for the escape of molten rock. If this is true it must have been an explosion of nuclear proportions.

The fires which once turned the Pinacate area into a volcanic inferno have long since burned out. The reports of Lumholtz, W. T. Hornaday, Godfrey Sykes and others who explored the Pinacate lava a half century ago estimate that no action has taken place there in thousands of years.

I counted more than 100 mature saguaros in the bottom of the crater. Many other well-known members of the Sonoran plant family were there—ironwood, palo verde, creosote, jumping cholla, tree cholla, encelia and senita cactus.

In mid-afternoon McKenney announced that he was heading for the top. "I would rather be on my way," he said, "than stay down here and become a dried-out mummy." Sherrill and I decided to wait until the sun had dropped below the rim. Sherrill was suffering from nausea, one of the symptoms of excessive dehydration. I was revolving pebbles in my mouth to stimulate the flow of saliva.

One of the popular yarns in desert mythology relates to the thirst-quenching virtue of the juice of the bisnaga cactus. But bisnaga offered no relief from the dilemma in which Bill Sherrill and I found ourselves. There were none in the crater. I knew the bitter sticky sap of the saguaro would not solve our problem, and I turned to the senita—the "old man" cactus of the Sonora desert which was plentiful on the floor of the crater. It was like green cucumber. It soothed our parched lips, but our palates rebelled against its vile tasting pulp.

As soon as the sun dipped below the rim Bill and I began our ascent. We found a slope of talus which offered better footing than the place of our descent. In our state of dehydration it was slow going. It took us almost to the top of the escarpment and there, just before dark, Arles Adams was waitiing for us with a rope, a flashlight and two canteens of water.

I had learned that the descent into Elegante, and the return, involved no great climbing difficulties—but I do not recommend it in 132-degree weather.

That night we camped beside an old Indian waterhole at the base of Pinacate Mountain. The pool near which we cooked our meal was one of a series of natural tanks known to the Papagos as "little pools." We slept on top of our sleeping bags, for the temperature was still over 100 degrees.

Having explored Elegante crater, our next goal was to find the Sacred Cave of the Papagos, a cavern which according to legend was the dwelling place of the god Iitio. The tribesmen believed that the cave extended along an underground passage to an island in the Gulf of California, where the wife of the god lived. The Lumholtz party had been guided to the cave-shrine by Quelele, an aged Papago. Since these tribesmen had migrated to more fertile lands to the north following the capture of Geronimo and the dispersal of his Apache warriors, Quelele had not visited the cavern for many years, but the preparations he made for the return indicated it was still regarded as a sacred shrine.

The sacrificial offerings which the old Indian had brought along to be deposited in the cave included an arrow, as a mark of respect and for the use of the god; a prayer stick colored by red pigment with a small eagle plume tied at the top; a bunch of yucca fibre tied in a knot, and a blue glass bead necklace. As the gifts were being deposited in niches among the rocks inside the cavern, the old Indian faced the west, blew smoke in the same direction and chanted a prayer in his native tongue.

Since we had only a general idea as to the location of the sacred cave, members of our party separated next morning, each of us going in a different direction. It was another hot day, and toward noon, with our canteens empty, Arles, Bill and I returned to camp. Two hours later Wilson McKenney arrived with a painted prayer stick in his hand. Following an old Indian trail up the lava slope toward Carnegie peak, he had spotted the entrance to the cave. He reported that it extended under the lava flow nearly 200 feet, and that there were many prayer sticks and other sacrificial objects scattered on its floor and among the rocks.

As soon as Wilson returned we packed our jeeps and headed back to the paved road which would lead us to Rocky Point, or Punta Penasco as it is known to the Mexicans, thirty miles away. We would have no time for fishing, but a dip in the surf would be refreshing after four days in that land of black lava and burning sun.

The once primitive coastal village of Punta Penasco has become a boom town—Mexican style—following the completion of the paved highway to the Gulf at this point. Modern hotels and motor courts were being built, and charter boats made available for visiting fishermen. Mexican towns generally are well policed, and Rocky Point was no exception. The chief of police not only kept the town in order, but he was serving as a sort of chamber of commerce and information bureau.

The busiest place in the settlement was the shipyard. I counted 36 boats under construction for commercial shrimp fishing and charter excursions. The keel and the framework of the boats were being hand-hewed out of mesquite wood. Labor was cheap here, and the mesquite trees which grew along the Sonoyta River lent themselves admirably to the timber work in boats.

Because of the fine fishing in Gulf waters, Punta Penasco probably will become a sophisticated seashore resort in the years ahead, but I am sure the traffic out across the grim scorching lava beds toward Crater Elegante will never become congested. That is a region only for hardy adventure and scientific research.

SAGA OF A NOMAD ARTIST · VIII

Say that I was starved; that I was lost and weary;
That I was burned and blinded by the desert sun;
Footsore, thirsty, sick with strange diseases;
Lonely and wet and cold—but that I kept my dream.
            From EVERETT RUESS' *Wilderness Song.*

IT WAS in fulfillment of his dream that twenty-two-year-old
Everett Ruess, vagabond artist of the desert trails, left the little
Mormon town of Escalante in southern Utah with his two burros
November 12, 1934. He had written his parents the previous day:
"Tomorrow I take the trail again, to the canyons to the south."

That was the last message Christopher and Stella Ruess in Los Angeles ever received from their son. Nor do the members of the family and friends know to this day what may have been the fate of this gifted lad who turned his back on the city to follow lonely trails in one of the most desolate regions of the United States.

Everett had written: "I may not have a postoffice for a couple of months. I am taking an ample supply of food with me." The parents were not apprehensive, for this was the kind of life their youngest son had been living for nearly four years, since he was graduated from high school. Artist, poet, music-lover and dreamer, he found his greatest happiness in the solitude of remote mountains and desert.

To his brother Waldo, he also had written from Escalante: "As to when I shall revisit civilization, it will not be soon, I think. I am not tired of the wilderness, rather I enjoy its beauty and the vagrant life I lead more keenly all the time. I prefer the saddle to the street car, and the star-sprinkled sky to the roof, the obscure and difficult trail leading into the unknown to a paved highway, and the deep peace of the wild to the discontent bred in cities. Do you blame me then for staying here where I feel I belong and am one with the great world about me? It is true I miss intelligent companionship, but there are so few with whom I can share the things that mean much to me that I have learned to contain myself. It is enough that I am surrounded with beauty and carry it with me in things that are a constant delight, like the gorgeous Navajo saddle blankets and the silver bracelet on my wrist, where three turquoises gleam in the firelight."

Everett had left home April 12 on his fifth and last trek into the lonely places. Waldo drove him with his camp outfit and artist's supplies to Kayenta, Arizona, where he was to take off. At Kayenta he obtained two burros, Cockleburs to ride and Leopold to carry the pack. Then he gypsied leisurely across the Navajo reservation to Chinle and Canyon de Chelly, and thence into the timbered Lukachukai Mountains.

Returning to Kayenta in May he trekked past the towering landmark known as Agathla Peak through Monument Valley to Navajo Mountain, which is one of the sacred places of the desert tribesmen. After camping a few days at War God Springs he turned back to Kayenta and continued through the Hopi pueblos to Gallup, New Mexico. Returning to the Hopi Mesas he lost his pack burro Leopold in the canyon of the Little Colorado, but obtained another donkey, Chocolatero, from the Indians, and trekked westward toward Grand Canyon, by way of Flagstaff.

He crossed the Colorado River by way of Bright Angel and Kaibab trails and visited Zion and Bryce National Parks before reaching Escalante, where he wrote his last letter to his parents the day before his departure for new adventures in the vast labyrinth of canyons where the Escalante River flows into the Colorado.

Everett's parents waited two months, as he had directed. They hesitated to begin inquiries because he was sensitive to any concern as to his welfare. Finally, on February 7 they wrote to Mrs. H. L. Allen, postmistress at Escalante. Letters followed to postmasters in all the towns and settlements in the desert country where Everett visited. They wrote to sheriffs of the counties of the region, to Indian agents and Forestry and Park officials, to newspapers, radio stations and to all individuals he had mentioned in his letters.

While none of those who replied could give any clue as to Everett's whereabouts, they were all reassuring. They were confident he was safe, for he was trail-wise, experienced, and capable of taking care of himself.

On February 28 a mining man from Hanksville, in southern Utah, visited the Ruess home in Los Angeles and suggested hiring three Navajo trackers to search the Navajo Mountain country. Christopher Ruess was ready to underwrite such an expedition—but nothing came of it.

On March 3, H. J. Allen, husband of the Escalante postmistress, wrote to the Ruesses offering to organize a search with volunteers from that community. "We will search for him as if he were our own son," Allen wrote. These volunteer posses covered the canyon country in the area near the confluence of the Escalante and Colorado Rivers. On March 7 they found Everett's two burros in Davis Canyon, a tributary of the Escalante. In a cave they found prints of boots the size Everett wore, and a small pile of potsherds he may have collected, but nothing more.

The people of southern Utah did not want to believe that in their part of the world a human being could vanish without trace. The Associated Civic Clubs of Southern Utah, representing fifteen communities, equipped another expedition under the leadership of Capt. P. M. Shurtz. These volunteers combed the area on foot and horseback for ten days, and found what was believed to be Everett's last camp—in a cave not far from where the burros had been impounded in a natural corral. On the wall was carved the inscription "Nemo 1934." A mile away the same legend was incised in the doorstep of a long-abandoned Moqui Indian pueblo.

In answer to a letter to Christopher Ruess inquiring as to whether the word "Nemo" might be identified in any way with his son, the father wrote: "In all probability it is an echo from repeated reading of Jules Verne's *Twenty Leagues Under the Sea.* Everett's copy is well worn. Everett had read much of Lawrence of Arabia, man of the desert, who had won the Moslems for Britain and the Allies in the first world war. Especially, he read Lawrence's translation of the *Odyssey* of Homer, the earliest novel. In this is the story of *Nemo,* Latin for Odysseus, or *Oudeis,* meaning 'No One'."

In the hope of finding some new clue, the parents in June made an extended trip through the Indian country of northern Arizona and southern Utah. This was the region most favored by their son for his wanderings, and he had made many friends there. They talked with John and Louisa Wetherill at Kayenta, the Buck Lowerys at Marble Canyon, Chief Ranger and Mrs. Donald Jolly at Zion Park, Chief Ranger and Mrs. Maurice Cope at Bryce Canyon, and President Frank Martinez and Secretary Ray Carter

of the Associated Civic Clubs at Panguitch, Utah, and members
of the searching party the Club had sponsored. At Escalante
they visited the H. J. Allens, who had known Everett personally,
and had organized the first volunteer search for him.

Several clues were investigated: A burned skeleton near Gallup; a hint that Everett was working near Blanding, Utah, under
an assumed name; that he was living with a Ute family in a
remote sector of the Navajo Mountain region. But these all proved
to be false leads.

In August, the *Salt Lake Tribune* sent Capt. Neal Johnson and
a star reporter to southern Utah to make a further search, and
secure pictures and information for a series of illustrated feature
stories bringing to light all data bearing on the mystery. Out of
this study came the hint that Everett may have been murdered
for his pack outfit. It was suggested that the State of Utah equip
and finance an expedition to investigate the murder theory. However, many of the residents in an area where no murder had been
committed in half a century scoffed at the proposal, and nothing
came of it.

Many theories were suggested in letters received at the Ruess
home. One writer thought Everett may have constructed a crude
raft and had been drowned while trying to cross the Colorado
River. John Wetherill of Kayenta, who helped Everett chart his
last journey, expressed an opinion shared by others in that region—that Everett may have fallen from one of the prehistoric
cliff dwellings which he liked to explore, and his body and outfit
covered by blow sand.

One of those who feared Everett may have met with accidental death was Clayborn Lockett, an archeologist with whom
young Ruess had worked for a brief period in excavations at Basket-Maker Cave on Skeleton Mesa in Arizona. Lockett wrote: "I
had an excellent chance to know Everett . . . he spent much of
his time in this burial cave with me . . . we had many talks together and I know Everett was always anxious to get into situa-
tions which provided thrills and excitement. When these situa-

TO KANAB

TO KAYENTA or TUBA CITY

PANGUITCH

ESCALANTE?

ESCALANTE R.

DAVIS CANYON
WHERE WILD
BURROS WERE FOUND

KAIPAROWITS PLATEAU

SAN JUAN R.

NOKAI CAN.

PIUTE CAN.

NAVAJO MTN.

COLORADO R.

RAINBOW BRIDGE

RAINBOW LODGE

NAVAJO CAN.

PARIA R.

UTAH
ARIZONA

GRAND CANYON BRIDGE

TO KANAB

BRYCE CAN.

N

tions arose he would think about them, write about them, or often paint them. One time in camp he stood on the edge of a 400-foot cliff during a rainstorm and did a water-color sketch of a waterfall. I remember this very clearly because I personally was scared to death just watching him perched on the edge of the cliff. It is my idea that while climbing a cliff . . . he may have fallen to his death."

Everett's disregard for his personal safety was revealed in a page from his personal notes, made public following his failure to return from the Utah wilderness. Following his graduation from high school he spent much of the fall, winter and spring of 1931-32 following the desert trails and in the High Sierra of California. Then, urged by family and friends, he entered the University of California in Los Angeles in the fall of 1932. His studies included geology, philosophy, English, history, gym and military drill. At the end of the school year he wrote: "I'm glad I went, but I'm glad it's over. College was a valuable episode, but it did not get a strangle hold on me." It was during this year in school that his pattern for the future was revealed. He wrote:

"One night, long ago, while I tossed restlessly upon my bed, an idea crystallized within me. In the cool of the night breeze I lay suddenly still, taut, and filled with a tremendous superabundance of energy that demanded outlet. My brain was busied with tense imaginings of adventure in far places.

"In my mind I conjured a thousand forgotten cities, left behind by the years; sheer gray mountains; mile upon mile of bare unfriendly desert; cold lakes unrippled by any breeze, with depths unfathomable, jungles filled with deadly snakes, immense butterflies, brilliant colors, fever, and death. I swam in the blue seas, and in

MAP ON OPPOSITE PAGE—*In the precipitous canyon country where the Escalante River flows into the Colorado in southern Utah Everett Ruess was last seen. His burros were found in an improvised cattlemen's corral in Davis Canyon, a tributary of the Escalante.*

coral-tinted waters. Through insufferable heat and incessant flooding downpours I plodded forward.

"On bleak, windswept coasts bordering the Antarctic, and on the broad endless pampas of the Argentine, I pitched my camps. On the banks of the sluggish Amazon I built my fires, which glowed like earthly stars, gleaming far across the turbid waters at night. I tramped alone through wilderness, with my food supply dwindling, and hostile forces of nature combining against me. I felt the ominous rumble and swift shock of volcanos bursting out. The ground trembled beneath my feet as earthquakes made red ruin. On storm-lashed islands I stood, surveying far-off mountain peaks. Then I camped beneath them in shadowed valleys, watching at sunset the last bands of light that gleamed on the highest mountain tops and wherever I journeyed strange people of a foreign tongue stared at me curiously.

"These are the things I saw and the experiences I lived through that night long past. Now it is night again —the night before I go. Once more I think of that which lies ahead.

"Bitter pain is in store for me, but I shall bear it. Beauty beyond all power to convey shall be mine; I shall search diligently for it. Death may await me; with vitality, impetuosity and confidence I will combat it. Not through cynicism and ennui will I be easy prey. And regardless of all that may befall, let me not be found to lack an understanding of the inscrutable humor of it all.

"Cuernavaca, Rio, Titicaca, Patagonia, Quetzalcoatl, Cotopaxi—they lure me, and I shall answer their call and and the call of the winding trail. Adventure is for the adventurous. My face is set, I go to make my destiny. May many another youth be by me inspired to leave the smug safety of his rut and follow fortune to other lands."

I did not know Everett Ruess personally, but I became interested in him and the mystery of his disappearance in the late 1930s when Hugh Lacy, a Los Angeles writer, submitted to the *Desert Magazine*, which I was then editing, a series of feature stories embodying many of the letters Everett had written to his family and friends during his wilderness treks. These stories were published serially in *Desert*, from January through November, 1939.

Some of the letters which came to my desk during the period when the series was running, suggested the possibility that Everett may have met death at the hands of the Indians whose lands he was traversing. On trips into that region I discussed this possibility with many Indian traders and others who had known Everett personally, and were intimately acquainted with the Navajo, Hopi and Ute Indians of the region. Without exception they discounted the idea that the tribesmen may have caused his death. They were sure of this for two reasons: Everett never carried arms. He was a friendly, likable lad, who would give offense to no one. He liked the Indians, and they were very fond of him. He had learned to speak some Navajo, knew some of their chants, and more than once had taken part in their sings. At Mishongnovi his Hopi friends had once painted him with the pigments of the clan and invited him to take part in their Antelope Dance.

As to the second reason: The traders generally share a conclusion expressed by one of them when he told me: "These Indians today are not killers. They value and respect human life perhaps even more than do the white races. They have a reverence for all life. That is part of their religion. If a death occurs on the reservation we traders always learn about it sooner or later. The Indians have an underground habit of communication which precludes secrecy where human tragedy is involved."

"Where I go I leave no trace." This prophetic line was contained in a letter Everett wrote from War God Spring on Navajo

Mountain to his friend Bill Jacobs, in June 1934, while on his long last trek. Everett wrote:

Dear Bill: A high wind is roaring in the tops of the tall pines. The moon is just rising on the rim of the desert far below. Stars gleam through the pine boughs, and through the filmy clouds that move across the night sky. Graceful, slim-trunked aspens reach upward through the towering pines. Their slender curving branches are white in the firelight, and an occasional downward breeze flickers their pale green leaves.

The beauty of this place is perfect of its kind; I could ask for nothing more. A little spring trickles down among the aspens and white firs. By day the marshy hollow is aswarm with gorgeous butterflies; tiger and zebra swallow-tails, the angelwings and morning-cloak and others. There are a hundred delightful places to sit and dream, friendly rocks to lean against, springy beds of pine needles to lie on and look up at the sky or the tall smooth tree trunks, with spirals of branches and their tufted foliage.

Two small bands of handsome bay horses, each with a bell-mare, water here. Often I hear from opposite directions the deep-toned music of their bells against the sharper tinkle of the burro bell. No human comes to break the dreamy solitude. Far below, the tawny desert, seamed with canyons, throbs in the savage desert sun. But here it is lofty and cool.

It is hard not to be sentimental about my burros; they are such droll friendly creatures. On the trail, particularly when they do the wrong thing in a tight place, I am often impatient with them, but when they stand up to their knees in wildflowers with blossoms on their lips, and look at me with their lustrous large brown eyes, cocking their furry ears and switching their tails at their fat sides—then who that knew them could help loving them?

I had to laugh a few mornings ago on the desert, when tracking the two foolish-looking pals, I saw their trail leading up to an abandoned hogan and heard a snort and scuffle inside. With all the spacious desert around them, they had chosen to bed down in that little hogan, which just comfortably contained the two of them.

We followed a steep trail out of Copper Canyon opposite No Man's Mesa. Near the rim it was just a scramble, and Leopold whom I was packing, in attempting to claw his way up a steep place, lost his balance and fell over backward. He turned two somersaults and a side roll, landing with his feet waving, about six inches from a yawning gulf. I pulled him to his feet. He was a bit groggy at first; he had lost a little fur, and the pack was scratched.

Now the moon swings clear of the tree tops. The wind is in the pine trees; what other sound is like it?

The perfection of this place is one reason why I distrust ever returning to the cities. Here I wander in beauty and perfection. There one walks in the midst of ugliness and mistakes.

All is made for man but where can one find surroundings to match one's ideals and imaginings? It is possible to live and dream in ugly, ill-fitting places, but how much better to be where all is beautiful and unscarred . . .

Here I take my belongings with me. The picturesque gear of packing, and my gorgeous Navajo saddle blankets, make a place my own. But when I go I leave no trace . . .

I made a cake in my frying pan this noon. It was a success. I wish you could have tasted it.

The beauty of this country is becoming a part of me. I feel more detached from life and somehow gentler. Except for passing flurries, it has become impossible for me to censure anyone.

Meanwhile I have used my body mercilessly, seldom giving way to it until forced, so that I should not wonder if it will turn traitor to me sometime. Anyway as Omar says, "If the soul can naked on the air of heaven ride, Were't not a shame for him in this clay carcass crippled to abide?" That is a big "if" but may the time never come when I have to minister to my body.

Now the aspen trunks are tall and white in the moonlight. A wind croons in the pines. The mountain sleeps. Peace to you.

(signed) EVERETT.

Everett wrote fluently, but his greatest pleasure was in his art work. His pack always included crayons, brushes, drawing paper and water colors. Also he was adept at making block prints —almost invariably in strong, bold strokes that depicted the canyons and fantastic rock formations of the mountainous terrain of his travels. Occasionally he sold a painting or print, and this, with a monthly stipend from his parents, was sufficient to supply the food and clothing which were his only needs. At the end of each long trek he would dispose of his burros. It was easy to acquire new pack animals in this Indian country, where burros are numerous.

The occasion and the impulse that prompted Everett to stop along the way and unpack his artist's tools were revealed in one of his letters:

Viljalmar Stefansson, the arctic explorer, says that adventures are a sign of unpreparedness and incompetence. I think this is largely right, nevertheless I like adventure and enjoy taking a chance when skill and fortitude play a part. If we never had adventure we would never know what stuff is in us. So last night I had quite a satisfactory adventure. (His burros had bolted in the night but he re-captured them.)

Then I rode on again, and for awhile I was very blithe, singing lustily into the wind and remembering some magnificent music. Then the sky grew inky and I urged the burros onward, shouting "Sintlo, Kelly, dilly ago!" We passed right under the towering bulk of Agathla, popularly called El Capitan, and I had to make a painting. It was a splendid rock, with spires and pinnacles of black volcanic stone. I did not trouble to finish the sketch, but even so it was almost dark, and it was five or six miles to a campsite. So I soon dismounted and drove both burros, shouting until they fairly loped.

Though not all my days are as wild as this, each one holds its surprises, and I have seen almost more beauty than I can bear. Many times in search of waterholes and cliff dwellings, I trusted my life to crumbling sandstone and angles little short of perpendicular, startling myself when I came out whole and on top. The burros are grazing peacefully now, like good little donkeys, and haven't strayed all day.

Twenty-seven years have now passed since Everett left the little community of Escalante to follow the historic Mormon trail that leads toward the Hole-in-the-Rock. Within a few years the rising waters of Lake Powell, the great new reservoir to be created behind the 573-foot Glen Canyon Dam now under construction in the Colorado River, will submerge the lower levels of the canyon-setting of Everett's last camp. Thus the possibility that the mystery of Everett's fate will ever be solved becomes more remote.

During my last visit with Waldo Ruess, I told him a story which has the ring of probability, although it is unlikely it can ever be confirmed.

One summer in the early 1950s I was a member of a camping expedition to southern Utah, and we spent a week looking for ancient cliff dwellings in the area where Everett's burros were found. It was a saddle trip, and our wranglers were Mormon cowboys who had resided for many years in Escalante, and knew the country intimately.

One evening as we sat around our campfire they told us their conclusions as to the fate of Everett Ruess. The names must remain anonymous for the story involves foul play and no evidence ever has been obtained that would support the arrest and prosecution of the men suspected. The story is this:

In the early 1930s some men, believed to be cattle rustlers, were camping in the wild country along the Colorado River not far from the Hole-in-the-Rock. This landmark was given its name by a hardy band of Mormon colonists who had spent nearly the entire winter of 1879-80 chiseling a trail through the rimrock down to the Colorado River where it was necessary to cross their wagons to reach their destination at Bluff, Utah. There a settlement was to be founded.

Ranchers, running cattle in the Hole-in-the-Rock area, where roundups were difficult and strays not easy to find, were convinced the men were outlaws engaged in putting their own brand on mavericks. The suspects posed as legitimate cowmen. Their identity was known, and they came to Escalante periodically for supplies, but it had never been possible to get positive evidence of their guilt.

In this situation it was arranged that a rumor should be circulated—and passed along to the suspected men—that the cattlemen had secured the services of FBI men, who would come into the region to investigate cattle rustling along the Colorado River. It was hoped this threat would end the depredations.

This was the stage setting into which Everett Ruess unwittingly projected himself. He was a lone wanderer, who went into the remote wilderness where the suspected men were operating their cattle business. Family and friends could readily understand the motives which impelled the youthful artist to do this kind of thing. But to guilt-conscious strangers who had been warned that the law might be coming their way, any explanation he might give would seem wholly irrational.

My informants were convinced that Everett had met with foul play. The fact that his burros had been safely corraled, but no trace ever found of his bedroll, notes, grubstake, artist's supplies, clothing and toiletries, could be construed as supporting this theory. Soon after public interest became aroused over the Ruess mystery, and posses began making a search, the suspected men abandoned their camp and left the area.

So convinced were my Mormon friends of the plausibility of this explanation, they went into the region some time later on an unannounced quest of their own, and spent several days seeking clues which might confirm their suspicions. They found nothing. Perhaps the secret lies buried in the broad, muddy waters of the Colorado a few miles away, or beneath the sand and rocks of one of the many almost inaccessible canyon recesses of the region.

Everett would have been twenty-one on March 28, 1935, the next birthday following his disappearance. He came from a good home. Stella Knight Ruess, his mother, is an accomplished and versatile artist; her work includes carving, modeling, bookplates and block prints. She has written and illustrated several books of poems and is a member of the National League of American Pen Women. Her home garden has a woodsy, oriental atmosphere, with tea house, fish pool and bamboo screening. Obviously, her artistry was an impressive factor in creating the environment mold of Everett's youth.

Christopher Ruess, at the time of Everett's last pilgrimage into the desert wilderness, was director of Education and Research for the Los Angeles County Probation Department. Later, following his retirement from public service, he became a counsellor for the American Institute of Family Relations. He held two Harvard degrees and on occasion had served brief periods in the pulpit of the Unitarian Church.

Waldo, the elder son, served the U. S. State Department in embassies overseas, including many years in China. He had come home a year prior to his father's death in 1954, later was stationed in Spain, and finally returned to Los Angeles with his Andalusian bride in 1958.

In his short span of years, Everett Ruess probably found more beauty, more soul-satisfying experience and more harrowing adventure than most human beings discover in a lifetime. Of material things, he sought only the simple necessities of daily sustenance. But in the realm of the spirit the range of his adventure was limitless. It was a warm and inspiring legacy he bequeathed to the youth of another generation, despite his tragic fate.

Perhaps it may seem a selfish role he chose for himself. But none can say it was a life of ease—of the self-indulgence that corrupts the spirit and ravages the body. Rather, he chose combat with the elemental forces of an untamed desert wilderness.

Everett was still in his teens when he dedicated himself to a strange unconventional pattern of life. He was a dreamer—but what a drab world this would be without those who seek the poetry in life! And who has not at some time shared the dreams that impelled this lad to go forth on his quest for the holy grail of beauty and adventure?

CLIFF-DWELLERS OF KAIPAROWITS   IX

ONE MAY MORNING eight of us climbed the steep trail which zig-zags up the northeast escarpment of 7000-foot Kaiparowits Plateau in southern Utah to learn what we could about the prehistoric Moqui people who dwelt on that isolated sky island a thousand years ago.

As nearly as archeologists can determine, the Moquis occupied this juniper and pinyon covered tableland between 900 and 1200 A.D. Then they left, for reasons which remain a mystery even to the scientists.

There is no road to the top of Kaiparowits. There are only a few clefts in the escarpment walls, where even a horseman can make the ascent. In winter the plateau is often covered with snow, and in summer the water supply is limited to an occasional small spring and a few natural catch basins which hold water for a few days or weeks following a rainstorm. And that probably is the reason why no white man ever has established a permanent home up there.

Sponsors of our expedition were Wayne and Lucile Hiser, who then owned an electrical equipment manufacturing business in Toledo, Ohio. For many years the Hisers spent their summer vacations trekking through the Indian country of the Southwest, with photography as their hobby. Between trips they gave illustrated lectures to service clubs and civic groups in Toledo, and contributed the proceeds to charity, mainly for the purchase of clothing and schooling for Navajo children.

The mentor of our party was Dr. Jesse Jennings, professor of anthropology at the University of Utah, whose department for many years has conducted a state-wide survey of ancient Indian sites in his state, and who welcomed the opportunity to extend his research to Kaiparowits.

Details of transportation, commissary and camping equipment were by Burnett Hendryx and Kelly Cameron of Panguitch, Utah, who accompanied us. They secured the services of Edson Alvey, science teacher in Escalante public school, as guide, and Delane Griffin, cowboy and rancher, as packer.

Our party assembled at the Cameron Hotel in Panguitch, and the following day motored past the entrance to Bryce Canyon National Park and over the Escalante Mountains to the town of Escalante. From there we followed an old Mormon trail to the base of the Kaiparowits massif. Here Griffin met us with the saddle and pack horses which were to take us to the top.

The sky was overcast, and I dug a trench around my bedroll that night. I rather enjoy the patter of rain on the waterproof tarpaulin which covers me, but I do not fancy a stream of cold water seeping in around the edges of my sleeping bag. Actually, it rained only a few drops.

Strung out in single file the next morning we followed a trail which gradually ascended a *bajada*—broken with ridges and gullies. The sandstone wall of the escarpment rose almost vertically above us, and we paused to cinch our saddle girths for the steep ascent.

The path zigged and zagged upward with hairpin turns. When the grade became increasingly difficult we dismounted and let the horses paw their way to the top, while we followed, much of the way on all fours. The Indians had discovered this route many centuries ago and had daubed red pictographs on rock faces along the way. Many years of weathering had left them only faintly visible.

We camped that night on the summit, in a pinyon-fringed little cove where there was a spring for stock water. We dipped our own water from small *tinajas* which had been eroded in a sandstone dike crossing an arroyo.

Cattlemen sometimes bring their stock up here for summer range, and had camped at these waterholes. The cowboys of the western range have sterling attributes, but good housekeeping is seldom one of them. The ground was strewn with tin cans. Our hosts from Toledo soon corrected this. Wayne dug a garbage pit, while Lucile recruited the rest of us as an anti-litter task force to dispose of the debris.

There followed many days of riding and exploring. We would rise soon after daybreak and after a seven o'clock breakfast the horses were saddled and Edson led the way in quest of Moqui houses. They were sunny days and, although the midday temperature generally approached 90 degrees, the dry atmosphere of the 7,000-foot plateau was exhilarating.

The geography books define a plateau as a high level tableland. But Kaiparowits is not exactly that kind of a plateau. The top surface is slashed by numerous arroyos. Domes and small-scale ridges and buttes outcrop in every direction. They rise

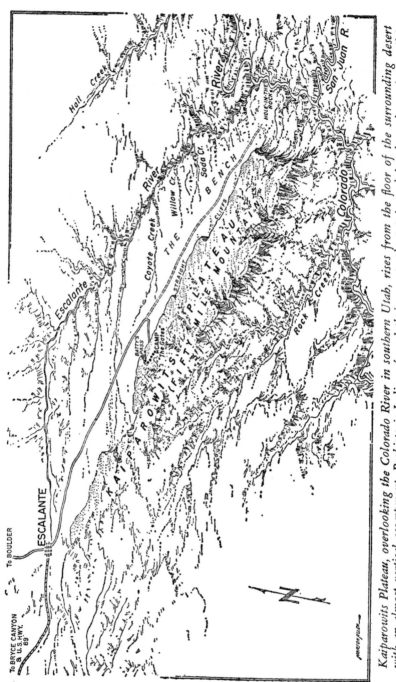

Kaiparowits Plateau, overlooking the Colorado River in southern Utah, rises from the floor of the surrounding desert with an almost vertical escarpment. Prehistoric Indians found their way to the top in a cleft where the ancient trail is used by an occasional visitor.

above the pinyon forest, which covers the plateau, like temples and fortresses of cream-colored Wahweep sandstone. Tens of thousands of years of rain and wind have eroded great caverns in the sidewalls of these buttes, and it is in these shallow caves, protected by the overhanging shelf above, that the aborigines built their homes of stone and mud. Edson previously had visited some of the cliff-dwellings in this area and he knew the best places to look for them.

The Moqui were thrifty house-builders. Their ideal site was beneath a low-roofed overhang where it was necessary only to lay up rocks for the outer walls. The back face of the cavern supplied one wall of the dwelling, and its ceiling was the roof of the cave. There was an abundant supply of small stones for the masonry, and these were laid with mortar of mud. Few of the dwellings remained intact after a thousand years of weathering. Rain beating on the exposed walls had dissolved the mortar, and many of them had collapsed.

Every cliff-dweller had built a granary for the storage of corn and squash grown around the springs, and pinyon nuts and seeds gathered from the landscape. Generally these storage vaults were placed in the most sheltered crannies of the cave, and many of them were well preserved.

Kaiparowits was given its name by John Wesley Powell during his Colorado River explorations in 1878-81. It is a Ute word variously translated, but the most common of the versions has approximately the meaning "Big Mountain's Little Brother."

Moqui is a word applied quite generally to the prehistoric Indians in this area. In the scientific world the tribesmen who dwelt on Kaiparowits were of the Anasazi culture, which embraced both the basket-maker and the pueblo periods of Indian occupation in the Four Corners region of Utah, Colorado, New Mexico and Arizona.

Until the 1890s the Hopi Indians of northern Arizona were known as Moquis. The Navajos called them Mogis, meaning "monkey," a term expressive of the contempt in which the Hopis were held by their plundering neighbors. Later, the Spaniards, who came into this region from Mexico, called them Moquis or Mokis. This term was used until 1895, when the Smithsonian Institution adopted the name Hopi, a contraction of Hopitu, meaning "peaceful people."

The fact that Utah people of this vicinity refer to the Kaiparowits cliff-dwellings as Moqui houses carries no proof that the ancestors of the Hopi Indians resided in these caverns. No one knows for certain who they were or where they went when they abandoned the plateau.

We found much broken pottery and many well-made arrow points. One small earthen bowl of rather crude workmanship was recovered intact from a niche in the cliff. Markings on some of the potsherds indicated these Indians had trading intercourse with other tribes.

Our camp cook was Kelly Cameron, a railroad passenger conductor on vacation. He had learned his cooking in the early days of his railroading in a freight caboose—and learned it well. The breakfast menu was always hotcakes. We all relished them except Spunk, the herd dog which followed his master, Delane, around like a shadow. Spunk evidently did not care for Kelly's flapjacks. He invariably buried them under a bush.

We spent the evening hours around our campfire talking over the day's discoveries, and trying to reconstruct the daily activities of the prehistoric tribesmen of the cliff houses. Dr. Jennings visualized the Moqui men as a little over five feet tall, the women slightly smaller. They subsisted on the fruits of a limited agriculture, and on nuts, seeds and the wildlife found here. Pinyon nuts probably were their staple item of food.

One evening the conversation turned to the glyphs—the petroglyphs incised in the rocks, and the pictographs painted with pigment. While it was possible to identify such figures as mountain sheep and deer, the archeologists have never solved the motivation of this Indian art. Members of our party were unanimous as to one conclusion—that the art of the ancients is no more baffling than are some of the modernistic creations being exhibited by contemporary artists today.

Botanically, the Kaiparowits exhibited specimens of both the Transitional and Alpine zones of life. The highest elevation we reached was 7410 feet. The plant life included Sego lily, the state flower of Utah, Indian paintbrush, and great fields of purple lupine just coming into blossom. In addition to the forest of pinyon and juniper there were aspen, manzanita, service berries, ephedra, scrub oak and one of the species of prickly pear cactus.

While there were many deer tracks, we saw only one doe. We observed one rattlesnake, a few jackrabbits, rodents and lizards, but wildlife is rather sparse, probably due to the limited supply of water during the summer season.

On the rim of the plateau we were looking down on the Escalante River basin and its many tributaries, and its confluence with the Colorado. It was into this area that Everett Ruess, twenty-two-year-old artist-poet-explorer, went alone with his two burros in 1934 to look for ancient cliff houses, and never returned. The Ruess story is told in another chapter of this book.

The use of ropes was necessary for security purposes in scaling some of the cliffs where the ancient dwellings were located. In one place we found where the Moquis had chiseled hand and toe notches in the sandstone wall to reach their home-in-the-cavern above.

In one area the ground was covered with chips of flint and obsidian. Evidently this was a workshop for the making of arrow and spear points. The stone for these weapons had to be brought from some distant deposits, for there is no rock on Kaiparowits suitable for this purpose. Edson picked up a beautiful turquoise bead, obviously brought in from elsewhere.

At the end of a week the three little *tinajas,* where we were dipping our domestic water, were nearly empty. Perhaps it was lack of water which caused the little brown men of the Moqui tribe to abandon their homes on top of the plateau. I am sure their departure was a matter of great urgency, for with an ample supply of food and water this truly was an ideal hideaway for peaceful tribesmen who preferred to live by toil rather than by plunder.

PALM HUNTER IN THE WASTELANDS X

TATTERED TROOPERS of General Stephen W. Kearny's Army of
the West had been straggling across the southern Arizona and
California deserts from waterhole to waterhole for weeks. Then
on November 29, 1846, an advance detachment following the
course of Vallecito Creek, which drains to the desert from California's Sierra Nevada, spied green foliage against the drab hillside in the distance.

Green trees on the desert could mean water, and when the
soldiers turned aside to investigate, they found a spring sur-

rounded by a group of trees which some of them were able to identify. Lieut. William H. Emory of the Topographic Engineers, accompanying the Army, records the incident in his diary, later published as *Notes of a Military Reconnaissance from Fort Leavenworth to San Diego*. Emory wrote:

> "A few miles from a spring called Oro Grande . . . several scattered objects were seen projecting against cliffs, hailed by the Florida campaigners, some of whom were along, as old friends. They were cabbage trees, and marked the locale of a spring and small patch of grass."

Many Floridans still call them cabbage trees, or cabbage palmettos, but to Californians they are palms—the *Washingtonia filifera*, which grows wild on the Southern California desert and south into Baja California.

Lieut. Emory's reference was the first recorded observation of California's native palms by an Anglo-American. The palms seen by the Kearny troopers are in San Diego County, and are located at the desert entrance to a canyon in the Laguna Mountains. The oasis is known today as Mountain Palm Springs.

I visited this oasis in 1931, and on this and subsequent camping trips in the area counted 57 palms in the group mentioned by Lieut. Emory, and an additional 238 palmettos in four other groups in the immediate vicinity. The Mountain Palm Springs oasis probably has changed little since General Kearny and his weary army came this way 115 years ago. The "cabbage trees" are still there—"green foliage against a gray hillside" where thirsty travelers may come for clear, sweet water and shade.

My interest in the wild palms of the Southern California desert dates back to 1920 when on a visit to my old prospector friend, Gus Lederer at Corn Springs in the Chuckawalla Mountains, I spent two days loafing in the shade of the palm fronds which formed a canopy over his one-room cabin. That was my introduction to one of the most interesting botanical phenomena of the Great American Desert. I have never ceased to be amazed and delighted at the paradox of palms growing wild in the arid desert, for this tree must have abundant water at its shallow roots.

The quest for these isolated palm oases became a hobby which has occupied literally hundreds of my weekend jalopy— and later jeep—outings during the last forty years. So far I have logged and photographed 88 separate groups on the American side of the international boundary, and I am confident the total will exceed 100. On the Mexican side of the border the palm canyons extend more or less intermittently the entire length of the Baja California peninsula.

There are few places where these palm oases may be observed from the paved highways. Generally they are in remote canyons and sometimes may be reached only after miles of hiking beyond the point where the terrain becomes impassable for a jeep. The clues to their whereabouts came to me from many sources: prospectors, hunters, cowhands and old maps. These trees thrive in both the Upper and Lower Sonoran botanical zones. At Dos Palmas spring, near the western end of Salton Sea, they are growing below sea level, and at another spring, also known as Dos Palmas, in the Santa Rosa Mountains, they are vigorous trees at the 3500-foot elevation. In my note book is reference to a report that a small group of the native palms are seen at 4200 feet in San Diego county—but that is a report yet to be confirmed.

On an old map accompanying the report of Col. J. W. Barlow of the U.S.-Mexican boundary survey of 1892-96, I saw a notation "palm spring" along a remote sector of the international border of Southern California. This region of ninety square miles is a blank white space on all published maps. During the next three years I made four trips into this area by jeep and on foot before I located them. There were 27 mature trees in the bottom of an obscure canyon in the Inkopah Mountains, watered by a trickle that flowed a few hundred feet from a spring, and then disappeared in the sand.

On the hunch there might be more palms in this little-known corner of the Colorado Desert, Arles Adams and I explored the area on a backpack trip in March 1946. Arles is a mill superintendent in El Centro, California, with the hands of a mechanical genius and an artist's delight in the primitive freedom of the unexplored wilderness. He has been my companion on many excursions into the unmapped geography of the Southwest.

We traveled light. Our sleeping bags, food for two days, and a quart canteen of water each added up to twenty-pound packs. Leaving U. S. Highway 80 near Mountain Springs, during the first hour we passed one small group of palms, and before noon had arrived at another where the blackened ceiling of a cave and a huge boulder with nine mortar recesses in its top surface were mute evidence that the site had been the home of prehistoric tribesmen. Later in the day we passed another group of 17 palms huddled together in a lovely picture that will remain in my memory as one of the highlights of the trip.

To the hiker, the desert escarpment of the Inkopah range is just a succession of ups and downs. We found it necessary to make a tedious detour around a 30-foot dry waterfall. A half hour later we were descending a 500-foot precipice of gray and white marble. It was a beautiful formation, but we were too busy clinging to the rocks and trying to find hand and toe holds to think much about the coloring at the time. On an almost vertical descent a twenty-pound pack, swaying with each movement, calls for rather critical balancing at times.

During the morning we had been able to refill our canteens at springs along the way. But as the afternoon shadows began to lengthen, water supply became our chief concern. When darkness came we found a little sheltered cove where there was enough dead ironwood for warmth. We were thirsty, but not painfully so, and made dry camp for the night.

The next morning we continued down the canyon and within an hour came to a series of *tinajas*, still holding water from the last storm. I use the Spanish term because I like the Mexican pronunciation of *Tená has* and it is a specific term whereas the English "natural tank" is neither exact nor accurately descriptive.

Now, for the first time since we had started our hike twelve miles to the north, I knew where we were. I had seen these *tinajas* on one of my previous trips into this region in quest of the palm springs. Unknowingly, we had crossed the international border and were in Mexico. The boundary monuments are far apart in this region.

We spent the day revisiting the palm spring and hiking back along the floor of the desert, at the toe of the range, to Coyote Well on Highway 80, where our car was to meet us. The two-day backpack trip had added three new groups to my roster of palm oases, and also the location of several prehistoric Indian sites, one of them identified by well-preserved petroglyphs on the rocks. We had seen no wildlife and few game trails, for this is indeed arid country, but all along the way we had been serenaded by the musical call of the canyon wren, which to me is the sweetest sound on the desert.

Owing to the sparsity of boundary markers in this remote area, I am not sure yet whether the little oasis to which I gave the name Boundary Palm Spring, to distinguish it from many other palm oases in Southern California, is in the United States or Mexico. However, on the map which I published in *Desert Magazine* at the time of the re-discovery of this little oasis, I gave Uncle Sam the benefit of the doubt. The other three groups are identified in my notes as Mortero Palm Spring, where we found the old grinding mortars, Juniper Palm Spring, and Mesquite Palm Spring.

On these palm-hunting excursions I always carry a mechanical counter to record the number of trees. While I have not yet completed the census, and the numbers change from year to year as scarred veterans topple before storm winds and new trees are constantly taking root, I estimate there are 11,000 native palms on the Southern California desert, and perhaps another 18,000 in Mexico within fifty miles of the international border.

There is one group of 57 Washingtonias on the Arizona side of the Colorado River in a precipitous canyon in the Kofa range. I learned about the Arizona palms from Albert Stitt of the U. S. Reclamation Bureau. He had seen them during a previous tour of duty with the U. S. Agricultural Station at Bard, near Yuma. He offered to serve as guide on a trip to the Kofa, and we arranged to go.

We crossed the Colorado River at Yuma, and then turned north over the suspension bridge which spans the Gila River. Just beyond this bridge a sign warns the motorist: "No water, no gas, no oil for 72 miles." The sign-maker might have added "no bridges." This is unimportant in dry weather, but the road crosses hundreds of arroyos between that point and the next service station at Quartzsite, and on those rare occasions when rain is falling these desert dips run full of water. I had once attempted this route after such a storm. At each arroyo I would wade out with a shovel to sound the depth of the torrent, while my companion drove the car. We navigated two of them, but at the third flood stream the handle of the shovel disappeared in the water. In this land of seldom-seen roads we had to make a 200-mile detour to reach our destination.

But we had fair weather for our trip to the Kofa, and camped that night at the base of the mountain which rises 2000 feet almost perpendicularly from the floor of the desert. The Kofa is a strange mountain, virtually without water. During many trips over and around the mountain I have never found a spring big enough to fill a canteen. There are *tinajas* which hold water for a few weeks after a rain, but during long periods of drouth the Kofa massif is as dry as the Sahara. Yet despite this apparent lack of moisture, every tiny ledge and crevice has luxurious green vegetation the year 'round. Evidently the huge block of volcanic rock which comprises the bulk of the mountain is shattered and porous, and stores great quantities of storm water within its mass. Dr. L. H. Bailey, the eminent botanist at Cornell University, who had visited the palm canyon, referred to it as a "fantastic mountain."

The name Kofa is derived from the King of Arizona, a long-abandoned mining property near the southern base of the mountain. The old prospectors had another name for it—one that could hardly be used in polite society. They called it S. H. Mountain, and that name appears on some of the old maps. When one drives along the Yuma-Quartzsite road with the mountain outlined against the eastern sky, there is observed a conspicuous butte which suggested the descriptive term used by the old-timers.

The palms grow in a narrow slot of a tributary canyon, accessible only by hand and toe ascent. There must be water at their roots, otherwise the palms would not be there. But it would require the pick and drill of a hard rock miner to get a drink there. The scarcity of water probably explains the absence of potsherds, petroglyphs or other evidence of previous Indian habitation near the mountain.

The daddy of the palm oases in California is the widely-publicized Palm Canyon, near the resort city of Palm Springs. There are approximately 3000 trees in this group, extending along the floor of the canyon for several miles, and fed by a live stream of water. They are multiplying, as is true in nearly all the oases where there is running water. Palm Canyon is on the agenda of the National Park Service as a possible national monument, but little progress has been made toward the acquisition of the oasis for this purpose because most of the palms are on the reservation lands of the Cahuilla Indians. The Cahuilla Tribal Council derives considerable income from a nominal charge for entrance to the canyon.

One circumstance which confirms the conclusion that the wild palms are increasing in numbers is that the old-timers who were responsible for the original naming of many of the oases frequently referred to them by number. For instance, Twenty-nine Palms, near the town of that name and the headquarters for the National Park administration of the Joshua Tree National Monument, was given the name by Col. Henry Washington, chief of the survey party which established California's San Bernardino Base and Meridian in 1852. Today only fourteen of the original palms are still standing, their age evidenced by the deep fire scars and the stooped angle of their trunks. However, young trees have more than replaced the fallen veterans. Incidentally, this is the northernmost of the wild palm groups in California. A few miles away, within the Monument, is another group known as 49 Palms.

Prospectors, who tramped this desert nearly a century ago, probably were responsible for the original naming of 17 Palms in the Borrego Badlands sector of the Anza-Borrego State Park. The popularity of this historic waterhole is attested by the old foot-trails which approach it from every direction. The last time I visited this oasis only five of the original trees were standing, but I counted 25 young trees ranging from two to 25 feet in height.

At Dos Palmas spring, on the desert slope of the Santa Rosa mountains, the original two palms has increased to five, with several additional trees down-stream below the spring. At Dos Palmas, on the old Bradshaw freight route, there are now 27 trees.

The native palms of California are all of the fan type, the species *Washingtonia filifera*. The scientific name was given by a German horticulturalist, Hermann Wendland, in 1879. He saw young trees growing in a hothouse at Ghent, Belgium, from seed brought from the United States. The name was given to honor George Washington, leader of the American revolution, and first president of the U.S.A.

In later years, other botanists added four other species to the genus *Washingtonia*. These were *W. gracilis, W. sonorae, W. robusta* and *W. arizonica*. The latter classification was given in 1923, by O. F. Cook of the U. S. Department of Agriculture, to the palms in Arizona's Kofa mountains. The other three species are natives of the states of Sonora and Baja California in Mexico.

In 1936, Dr. Bailey of Cornell published a monograph in which he suggested that the variations in *robusta, gracilis, son- orae* and *arizonica* were so slight it would greatly simplify the identification of the four if they were all reclassified as *robusta.* Thus, on the authority of the Cornell scientist, we now have but two species in the genus *Washingtonia, robusta* and *filifera.* The two are readily distinguished. Robusta is a tall slender tree some- times reaching a height of 50 or 60 feet. It is widely planted as an ornamental tree in the Southwest. Filifera is a thick-trunked tree seldom growing higher than 35 or 40 feet.

Along the desert escarpment of the Sierra Juarez range, just south of the international boundary in Baja California, is another fan palm distinguished by the bluish cast of its fronds, and, when in fruit, by its seeds. It grows large clusters of marble-sized seeds compared to the pea-size of the Washingtonia genus.

During trips to the canyons of the Sierra Juarez many years ago I noted this strange palm growing in the same canyons with the Washingtonias. Later I brought out some of the seeds and sections of the frond stems and sent them to botanist friends for identification. Evidently they were passed along to Dr. Bailey for I received a letter from him asking for information as to the habitat. A year later, the scientist sent word that on his next trip West he would like to visit one of the canyons where the trees were growing. The trip was arranged, and it proved to be one of the most delightful experiences in my years of palm hunting. The eighty-year-old botanist revealed amazing stamina during the four-mile hike along the rocky trail into Taos Canyon. Along the way he entertained members of our party with his experi- ences around the world in assembling the fine herbarium at the Cornell campus. When we reached the palms he immediately confirmed his previous conjecture that they were one of the blue palm species, the *Erythea armata.* This species is found within 25 miles of the American border, but I have never found a single tree north of the boundary.

Visitors to Palm Canyon, near Palm Springs, note there is considerable variation in the thickness of the trunks of mature trees, some of them approaching the graceful lines of the robusta species. Where the water supply is ample and the trees grow in a dense forest, as in the natural park above Hermit's Bench in this canyon, the trunks tend to be more slender than where the growth is scattered or the water supply more limited.

As the tree grows and puts out new fronds at its crown, the lower fronds die, but do not pull loose from the trunk as do the leaves of most other trees. They hang close to the trunk, forming a thick skirt. These skirts are highly inflammable, and generally on the older trees have been burned away. Sometimes the fires are started by campers, and at other times by lightning. Prehistoric Indians who camped at the palm oases are said to have burned the dead fronds because they believed the thatch was the hiding place of evil spirits.

I have slept on the ground beneath these wild palms many times, and I can understand the reasons for the Indian superstition. Bats, wrens, insects and even rodents sometimes find shelter among the dead fronds. More than once I have been awakened by a faint rustling in the dry skirts overhead.

During the late spring and early summer the mature trees throw out creamy plumes of blossoms among the living fronds. These develop into tiny seed berries and by October great clusters of the dark brown seeds dangle from the foliage. The berry consists of a hard seed covered by a thin sweet skin. The Indians crushed these seeds in crude mortars and made them into a porridge. In Guadalupe Canyon, in Baja California, I once came upon a hermit cutting the tender crown out of the young trees for food. I have never found evidence that the Indians did this. To them the tree was too valuable a source of food and shelter to be destroyed in this manner.

In seeking out the location of palm groups when I had no other clues for guidance, I learned a lesson from the prospectors. In their search for free gold they not only panned the sand of the arroyos, but they kept a sharp eye for float—for pieces of ore which may have broken loose and been washed downstream from a ledge higher up on the mountain. And so I learned to scan the creek beds of the lower canyons for palm float—a bit of frond, a seed stem, or perhaps a section of trunk washed down the canyon. Such evidence unfailingly led to living palm trees higher up.

Whence came these wild palms to the Southern California desert? No one can answer with certainty. It is not true—as some unknowing persons have suggested—that they were planted by the Spanish padres who first came to this region. Undoubtedly the Franciscan fathers, who first established missions in the Californias in the 18th century, planted seeds and grew palms in their settlements. But the palms were here many thousands of years before the white man came to this western hemisphere. Probably they were here before primitive man inhabited the earth. The *California Highway and Public Works* magazine reported in January 1932: "Near Bridge Canyon north of Castaic school the fossilized imprint of a palm leaf was found embedded in limestone. The depth at which the fossil was found was estimated at from 25 to 30 feet below the present surface of the ground."

The Los Angeles museum has a fossil imprint of a palm frond, presumably a fragment of Washingtonia, collected at Austin quarry, Calabasas, California, which scientists believe dates back to the Miocene period. Baja California's palm trees were mentioned by Father Juan Crespi, historian of the Portola expedition, as long ago as 1769, and Father Junipero Serra, who founded the California missions, recorded seeing them the same year.

There is good reason to believe the trees date back to a period when the desert as we know it today was partially inundated, or threaded with swamps and bayous, for there is no escaping the fact that the palm is a water-loving tree. Its shallow root system bears out the conclusion that it has made no evolutionary progress in adapting to dry arid soil or deep water tables, as have the smoke tree and other desert shrubs with long tap roots. Its fronds thrive in the desert sun, and its trunk conserves moisture—but its roots must have a generous supply of water.

My study of the desert palms has convinced me that the original trees in this area survived along the fault lines which more or less parallel the Salton Sea on both sides. These fault lines, where water rises close to the surface of the ground, may accurately be followed from an airplane overhead by noting the extra growth of vegetation which marks them. These stringers of vegetation often include palm trees.

The palms in the canyons, where the greater numbers are found, are migrants from the floor of the desert. Their seeds from the parent trees along the fault lines were brought into the canyons by Indians and coyotes, and possibly, in the case of Kofa Palm Canyon, by birds. The Indians carried them, as they did mesquite beans and chia seed, for food. The coyotes eat the fruit as it falls to the ground, but digest only the sweet skins. Undigested palm seeds may be seen in coyote dung in nearly all the desert canyons where there is water. The coyote is despised as a chicken thief and camp robber—but I believe this wild dog of the desert must be credited, more than any other agent, for the fine stand of palmettos in Palm Canyon and the many other canyon oases where the Washingtonia thrives today.

Since a palm tree has no growth rings by which its age may be determined, I have sought the answer in other directions. There are canyons where I can identify three different generations—all of them fully mature. The separate generations may be determined by the fire scars on the trunk, for all the aged trees have been burned, and by the length of the dead frond skirts. It is not uncommon to find a fire-scarred veteran of perhaps 150 years growing close beside another tree which has a full skirt of dry fronds. Considering the inflammability of the dead fronds, it is obvious the older tree reached full maturity before the adjacent tree had sprouted.

Fortunately, the fire which strips the palm of its dry fronds seldom kills the tree. The outer surface of the trunk may be charred and the green fronds at the crown singed until they wilt and die, but within a few weeks a new growth of fronds emerges and the vitality of the tree appears in no way impaired by the flames. Actually, the burned tree almost invariably grows a heavier crop of seed the following season—as if Nature had stepped up its reproductive process to compensate for any destruction that may have been caused by its flaming enemy.

The effect of water supply on the growth of the Washingtonia has been demonstrated by trees I have grown domestically. Twelve years ago I transplanted some native seedlings given me by Paul Wilhelm of Thousand Palms Canyon. They were three years old and 2½ feet high. Part of them were planted where they received only a weekly irrigation. They now average less than six feet in height. Others were planted where for six months of the year they received daily irrigation of warm water, the waste from a refrigeration cooling system in a nearby building. These palms are now twenty feet high.

The root system of the tree consists of hundreds of small rootlets, each no thicker than a lead pencil, which spread through the ground immediately below the surface. The sap flows from roots to crown in the porous heart of the tree. It is this characteristic of the tree that enables it to survive even when the bark—if the outer covering of the trunk may be called bark—is blackened with char.

Why does a person, presumably in his right mind, spend his weekends for many years hunting for palm trees? I can only answer that by suggesting other questions: Why do men and women climb mountains, or run the treacherous rapids of the Colorado River in wooden boats?

To active-minded human beings life would be meaningless without goals. They cannot all set out as did Christopher Columbus in quest of a new world, or Admiral Byrd in search for the South Pole. Most of us have to be content with more modest projects. But in nearly every member of the human species there is the built-in urge for conquest—for exploration. This is especially true of youth. And so we embark on whatever form of adventure our environment will suggest and our circumstances will permit.

Oh, I know, the psychologists have a more scientific—and incomprehensible—explanation for human impulses than I am suggesting. But the basic urges in human nature really are not as complicated as some of the minds in the ivory towers would have us believe. If parents and teachers and law-makers better understood the basic emotions which are the dynamo of human conduct I am sure there would be less alcoholism, fewer love triangles, and certainly less crime and juvenile delinquency than plague our society today.

I am sure no winner of the Indianapolis Sweepstakes or the Open Golf championship or the Kentucky Derby ever experienced a deeper sense of achievement or a more lasting satisfaction than came to me the day, after six fruitless weekends spent scaling the rocks and plodding up the sand canyons of the Inkopah Mountains of Southern California, I finally got my first glimpse of the pretty palm oasis near the fantastic rock formation known as Dos Cabezos.

CHAPTER III. *Flag flying and steam engine belching smoke, the stern-wheeler Explorer departs from Yuma landing on its great adventure—to determine officially if the Colorado River could be a navigable stream.*
—Old lithograph made from sketch by H. B. Mollhausen.

161

The rusting iron skeleton of the historic steamboat was discovered, partially buried in the silt from the Colorado River, seventy years later.

CHAPTER V. *Seventeen Palms in the Borrego Badlands of Southern California. The fabulous and long hunted Lost Pegleg nuggets are believed to be somewhere in the region surrounding this lonely oasis.*

Superstition Mountains in central Arizona. For seventy years treasure hunters have been seeking the Lost Dutchman mine in these mountains

—*Josef Muench photo.*

CHAPTER VI.   *Death Valley Scotty, center, with Bessie and Albert John-*
son in the lounge of the fabulous Castle they built in the Death Valley
desert. Johnson bequeathed the Castle to the Gospel Foundation of Cali-
fornia where it is open today with guided tours for its many visitors.

—*Top photo, Frasher's Inc., Pomona, Calif.*

163

Chapter VIII.

EVERETT RUESS

To the left—Everett in Canyon de Chelly as sketched by G. A. Randall

Chapter IX. *Kaiparowits Plateau in southern Utah where the ancient Moqui cliff-dwellers built their stone and mud houses in recesses high in the cliff walls—and then for unknown reasons abandoned the area.*

165

CHAPTER X. *Hidden Palms oasis in the Mecca Hills of Southern California. Hemmed in by cliff walls of an obscure side canyon, this spring more often quenches thirst of deer and other wildlife than human beings.*

—Dick Freeman photo.

CHAPTER XIII.   *The Monument Valley—the Graveyard of the Gods—here gigantic pinnacles and domes of red sandstone rise from eight hundred to twelve hundred feet above the floor of the desert.*

A Navajo medicine man and his helper create one of the sand paintings which are an essential part of many of the tribal healing ceremonies.

—*Josef Muench photos.*

CHAPTER XIII. *Into this fantastic setting where the blue of the distant horizon is punctured in every direction by protruding spires, turrets, domes and embattlements, came Harry and "Mike" Goulding in 1924 to establish a trading post for Chief Hoskininni's irreconcilable Navajos.*

—*Josef Muench photos.*

CHAPTER XIV. *Two of the Snake priests, writhing reptiles in their mouths, who participate in the famous Smoki dances at Prescott.*

—Harry Vroman photo.

169

Climaxing the Smoki Snake Dance, Snake and Antelope priests form a circle and hold aloft their "Little Brothers" before dispatching them as messengers to the gods of the underworld.

—Photo courtesy The Smoki People.

Chapter XVI. *Land of the Standing Rocks in southern Utah. Members of the author's party reached this almost inaccessible region in three jeeps. This wild area was once the home of prehistoric Indian tribesmen, and later was one of the hideaways of Butch Cassidy and his outlaws.*

CHAPTER XVI. *Palm Canyon in Southern California, having an estimated 3000 native trees, provides recreation for both riders and hikers who visit Palm Springs.* —*Chuck Abbott photo.*

CHAPTER XVI. *Described by Secretary of Interior Stewart Udall as "the most awe-inspiring work of natural sculpture in the United States," Rainbow Natural Bridge in southern Utah desert is accessible only by foot trail. Less than 14,000 visitors have signed its register since it became a national monument in 1913. The great bridge is 308 feet high and has a span of 270 feet.*

—*Josef Muench photos.*

CHAPTER XVI. *In Havasupai Canyon, in northern Arizona. The Supai children are eating a new sweetmeat—dates given them by the photographer. Below are Mooney Falls on the left and Havasu Falls on the right.*

CHAPTER XVIII. *Coachella Valley Mineral Society always takes its chuckwagon on a field trip. When mealtime comes the rockhounds don the garb of kitchen police. These pictures were taken at one of the Society's treks to a fire agate deposit in the Southern California desert.*

CHAPTER XIX. *Pictographs painted by prehistoric tribesmen on the wall of Horseshoe Canyon near the Green River in Utah.*

175

The Navajo medicine man is no less puzzled as to the origin and meaning of these petroglyphs incised on the rock in Monument Valley than are white men. —*Josef Muench photos.*

CHAPTER XX. *The sap of barrel cactus is bitter but thirst-quenching if one has the energy and tools to penetrate its wiry armor. Bill Sherrill, with a machete, and Arles Adams with handpick, solved the problem.*

—*Josef Muench photos.*

176

BAJA CALIFORNIA TRAILS   XI

WE WENT hunting for a palm canyon, and found a tribe of Indians. That, briefly, is what happened one weekend in April when four of us in two jeeps crossed through the Calexico-Mexicali port of entry for an exploring excursion in Baja California. My companions were Bill Sherrill of the U. S. Immigration Border Patrol, Arles Adams, and his son Tony.

One of the Mexican workers in his flax processing crew at the mill in El Centro, California, had told Arles about a remote canyon south of the border with *muchas palmas* and many springs of water. That was to be our destination. The directions for reaching the cliff-walled oasis in this unmapped land of few roads were rather hazy but with jeeps for transportation the search would at least be an interesting adventure.

For the information of those unfamiliar with the geography of this region, the great Sierra Nevada range, which forms the backbone and runs the full length of California, separating the coastal plain from the desert interior, also extends deep into Baja California. South of the border it is known as the Sierra Juarez, and still further south, the San Pedro Martir range.

The canyon we sought was one of the many gorges which drain the desert slope of the Sierra Juarez and empty their storm water into the delta of the Colorado River or the Gulf of California. Many of them are palm canyons, and there are flowing streams in some of them in seasons of normal rainfall.

A few miles out of Mexicali an unimproved dirt road swings to the south and crosses the Laguna Salada, a great dry lake bed which at long intervals is filled with backwater from one of the delta channels of the Colorado. Even when filled it is a shallow lagoon, and following its periodic floods the water evaporates in two or three years. Then there is an interval of five, ten or twenty years when its floor is dry and hard, and soon becomes crisscrossed with the truck-tracks of Mexican woodcutters who chop down the ironwood, palo verde and mesquite trees around its shores to stoke the wood stoves of Mexicali. The lake bed, or playa as it is known to the Mexicans, is barren of vegetation.

For sixty miles we rolled along the smooth floor of the playa, and then climbed a gentle *bajada* to a plateau that parallels the base of the Sierra Juarez. We assumed we were on a woodcutter's road, and continued another thirty miles until it crossed an arroyo and turned sharply into a canyon in the Sierra. The road came to an abrupt end before a rather spacious mud and thatch house beside a spring where two palm trees were growing.

There were women and children, goats, dogs and chickens in the dooryard, and beside a gnarled hitching-post an Indian was saddling his pony. Arles spoke to him in Spanish. He replied, hesitantly at first, and we were not sure we were welcome guests at this remote oasis. Both Arles and Bill speak the language of Mexico fluently, and they assured him we carried no firearms, and that our mission was friendly.

Ramon Arvallo was his name. He told us he was a brother of Juan Arvallo, the chief of a little remnant of the Catarina Yuma Indians, who still dwell near the top of the range at the site of the old Dominican mission of Santa Catarina de los Yumas. These Indians call themselves the Pai-Pai.

Arthur W. North, and other early explorers in Baja California, reported that they were hostile and thievish. This appraisal is borne out by historical records of the old missions, which reveal that Santa Catarina was the last of the missions founded by the Dominican Frailes. Built in 1797, the 1500 Indians in the mission parish were never peaceful. After several revolts, they finally killed or drove away the last of the padres in 1840, and burned the mission. It was never rebuilt.

During our two days with these Indians we learned there are now less than 100 of them, living in three settlements. In the adobe house, where our road ended, there were only Ramon and his family. Five miles upstream was a hot spring which had given this water course its name—Arroyo Agua Caliente. At the spring, Ramon told us, was another camp occupied by two families of the Pai-Pai. Remaining members of the tribe lived in mud and stone houses at the site of the old mission at the headwaters of the canyon on the ridge above.

Arles asked if we might continue up the arroyo to the spring. Ramon tried to discourage the idea, and we wondered if we might encounter hostility there. After some palaver, it became apparent his hesitancy was prompted by doubt that our cars could make it up the roadless canyon. We reassured him, but before we reached the upper camp we could well understand his skepticism. We followed a sandy rock-strewn horse trail, overgrown in many places with brush. We made it, but at times we had to thread our way carefully through great patches of agave, or mescal, as it is known to the Mexicans. No tire will resist the needle points on the mescal blades.

Soon after we left the camp Ramon caught up with us on his pony, and dispelled any doubts as to his goodwill by riding ahead and picking out the best route for the cars. Later, one of the Indians at the upper camp told us we were the first party of white Americans to visit them during the thirty years he had lived there.

As we bucked the sand, rocks and brush going up the arroyo there were little groups of native palms along the tiny stream of water. On a slope above the creek were gorgeous fields of wild-flowers in bloom. Hedgehog cactus was displaying its clusters of silky cerise petals, my favorite among all the desert blossoms. There were many colors, the bright red of ocotillo, the reddish brown of prickly pear, the ghostly lemon-yellow of the bisnaga, the dainty pink of fairy duster, which resembles a ball of thread that has exploded.

Nearing Agua Caliente spring we came to an impassable dike of rock, and there we would camp for the night. Our first concern was to establish friendly relations with the Indians at the spring. With Ramon as our guide we hiked along the creek through a vista of stately Washingtonia palms to the village. There, from Ramon and his sister, Benita, a very superior-type of middle-aged woman, we learned much about the life of this little band of Catarina Yumas.

Over a hundred years had passed since the mission on the ridge above had been burned and the Dominican fathers forced to flee for their lives, but the spiritual seeds they had planted had borne some fruit. Very few of the Pai-Pais have ever been in a church, yet they regard themselves as Christians, and Benita was wearing a rosary.

These tribesmen have a little cash income from two sources. During the cotton harvest on the rich delta land below Mexicali, younger members of the tribe ride eighty miles on their ponies

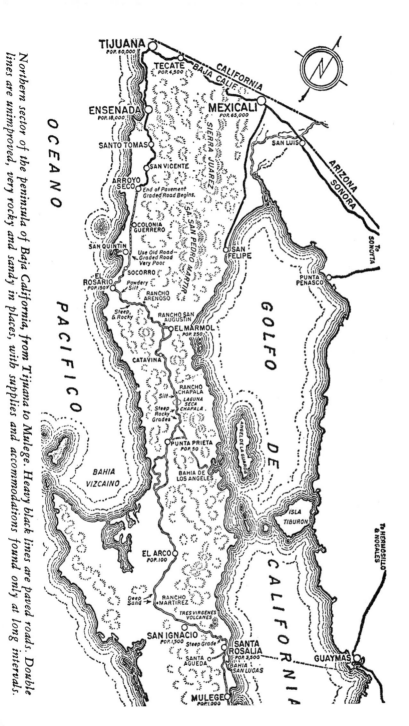

Northern sector of the peninsula of Baja California, from Tijuana to Mulege. Heavy black lines are paved roads. Double lines are unimproved, very rocky and sandy in places, with supplies and accommodations found only at long intervals.

and work as cotton-pickers for two or three months. Also, they run cattle on the desert range, and once a year drive a few steers over the mountain to Ensenada on the Pacific coast sixty miles away.

Much of their food comes from the natural landscape. They gather seeds from the chia species of sage in May, and in August go to the higher elevations for pinyon nuts and acorns. There is fresh meat or jerky from their own herds. In April, when the agave is in bud, they have roast mescal, and also eat the flower stalks, which have the sweetness and about the same texture as sugar cane. Tuna, or cactus apples, from the prickly pear, which grows luxuriantly below the spring, is another item of food, and they are quite adept at removing the tiny spines which cover the fruit. They mentioned certain other roots, and two or three species of wild seeds with which I am not familiar. Below the spring was a little orchard, fenced with ocotillo stalks, in which were fig and pomegranate trees, no doubt grown from cuttings or root-stock originally brought to the mission of Santa Catarina 150 years ago by the padres.

Tramping over the desert in previous years I had often come across mescal pits—small cavities in the ground lined with rocks—which had been used by prehistoric tribesmen to roast one of their staple foods, the heart of the agave plant. This was my first contact with the Indians who still depend on agave for food, and since this was the season when the plant was in bud, here was an opportunity to learn something about the culinary art of roasting mescal.

The Indians were quite willing to cooperate, and at sundown I went up on the hillside and selected a bud a few inches high. It resembled a thick stalk of asparagus just emerging from the center of a roseate of dagger-like blades. The Indians in the old days would gouge the bud out of the center of the plant with a sharp stick. Our time was limited and I modernized the operation by getting a machete out of one of the jeeps. The Indians liked the new tool. While they were separating the bud stalk from its cluster of armored blades, I began digging the pit. When it was two feet deep, and eighteen inches wide, I laid down the shovel. One of the Indian boys promptly picked it up, and when he had finished, the hole was nearly three feet deep and three feet in diameter. I had flunked my first lesson.

Then, at the direction of Ramon, we all began bringing in small boulders, and while he lined the cavity we gathered fire-wood. A huge fire was built in the pit, and when it had burned down to a bed of embers, he tossed the mescal—about the shape and twice the size of a pineapple—into the center of it. More hot rocks were pushed in around the mescal, and then a foot of sand spread over the top.

Scene II of the mescal roasting party was at nine the next morning, when the Indians came down from their camp to uncover the pit. The entire tribe was there. After much sand and many rocks had been removed, we found the charred "pine-apple" shrunken to about half its normal size. The Indians stripped off the husks, much as one would go about eating an artichoke. The meaty core in the center was split open with a hunting knife, and it was a delicious morsel, about the shade of ripe cantaloupe. Ramon told us it would have been better to have been left in the pit a few hours longer. Then the center would have been about the color and consistency of a cooked yam—sweet and gooey.

More than anything else it tasted like sweet potato, and the cooking job could not have been too bad, for after we visitors had each eaten a sliver, the Indian women finished it with relish. Later in the day we bade our Indian friends goodbye, leaving them most of the food in our grub boxes.

The Pai-Pai are one of the few tribal groups surviving out of an Indian population estimated at more than 40,000 when the Jesuit priest Juan Maria Salvatierra established the first Baja California mission in 1697. The Indians of that period depended entirely on the game, and native plants of this arid land, and such sea food as could be caught with crude implements. They were always near the point of starvation. The drastic reduction in native population during the last 300 years is attributed partly to a birth rate which had overtaken the natural carrying capacity of the land, and partly to epidemic diseases brought in by Spanish soldiers and sailors.

The Baja California peninsula today, extending from the California border over 800 miles south to Cape San Lucas, is for the most part desert. The only variations in the prevailing aridity are the higher levels of the Sierra Juarez and the San Pedro Martir ranges where coniferous trees grow above the 6000-foot level, and a zone of tropical rainfall and vegetation at the southernmost tip south of La Paz.

However, it is a luxuriant desert, much of it covered by flowering shrubs and trees of drought-resistant species which are a delight to the botanist and a source of great interest to those hardy motorists who venture beyond the paved roads. As funds are available, a macadam highway slowly is being extended down the peninsula and has now reached a point 140 miles south of the California border, along the Pacific coast. Beyond this point graded roads are under construction, but the distance from Ensenada to Santa Rosalia is 541 miles, and some of it too treacherous to be undertaken by a heavy stock model automobile. From the old mining town of Santa Rosalia on the Gulf coast it is another 352 miles to La Paz. From this pearl fishing port on the Gulf coast there are two routes to San José del Cabo near the tip of the peninsula, the distance about 130 miles.

For the American motorist who travels for pleasure and prefers paved roads and frequent service stations, Baja California is still a raw frontier, and the long trip down the peninsula an adventure to be postponed to a future day. The Mexican administration is fully cognizant of the value of tourist travel, and is looking ahead to the day when good highway facilities will be provided the full length of the peninsula—but that will be mañana.

However, there are two paved highways in Baja California which may be traveled in comfort and without hazard. One of these parallels and is never more than 25 miles south of the California or Arizona borders, extending from Tijuana opposite San Diego, through Mexicali and San Luis to Sonoyta in the State of Sonora. This well-engineered road, starting from sea level at Tijuana, climbs over the Sierra Juarez at an elevation of approximately 5000 feet, then descends to sea level again at Mexicali in the great delta of the Colorado River. Mexicali, with a population of over 100,000, is a thriving agricultural city, typically Mexican in many respects, yet providing excellent accommodations for the motorist, and the native handicrafts sought by souvenir hunters.

The other Baja California road popular with American motorists is the paved highway from the Mexicali port of entry to the little fishing village of San Felipe on the Gulf coast 130 miles to the south. This highway passes through the cultivated farm lands of the Colorado delta, then skirts an expansive salt flat at the head of the Gulf, and finally follows the Gulf coast to the bay of San Felipe, where a primitive town of 1000 Mexicans derives its income from fishing and tourists.

The Gulf waters are famed for their abundant supply of sea food. Sea bass and shrimp are trucked from here to the Southern California markets. There are charter boats available for visiting sportsmen, and comfortable motor court accommodations.

Permits may be obtained at the border or from Mexican consulates at nominal cost, with a minimum of red tape. Mexicali and Tijuana are free zones and there are no passport requirements for visitors who enter Mexico only for a day of sightseeing in the border towns. Americans carrying foreign-made cameras or other equipment manufactured outside the United States, should register these at the custom house on the American side of the line before leaving the country.

For more than forty years I have been crossing the international border into Baja California, including fifteen years' residence in Calexico, and I have acquired a great fondness for the Mexican people. They are friendly and cooperative when their laws and their dignity as human beings are respected. They have intense pride—but also a fine sense of humor.

As in every part of the desert Southwest, the rugged land beyond the terrain which borders the paved roads is always a fascinating challenge. This is especially true in the Baja California immediately south of the international border because of the inaccessibility of this region. My unplanned intrusion into the camp of the Pai-Pai Indians merely is one of many delightful experiences in the exploration of this region. I got my first glimpse of Laguna Salada in 1922, then a lake 60 miles long and 18 miles wide. Since then this lake has gone through three cycles of overflow and total evaporation. When the construction of Hoover Dam in the Colorado River near Las Vegas in 1936 ended the great seasonal floods following the melting of snow in the Rocky Mountain watershed, many of us assumed that the factors of silt deposit and erosion in the delta of the river which had caused the filling of the inland basin would no longer operate. We were mistaken. Laguna Salada, like desert weather and the peregrinations of burros, is unpredictable.

This region has a special interest for those who like to follow the desert byways. On one trek along the rocky *bajada* which rises in a gentle slope from the lake shore to the toe of the Sierra Juarez, I came upon great piles of driftwood. Palm logs were heaped in confusion—many hundreds of them. Tracing the dry water course to the mouth of the canyon from whence they had come, and following the gorge upstream to a beautiful waterfall, I found additional evidence that a cataclysmic torrent at some unrecorded date had swept down from the slopes and completely transformed the character of this mountain chasm. The story was not hard to visualize. The little creek in the floor of this canyon had been lined for a distance of three miles with a dense forest of native palm trees.

There had occurred one of those torrential cloudbursts—
"hundred-year floods," the engineers term them because of their
infrequency—which sooner or later come to nearly every desert
community situated along the dry channel of a main water
course. The flood not only had swept away the entire forest, but
had rolled huge boulders down from the mountainside and so
clogged the canyon it was difficult to make my way over, around
and under them. A few veteran trees, growing on ledges high
up on the side of the canyon, had survived the flood. A new
generation of young palms growing among the boulders in the
floor of the canyon indicated this flood had taken place in recent
years, for none of these trees were more than 25 years of age.

This was one of the many unnamed canyons in Baja California, and with some coaching from my Spanish-speaking companion I recorded it in my log book as Cañon de los Torrentos—
Cloudburst Canyon.

Cloudburst Canyon is one of a score of deep gorges which
slash the desert slope of the Sierra Juarez, and empty their occasional flood streams into Laguna Salada. One of these is Guadalupe Canyon where hot and cold springs emerge from the rocks
within a short distance of each other. Guadalupe derives its
name from a conspicuous pinnacle on the skyline above, a spire
of rock which so resembles a human figure the Mexicans named
it for the Virgin of Guadalupe.

In nearly all these canyons the *Washingtonia filifera* of the
California desert grows side by side with the blue palm, *Erythea
armata*, both members of the fan palm family. Farther south on
the peninsula are other species of wild palms, the most conspicuous of which is *Washingtonia robusta,* easily distinguished from
its cousin the *filifera* by its great height and slender graceful
trunk.

In all these canyons are relics of ancient Indian habitation.
One often sees petroglyphs on the walls, *morteros* or grinding
holes in the rocks, and occasionally a smoke-blackened cave. The
shards of Indian pottery are common-place, and old trails lead

to the top of the Sierra Juarez where the desert tribesmen went for pinyon nuts.

The high adventure of my Baja California exploration was the ascent of Picacho del Diablo, or as it is recorded on some of the old maps, La Encantada. This peak in the San Pedro Martir range has an elevation of 10,136 feet and is the highest on the peninsula.

Malcolm Huey and I attempted to reach this summit in 1934, but we had underestimated the climbing difficulties. Our route was up Providencia Canyon, which seemed to provide the most direct route to the peak, fifteen miles away. Starting from the floor of the desert, at an elevation of 1500 feet, we spent an entire day wading pools, scaling or detouring waterfalls and bucking heavy brush in the floor of the canyon, and reached only the 3800-foot level. We found shelter that night in a cave when rain began falling. The next morning the slopes above were covered with snow. After two hours of slow progress over slippery rocks we realized the two days' provisions we carried in our packs were not enough, and turned back.

A year later a second attempt was made with Huey, Wilson McKenney and Paul Cook as my companions. At the end of the second day we camped at the 7000-foot level. From here we spent another day exploring possible routes and eventually reached a secondary peak separated from the highest summit by a deep chasm. Again, lack of time forced us to turn back without attaining the goal.

In April the following year, Norman Clyde, veteran mountaineer from the High Sierras, came down to the desert to join me in the attempt. Taking advantage of the lessons learned on previous expeditions, we reached the top late in the afternoon of the third day, and stood on the one point on the peninsula where it is possible to view both the Gulf of California on the east and the Pacific Ocean, where the sun was setting in the west.

We bivouacked that night in a sheltered cove just below a snowbank near the summit, and spent two days returning down

Providencia Canyon. On the return we roped down over several waterfalls we had detoured on the ascent. At one place in the upper canyon is a series of ten natural tanks, one above the other, eroded in a 500-foot slick rock face of granite, each of them a lovely pool of water separated by waterfalls. This formation required a long and treacherous detour—treacherous because the slopes on both sides of the canyon are overgrown with dense gardens of agave, commonly called century plant. The needle-like points on the thick stiff blades of this succulent are hazardous to both man and wildlife, and I attribute the absence of the spoor of deer or bighorn sheep on the desert face of the San Pedro Martirs to the extensive growth of this plant above the 2500-foot level.

In a cairn at the top of Picacho del Diablo we found records of two previous ascents of the peak from the Pacific side by members of the Sierra Club of California. There was no record of a previous ascent from the desert, but several mountaineers have made the climb since then, and have found a more feasible route than that followed by Clyde and myself.

If there had been greater foresight in the halls of Congress in 1854, when the James Gadsden proposal for the purchase of a large parcel of desert domain from Mexico was under consideration, it might have been possible for Uncle Sam to acquire the entire peninsula at a nominal cost.

But 107 years ago no one envisioned the impact of increasing population and industrialization on the geography of this nation. And who would have dreamed that the desert Southwest would some day compete with Florida as a lure to winter vacationists? There was opposition even to the acquisition of the 30,000 square miles in what is now southern Arizona and New Mexico, which became the Gadsden Purchase.

It is too late now, and perhaps we should have no regrets. Under the impact of Yankee commercialization it seems inevitable that the 2000-mile shoreline of the narrow peninsula, with its lovely bays and beaches, would have become dotted with sophisticated bathing and fishing resorts. Perhaps a swanky hotel, overlooking the scenic waterfalls in Providencia Canyon, would be competing with the Seven Falls of Colorado Springs as a tourist attraction. So far, the peninsula has been spared the ignominy of thousands of miles of highway roadsides cluttered with beer cans and other debris, as in *Alta* California.

Baja California, for the most part, is still a desert wilderness —a great natural botanical garden of beautiful and sometimes grotesque members of the plant world. Unwittingly Congress in 1854 assured the preservation of the natural charm of this land for at least another century.

In the face of expanding population it cannot always remain so, but those who would bequeath to future generations at least some portion of the virgin landscape as the Creator designed it, will hope the day of exploitation will be postponed until that time when both Mexicans and *Norte Americanos* will have learned to regard the good earth and its plant and wildlife with a deeper sense of reverence than prevails in the United States today.

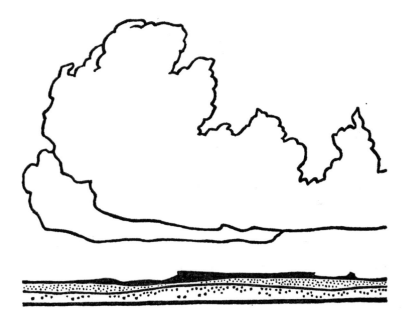

HOGAN OF A MEDICINE MAN   **XII**

A WINDING dirt road that led deep into the pine forest of northeastern Arizona brought me late one afternoon to the hogan of Ayoo'anlh nezi, medicine man of the Navajo Indians. My companion and guide was Richard F. Van Valkenburgh who at that time was stationed at Fort Defiance as ethnologist for the U. S. Bureau of Indian Affairs.

Van had invited me to accompany him on this trip. He wanted to take pictures to illustrate a story he was writing for the *Desert Magazine* about a well-preserved multiple cliff dwelling known as the House of the Three Turkeys, which he recently had seen. It was his friend Ayoo'anlh nezi who had first revealed the location of this prehistoric cliff dwelling to him, and we were to camp that night at the medicine man's hogan.

Van Valkenburgh had lived among these people for many years and was learning their language. His friendship for them was genuine. They sensed this, and while the greeting we received was reserved, it was friendly and sincere.

During the 24 hours we were at the camp I got a rather intimate glimpse of the daily life of the Navajo singer and his wife and two children, from the butchering of a sheep to provide broiled mutton for the evening meal to the weaving of a rug which, when completed, would be taken to the trader to exchange for sugar, flour and cotton goods.

That evening we sat on the ground around the outdoor fire and ate our mutton and fried bread, with some added delicacies from our own grub box. The medicine man spoke some English, but the conversation was carried on mostly in Navajo which was interpreted for my benefit. Van told me our host knew the ways of the white men better than a majority of the elders of the tribe. In his younger days he was a skilled silversmith and was one of a group of Indians taken to the Panama-Pacific International Exposition in San Francisco by the Indian Bureau in 1915 to demonstrate craftsmanship of the tribesmen.

Ayoo'anlh nezi was sixty-nine at the time of my visit. His grandfather, Chalisani, was a medicine man, and had begun teaching his grandson the Indian chants and sacred prayers as soon as he was old enough to talk. At the age of twelve he began to learn the Life chant, and was taught how to identify and gather the plants and herbs used in healing ceremonies. Then followed lessons in the making of sand paintings, which are an essential part of every sing.

Later in the evening members of the Indian family retired to the hogan, where their beds were sheepskins on the dirt floor, and Van and I spread our bedrolls outside. But before we retired, the little girl—I would not attempt to spell her Navajo name—had a new experience, and so did I. There was a box of marshmallows in my grub box and I taught her how to toast them over the campfire coals at the end of a juniper stick. She accepted the first one gingerly, but after tasting the candy her eyes twinkled with enjoyment, and soon she was toasting marshmallows for the group.

We were up at daybreak the next morning, and while the mother was preparing fried bread for breakfast, the father and daughter knelt on the ground, where she untied the bandeau around his head and washed his hair in suds made from yucca roots. After the meal the girl and her older brother turned the sheep out of the corral and followed them through the woods for the day's grazing. We did not see them again until they returned as the sun was setting.

White parents would marvel at the industry and obedience of these Navajo children. One of the reasons for this discipline, I am sure, is related to the gentle manner in which the Indians address each other. During the time I was at the hogan I never heard a voice raised in impatience or command—not even when a battle-scarred old rooster annoyed the eleven-year-old girl with his persistent efforts to rush in and grab a bit of dough from the pan in which she was making bread. She shooed him away with a soft-spoken Navajo word that I would have taken to be a term of endearment under any other circumstances.

With Ayoo'anlh nezi leading the way, Van and I set off through the forest toward the canyon where the cliff house was located. Soon we were following the bed of a meandering arroyo. Gradually, the walls on both sides closed in and as we continued downstream the canyon became deeper and our glimpses of the sun less frequent. Occasionally we saw crumbling hogans perched high in recesses in the canyon walls. Our guide told us these were the former homes of his relatives, who as fugitives, had hidden in the canyon to escape capture by the soldiers of Kit Carson during the Navajo roundup in 1863.

It was mid-morning when the medicine man stopped, and I followed his gaze to a point high in the cliff wall where in a vast recess beneath a great overhang of sandstone was the most perfectly preserved group of cliff dwellings I had ever seen. We sat in the shade of an oak tree to study the picture. We estimated there were at least twenty rooms in the sprawling pueblo. They were built of sandstone slabs laid with adobe mortar. The circular walls of a plastered kiva or ceremonial chamber rose above the cluster of buildings.

And there, on an upper wall, were the three turkeys which identified this abandoned cliff dwelling. They were painted in brown and white pigment. We judged them to be at least six feet high, and they were grouped close together. The pigment with which they had been painted at least 300 years previously was in a fine state of preservation.

In imagination, we went back to the period of long ago when tribesmen of unknown lineage, presumably for defensive purposes, had selected this almost inaccessible cavern for their abode. It must have taken months, perhaps years, for a colony of a hundred or more men and women to carry the stones one by one up the almost vertical wall to the site fifty feet above the floor of the canyon. Some badly-eroded hand-and-toe steps were visible in the wall. Perhaps notched logs were used for ladders, with yucca fiber guide ropes in the steepest places. As an added measure of defense, or perhaps to keep the children of the tribe from falling from the cliff, a stone and mud parapet had been built on the sloping edge of the cavern floor just below the dwellings.

Modern anthropologists regard it as quite obvious these cliff dwellings were built in almost inaccessible places as a measure of protection against hostile tribesmen. But among the Navajo the answer is not as simple as that. When Van asked the medicine man why the prehistoric Indians selected such a place for their home he replied:

"These old people whom the wind, rain and lightning destroyed and whom we call the Old Ones, lived in this country before the Navajo. Only our gods and holy people dwelt here then. But there were also evil gods who would come and sit at the base of the rock and taunt the cliff people and try to get them to come down from their high places so they could carry them away."

It was hard to realize this well-preserved cliff settlement had long been deserted. Wood smoke should have been coming from the roof vents. Naked children should have been playing on the mud housetops, and women should have been climbing the sheer hand-and-toe trail with grain and squash from fields somewhere below, slung from their shoulders in nets of yucca fiber.

We explored the possibility of climbing the wall, but the old finger holds were too badly eroded. The ascent could be made only with ladders or other special equipment. However, when Van Valkenburgh reported this find to the Museum of Northern Arizona at Flagstaff, he was advised that the House of the Three Turkeys was known to them and had been explored by their archeologists.

My first visit to the Three Turkey House, or *Tatazih bekin* as the cliff dwelling is known to the Navajo, was 23 years ago. My friend Richard Van Valkenburgh and the medicine man Ayoo' no longer are living. But in the intervening years I have had the opportunity to become much better acquainted with the Navajos. This acquaintance has derived less from personal contact than with Anglo-Americans who have been closely associated with them over long periods of years, such personages as John and Louisa Wetherill. John was one of the original discoverers of the Mesa Verde ruins in Colorado, and Louisa spoke Navajo fluently and made a special study of the ethno-botany of these people. The Wetherills had a trading post at Kayenta, Arizona, for many years before their death.

Then there were Harry and Mike Goulding of the Monument Valley trading post; Cozy McSparron of the Thunderbird trad-

ing post at Canyon de Chelly; Joe Kerley, trader for many years
at Tuba City; Gladwell Richardson, who grew up in a family of
traders at Inscription House, Arizona; Shine Smith, most of
whose life has been dedicated to free lance missionary work
among the Navajo; Lorenzo Hubbell, Jr., at Oraibi in the Hopi
country; and Sandy Hassell, long-time trader, who in more recent
years has been a dealer in Indian goods in Santa Fe and Denver.
I am also indebted to M. L. Woodard, for many years secretary
of the Indian Traders' Association and later manager of the annual Inter-Tribal Indian Ceremonials at Gallup, New Mexico.

From these and many other friends in the Indian country of
Arizona, New Mexico and Utah, I have gained an understanding
of Navajo character and custom which, although not always
flattering to them, has convinced me these Indians have the
same potential for honor and dishonor as do humans everywhere.
Their religion is a strange medley of superstitions, which, to the
Anglo-American mind, seem quite irrational, and yet I have found
in no religious creed a more admirable passage than the prayer
of a devout Navajo as he departs on an important mission:

> *With beauty before me, I walk;*
> *With beauty behind me, I walk:*
> *Grant me fidelity in my journey.*
> *In beauty I walk.*

The older Navajos have great pride in their tribe. Traditionally, like many other races of men, they regard themselves as
favored children of the earth. They refer to themselves as *Dineh,*
meaning The People.

Louisa Wetherill once gave me what I have always regarded
as the best formula for dealing with them: "As a guest in a land
where most white people are regarded with suspicion, always
remember that your acceptance by The People will depend on
your ability to accept with dignity, sympathy and honesty the
Navajo way of life. Treated right, the Navajos become humorous, dignified and loyal friends."

From Van Valkenburgh and Sandy Hassell I learned much about their customs. "My first rebuff from a Navajo," Van Valkenburgh once told me, "was when I learned that asking personal questions of a strange Indian is not good manners. Invariably, the Navajo will reply '*hola*', meaning 'Who knows?' Even a slight acquaintance does not give one the privilege of being inquisitive.

"The best approach to a Navajo is through a trader whom the Indians respect. With a long tradition of service to The People, such as dispensing medicine, giving first aid, mediating family troubles, interpreting and writing letters, creating markets for Indian crafts work, extending credit and burying the dead, the Indians look to a veteran trader as both friend and protector insofar as his dealings with the white man's world are involved."

Van recalled an experience with the tribesmen soon after his assignment to the Indian Agency headquarters at Fort Defiance. "I was sent out to do some archeological work in the Wupatki Basin, 40 miles northeast of Flagstaff. Here the members of a big tribal family known as the Peshlakai lived in hogans and grazed their sheep in a jumbled terrain of malpais, volcanic cinders and sandstone boulders.

"I had been told the Peshlakai were unfriendly to the whites. The grandfather of the tribe had become embittered many years previously when he was forced to vacate some mesa land outside the reservation where he had squatted in the 1870s.

"During the first few days after we moved in, even though the Peshlakai flocks were being watered at Wupatki Spring near our camp, we were ignored as completely as if we had been slabs of sandstone. But one evening when the Indian children were watering their sheep at the spring, I noticed they were suffering from a skin infection. From my first aid kit I obtained a can of healing salve, and showed them how it was to be rubbed on the skin, not eaten. Shying away from my attempts to apply the salve, one of the children finally came close enough to grab the can and then scoot off through the cinders toward home.

"Early the next morning a Navajo wagon drove into our camp. The father of the children climbed down from the seat and extended his hand. The Navajo handshake is not a hearty pumping, but a gentle handclasp. With him was one of his older daughters who evidently had been in school for she spoke fair English. She approached me shyly and said: 'My mother says it is good to give the children healing medicine. Sleep came to their eyes last night. This morning we came to tell you a thing. Should you come to our hogan beyond the Twisted Rock welcome will greet you.'

"Through this contact all the Peshlakai soon became my friends. I might add that candy for the children, trinkets for the women, tobacco for the men and rides in my car to the trading post at Luepp helped cement the friendship. I soon learned that personal names must be obtained indirectly, never by direct question. Generally a Navajo has three or four names: The nickname given by the trader, the name that goes on the federal census roster, the family name, and the ceremonial name. For instance, the father who first brought his daughter to our camp was known to the traders as Cal. To government officials he was Mark Anthony. To members of his family and friends he was *Peshlakai atsidi alangi begay,* meaning the Eldest Son of the Silversmith. I never learned his ceremonial name for this is secretly given by the mother in early childhood, and is seldom revealed, for knowledge of this name might give to some person of evil intent the power to do harm."

Van Valkenburgh once gave me a brief outline of the Navajo religious faith as related to him by Ayoo'anlh nezi: "We Navajo believe in a supreme power, not a supreme being," the medicine man said. "We call it *Etnit.* We have many gods, among them Talking god, House god, Fire god, Changing Woman, and White Shell Woman. They are all children of *Etnit.* We do not fear the things of nature—lightning, the bears, rattlesnakes, whirlwinds. It is the power of *Etnit* back of them that may bring harm. One feels it, knows it, but cannot see it. This universal power can be dangerous to man or helpful to him. Medicine men are the mediums through which this power can be utilized by the Navajo for good, and for protection against evil. Through prayers and offerings of turquoise, white shell, mother-of-pearl and jet, the power of *Etnit* can be enlisted to bring beauty to physical things and to the mind.

"When a Navajo sends for a medicine man he must have faith. He must believe that we medicine men are the agents through whom *Etnit* restores health and drives out evil. For over 50 years I have been healing The People who are sick in mind and body. I know the power of religion."

The Navajos have a keen sense of humor, and their own code of justice. Insofar as their personal and family relations are concerned they prefer to settle their own affairs without recourse to the laws of the *Bilakana* or white race. Sandy Hassell once told me an experience which is quite revealing. The names I am using are fictitious, but the story is true:

> Slim man was bothered with a cough and he was tired much of the time. But within his physical limitations he was a faithful worker and often was employed by the trader for odd jobs. This way he was able to provide most of the groceries for his hogan.
>
> But he was having trouble with his wife. He learned that the gambler Many Horses sometimes visited his hogan when he was away. And his wife would go out in the evening and not come home until very late. He was sure she was not visiting with relatives for they lived many hours away. Finally she left to visit with her mother, and there was talk that Many Horses had gone with her. After a few days Slim Man followed and found her living with the gambler. She would not return with him. She said Many Horses was now her husband.
>
> Slim Man talked with the headmen where he lived and it was decided there should be a trial. The day of the hearing was settled. No one was appointed to notify

Many Horses. But this was not necessary. Everyone knew when trials were held and all the principals were there. They gathered in the back room at the trading post. They liked to hold their trials here for it was warm, and if there was a dispute they could call on the trader to tell them what was right. It was known he always agreed with the headmen.

The trial lasted nearly three hours. No one in the room was called upon to testify. The headmen gave all the evidence, discussed the case and agreed on the verdict without asking anyone for comment.

Many Horses had taken Slim Man's wife, and of course he could keep her, but Slim Man should be paid for his loss. Before they could decide the amount of the payment it was necessary to review the wife's good and bad points. Nothing was overlooked. They wanted to be fair and impartial.

Her disposition came first. That was above reproach. She laughed much and was never ill-tempered. She did not complain or nag her husband. Her fried bread was excellent and she always washed her hands before patting the dough. She made good coffee and was not stingy with the sugar she put in it. Her rugs brought a good price, for she was a careful weaver. She kept her hair tidy and never came to the trading post and talked in a loud voice. No mention was made of her morals for they had no bearing on the case. If they had, they would have been discussed as freely as were the other details of her life.

It did not take long to discuss her shortcomings. She had no children and none could be expected. She had no sheep, but that was not too bad for there were no children to look after them. Like Slim Man, she had a cough and neither the medicine man nor the white doctor had been able to help her.

After all her good points and shortcomings had been reviewed by each of the four headmen who were conducting the trial, they then discussed the ability of Many Horses to pay. In the end it was decided he should compensate Slim Man with twelve monthly payments of $5.00 each, or $60.00.

Now the trial was over and everyone was free to talk. Good manners and self-restraint had caused Slim Man to remain silent until now. He did not want to influence the judges, but now he was entitled to express an opinion. He arose and looked at each headman as he spoke in a low voice. "I know that all of you are smart men, smarter than I am, and have tried to be fair in your decision. But I think I know better than you how much this woman is worth for she has been my wife. I think $50.00 is enough.

The Navajos, like all desert Indian tribesmen, subject themselves to many social and religious taboos. For instance, among the longhairs of the tribe—that is, the older generation—there is the superstition that ill fortune will befall if a young groom looks at his mother-in-law. The younger Indians are breaking with some of these ancient taboos. But while freedom from superstition may be regarded as a desirable goal, this is not always true of primitive people. Superstitions are their tribal religions. They impose disciplines—not always admirable disciplines perhaps—but they serve to restrain and restrict the conduct of the pagan believer to a code which seems to be in the best interests of the tribal society as a whole.

The tragedy of the Navajo reservation today, and this is true on the Hopi Mesa and to an increasing degree in our own Anglo-American communities, is that the religious disciplines of the fathers are eroding away before a new and more enlightened faith is evolved to replace the old. The resultant is a moral vacuum in which cynicism replaces faith.

The communal life of the Navajo is essentially domestic. I believe the secret of their success in preserving their democratic way of life is in the rigorous self-discipline taught the children almost from birth. There is kindness, but no coddling. People who discipline themselves do not need books of law or dictators to rule them.

The Navajos have attained a remarkable degree of self-discipline. They seldom lose their tempers. They patiently discuss their differences in quiet even voices. To lose one's temper, in their creed, is a weakness not soon forgotten or forgiven. My friend Joe Kerley learned this lesson the hard way. He recalled an experience of many years ago when he first became a trader on the reservation. He had been cautioned to expect some severe heckling from some of the tribesmen. That is one way they test the fiber of a newcomer.

One of Joe's customers was a wealthy Indian who came to the trading post periodically with big bags of wool from his sheep. He had a good income for a tribesman, and when he cashed his wool he spent the money generously on his two wives.

One day when this customer was in the store a young Indian who was loitering in the room began making disparaging remarks: "This new trader is stingy," he said to the older customer. "He is a cheat and a liar." Then he raised his voice so all might hear and addressed Kerley: "You are not a good trader like the other one. He gave us tobacco and coffee. Pretty soon no one will be trading here."

Kerley restrained himself, and others in the room did not seem to be paying much attention to what was being said. While this was going on, one of the best weavers came in and laid a beautiful rug on the counter. Before Kerley had an opportunity to tell her what the payment would be, the heckler broke in: "This trader does not want rugs. That's why he pays so little for them. Take your rug to some other post where they will pay you more."

To the trader's dismay, the woman picked up the rug and left. Kerley could take it no longer. He jumped over the counter, seized the scoundrel by the collar and shoved him through the door. Then he returned to serve his customer. The old Indian was deeply disturbed.

"I am sorry," he said sadly. "I thought this new trader was a man, but he's only a child. I heard all the Navajo was saying, but I paid no attention. Why did the trader lose his head? I am ashamed of him.

"That is the day I began learning the fine art of trading with the Navajo," Kerley told me. "Until then I was just a tenderfoot in this business. The Navajos have great patience and restraint, and they have respect only for others who share these traits.

"If that incident happened today I would dispose of the heckler very quickly by ridiculing him. I would answer him, 'Everybody knows you skin coyotes,' or 'When did you look at your mother-in-law last?' Such remarks would have turned the tables. They would have put the Indian on the defensive. All the Indians who come to the post soon would have known how the new trader outwitted one of their number, and there would have been no more heckling."

Today on the Navajo reservation, as among other desert Indian tribes and all around the world, there is the foment of rapid change. The incidents I have quoted represent a way of life that is passing. The young Indians are going to school, and while they study the white man's language they also are acquiring, for better or for worse, his sense of values.

This is a time of transition, and the critical need in such a period is for strong, enlightened leadership. The genes of character, wisdom and the capacity for leadership recognize no racial or color boundaries. The Navajo tribe has been fortunate to have, and to recognize in its membership, a few men whose vision, understanding and integrity would do honor to any race of men.

For nearly a half century the leader of these people was Henry Chee Dodge, a man loved by his own tribesmen and respected by Anglo-Americans who knew him personally or by reputation. Chee Dodge was a boy of three when Colonel Kit Carson was sent to Arizona in 1863 to put an end to the ruthless warfare the nomad Navajos were waging against neighboring tribesmen of the pueblos and American and Mexican settlers. Col. Carson, with a battalion of soldiers, solved the problem by rounding up the Navajos at Canyon de Chelly, confiscating their livestock and destroying their hogans, and marching them 800 miles overland for internment at Fort Sumner, New Mexico.

Four years later the tribesmen were ready to acknowledge and submit to the authority of the Great White Father in Washington. A treaty was signed in 1868 whereby the Indians would be returned to their own country and given agricultural implements and financial help until they could reestablish themselves as peaceful members of Uncle Sam's community.

Chee Dodge and his mother—his father had been killed by Mexicans before the internment—returned with the others and settled near Window Rock, where the boy could go to one of the schools provided under the treaty. In 1884 he was appointed interpreter for the Indian Agency, then at Fort Defiance. A few years later he was elected chairman of the first Tribal Council formed by the Indians to conduct their internal affairs. He held this post almost continuously until his death in 1947 at the age of 87 years.

The Navajos fulfilled their treaty obligations more faithfully than did Uncle Sam. One of the provisions of the treaty was that there would be schools for the Indian children, with teachers provided by the Bureau of Indian Affairs. With the patience characteristic of his people, Chee Dodge spent much of his life pleading for the fulfillment of the pledges contained in the treaty.

In September 1945 the Tribal Council awarded him an achievement medal in recognition of his faithful service in behalf of the advancement of his tribesmen. Responding to the award he wrote: "I am an old man. In my time I have seen much of the history of my people. As a boy I was rounded up with the Navajo by American soldiers, taken for the Big Walk to Bosque Redondo (Fort Sumner), and imprisoned for almost four years. Then we signed a treaty with the United States and were told that if we would behave we could have our land back, could have a teacher for every 30 children and many other things.

"The government then put us on a reservation which was like putting us in a little corral. As the Navajo increased the corral was made a little bigger, but never big enough that there was land for the Navajo as they grew up. If we could get half of all that was promised us in the treaty we would be happy . . .

"The greatest of all Indian needs is education. We need boarding schools with a hospital at each and doctors and nurses. At one time we opposed having our children forced into schools. Now most Navajo favor compulsory education. There is not room enough on the reservation for all the Indians. They want to do something for themselves now, but most of them do not know how. Education is our great need."

It is only within the last ten years that Congress has provided funds to carry out the pledge that every Navajo child should have the opportunity to go to school. Today the Indians need not only a common school education, but also training for technological and professional employment. For much of their reservation is arid land, suitable only for grazing and not enough of that to support the Navajo population of over 70,000.

Chee Dodge is gone, but other worthy Indian leaders have taken his place. Chairman of the Tribal Council today is Paul Jones. Associated with him as secretary-treasurer of the tribe is J. Maurice McCabe. These two men, heading the executive branch of the tribal organization, are fine, capable administrators thoroughly dedicated to the service of their people.

It is doubly important today that the Navajos have competent and honest men to manage their tribal affairs, for oil, gas and uranium leases on reservation lands are now bringing millions of dollars annually into the tribal treasury. By 1958 the Council had acquired a bank account of over $50,000,000. Individual members of the tribe who have title to personal land allotments also are reaping rich royalties from their holdings.

The Navajos are determined not to follow the example of the Osage Indians whose sudden wealth after the discovery of oil in Oklahoma fifty years ago was followed by a wild orgy of reckless spending. The response to sudden riches in Navajoland has been quite the opposite. The attitude generally shared by the tribesmen was expressed by Treasurer McCabe when he said:

"We Navajos are realists. We remember the hard past and look warily to an uncertain future. The oil and uranium may not last forever. We are going to conserve these funds for the benefit of all our tribe, and the best investment we can make is in education. Our boys and girls have herded sheep for generations. Now there is the opportunity for them to learn to be lawyers and doctors and business men. Others will become skilled electricians, machinists, nurses and stenographers. Also, we need hospitals and good highways and industries where our people may find employment. Not a dollar of this money is to be squandered for the personal enrichment of any member of the tribe."

The story is told of a young Navajo who had received $45,000 for his personal land allotment. He went to town to trade in his old car for a new pickup. The dealer knew of his recent windfall and proceeded to demonstrate the fine qualities of the most expensive car on the floor. The Indian remained silent until the salesman exhausted his patter. Then he answered in a quiet voice:

"This is a beautiful car, but it is of no good to haul mutton to my neighbor. The pretty paint is no good for travel through the sage bushes when I go out to get my pony. The other Indians see me drive along the road and say: '*La,* Hoski begay he spend his money like fool. Pretty soon he have no money like rest of Navajo.'

"No, I am not fool. I remember when my wife sick and no can weave rugs. And my children not go to school because they have no warm clothes. We have to pawn all our turquoise with trader for food. I come here buy pickup truck. You no show me truck. I go some other place."

Perhaps this untutored Indian unwittingly had dramatized a lesson in basic values. The salesman was accustomed to selling cars to white-skinned people for whom automobiles have become a symbol of status. Here was a young man who wanted a car for transportation. Maybe he was right. Perhaps it is more rational to buy automobiles for transportation than to flaunt them as tokens of appeasement to the god of personal vanity.

Chee Dodge, Paul Jones and Maurice McCabe have all stressed the importance of education for the Navajo people. But the education they envision is not the kind of schooling which produces status-worshippers—which creates customers for big fins, lavish chrome and push-button gadgets.

The American people, through their government, are duty-bound to provide better educational facilities for the tribesmen. But the education which will serve them—and ourselves—best is not a one-way road. We also can learn from these close-to-earth people. I recall a quotation from the Indian boy Rafael, one of the characters in Ruth M. Underhill's *Hawk Over Whirlpools.* He had been the victim of the inevitable clash between the primitive traditions of his people and the sophisticated civilization of the white man, and finally had envisioned a reconciliation between the opposing cultures. He said:

"Maybe we make something new. Not white. Not Indian. We keep what is good in our life—not throw away. Then we look to you. See what you got that we really need. Not hurry. Not money. Doctors, maybe. Machines—some. Water. We learn those slow, like you learned them yourselves. Like we learned the grinding stone and the bow and arrow. Then maybe you learn from us."

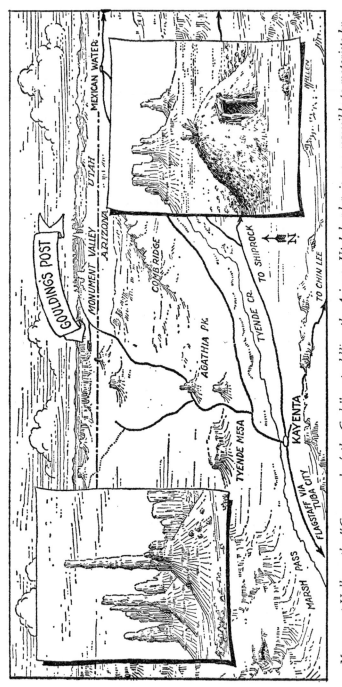

Monument Valley—the "Graveyard of the Gods"—straddling the Arizona-Utah border, is now accessible to motorists by a paved road. The paving of the last five miles between Tuba City and Kayenta is in progress in the fall of 1961, and this will make it possible for motorists to travel from Flagstaff or Tuba City through the Monument to connect with the Utah highway system at Monticello on a hardtop highway. The Goulding Trading Post and the Visitors' Center in the

GRAVEYARD OF THE GODS   XIII

ASTRIDE the Utah-Arizona state line, in one of the most arid regions in western United States, is Monument Valley. Here are 2400 square miles of Uncle Sam's domain where, scattered in weird formation over a landscape of sage and sand, great sandstone monoliths which might be the giant tombstones of a forgotten race of gods, rise in colorful splendor from the floor of the valley.

In this fantastic setting, almost as sterile as if it had been transplanted from the moon, the blue of the distant horizon is punctured in every direction by protruding spires, turrets, domes and embattlements created by millions of years of erosion following other millions of years of alluvial deposit. Here the book of geological history lies open for all to read. It is an illustrated book in technicolor, the reds and browns of its massive rock formations standing in sharp contrast with the golden sands that carpet the floor of the desert below.

My acquaintance with Monument Valley goes back to the 1930s when I left Kayenta, Arizona, to follow a corrugated sand road that leads north toward the Utah state line. As I bumped along the ungraded trail across this seemingly unproductive desert I wondered how it was possible for human beings to make a living in such a land.

But men and women and children do live here. This is Navajo reservation, and more than a hundred families of these nomad tribesmen eke out a meager existence grazing their sheep and goats between and around the majestic rock formations and adjacent canyons of this remote region.

And here also are Harry Goulding and his attractive wife Mike. The Gouldings have been Indian traders in this region since 1924. In more recent years they have added guest accommodations for the increasing numbers of travelers who come this way. Their trading post and lodge are located on a natural bench at the base of a 1,000-foot cliff of red sandstone, not far from a spring which was their original source of water.

It was during this first trip into Monument Valley that I became acquainted with the Gouldings. They were living in comfortable quarters above the store where the Indians brought their wool and woven blankets to exchange for flour and sugar, denim and yardgoods. At the invitation of the Gouldings I joined them that evening on the veranda of their apartment where we could look out across the vast expanse of Harry's "front yard." In the distance we could see the dim outlines of the Henry Mountains, 125 miles away in Utah. At closer range were the giant tombstones which gave the valley its name—Castle Butte,

Brigham's Tomb, Train Rock, Eagle Rock Mesa and many others.

On this and subsequent visits to the Goulding trading post I learned the story of these hospitable westerners who had the fortitude and faith to choose this lonely land for their life's endeavor. Harry, a tough lanky horseman, had become acquainted with the Navajos and their way of life while riding range for his father and uncle, New Mexico sheepmen. Mike, with the genes of pioneering ancestors, had come here as a bride. Her given name was Leone, but Harry had had trouble with the spelling, so he changed it to Mike—and today Leone is as seldom mentioned as is the ceremonial name of a Navajo.

Harry had acquired 640 acres of school land from the State of Utah for $320. Later the Navajo reservation was enlarged to extend entirely around his section. Their first trading post was a tent, where they camped while Harry, with the help of a prospector who happened to come that way, and the Indian neighbors, erected a permanent abode of country rock.

They began learning the Navajo language and cultivating the friendship of the tribesmen. At every opportunity Harry would saddle his horse and follow the sandy trails which led to the remote hogans scattered among the monoliths. There was always candy in his saddlebags for the children, and when he attended the sings a special gift for the medicine man.

Gradually, he was able to break down the distrust these people felt for the white race. For most of these tribesmen were the descendants of that little band of irreconcilables who were led to this almost inaccessible valley by Chief Hoskininni in 1863 to escape capture by Col. Kit Carson, when the Navajos were being rounded up at Canyon de Chelly for internment at Bosque Redondo. The old chief had passed away and his son, Hoskininni Begay, was now the leader of the fiercely independent tribesmen. Gradually the Gouldings were able to win the confidence of this venerable Navajo.

Harry saw that one of the most urgent needs of these people was roads. Every penny that could be spared from the working capital of the trading post was spent in clearing and dragging trails which could be traveled by Navajo wagons and by the doughnut-tired car which would enable him to keep closer contact with his friends and customers.

It was necessary in those days to make periodic trips to the closest railroad for supplies, to Flagstaff, 200 miles to the southwest, or Thompson, Utah, the same distance to the north. Eventually he was able to induce the Utah and Arizona state road departments to cooperate with the Indian Bureau in constructing a graded road from Kayenta through Monument Valley to Bluff, Utah. The improved road brought increasing tourist travel, and modest cottages were built for overnight visitors.

Long ago it became apparent to the Gouldings that the grazing of sheep and goats in a land as arid as Monument Valley could never provide more than a bare subsistence for the Navajos, and any increase in the population would reduce them to dire need. If the Indians ever were to attain even a modest living by American standards, then their economy must be expanded to provide income from other sources.

One of the long-range plans Harry and Mike envisioned to accomplish this goal was to break down the superstition of the tribesmen against being photographed. After passable roads became available Harry instituted a guide service for visitors who wanted to visit the hogans, see how the Indians lived— and of course take pictures of them. Eventually, through their complete confidence in the trader, the Navajos became reconciled to the click of the camera shutter. Today it is possible for photographers to go on one of the guided tours and obtain pictures of Navajo ceremonials and intimate close-ups of every phase of hogan life. The Indians expect only a moderate fee for their posing. It is a conservative guess that three-fourths of the Navajo photography distributed today by professional cameramen and news syndicates was taken in Monument Valley. And there probably is not a family in that area which has not enjoyed a few extras in the way of food or clothing, purchased with the tips from the camera fraternity.

Harry once told of an incident which reveals the superstitious reaction of these tribesmen to the white man's gadget for taking images of people. A visiting photographer wanted to get a picture of the sand-painting detail of a healing ceremony. The medicine man was making his painting on the floor inside a hogan, where poor lighting made a flash bulb necessary. This was a new experience for the singer, and when the flash went off the medicine man looked up in angry terror. It was a critical instant when there might have been a tragic sequel. But Harry knew the right answer. Before the old Indian could make a move, Goulding laughed and spoke in Navajo: "Ha ha ha, medicine man have powerful magic. Him break the white man's machine." The old Indian's fright instantly vanished, and his face registered the triumph of his profession.

Having persuaded the Indians that the white man's camera was a harmless plaything, Harry's next goal was to convince Hollywood that Monument Valley would be an ideal location for the filming of certain types of western pictures. After some preliminary correspondence he made several trips to the movie capital to interest directors in his plan. He even graded a landing strip on the valley floor below the trading post so the directors and location men could fly in to make their own appraisal of the scenic values and the availability of livestock, cowboys and Indians to play extra parts.

In 1938 when it became known that Director John Ford of United Artists was planning to feature John Wayne in a Class A western, Goulding went to Hollywood with a stack of Monument Valley photographs. It was not easy to get into the Director's office, but when Harry threatened to spread his bedroll on the floor and camp there until he could see John Ford, an interview was granted. Several hours later he was handed a check and told to return home and arrange food and accommodations for a hundred players and technicians. They would arrive in three days. It was a staggering assignment for a lone trader in a lonely land, but Harry and Mike were equal to the task. The picture, *Stagecoach*, won the Academy award, and Monument Valley was on the map as a locale for motion picture production.

John Ford was delighted with the cooperation he had gotten from the Gouldings and their Indian neighbors, and was responsible for bringing other productions to that location. He returned in 1946 to direct the filming of *My Darling Clementine*, and in 1947 to take location shots for *Fort Apache*. In 1948 the U. S. Cavalry picture *She Wore a Yellow Ribbon* was filmed there in technicolor.

All this proved to be a bonanza for the Indians who played extra parts or were employed on construction and other work. One company distributed $62,000 in local payrolls during several weeks on location there. Twentieth Century Fox and Argus built more or less permanent sets, including frontier type buildings, and then donated them to the Navajo Tribal Council.

The Navajo Indians, endowed with a fine sense of humor, quickly sensed the drama in the roles assigned to them, and responded like veteran actors. They are all good bareback riders, and were at their best in the roles of wild Apaches chasing the cavalrymen of the U. S. Army. So well did they perform that in 1952, when Universal-International selected Moab, Utah, as the location for the filming in technicolor of *The Battle of Apache Pass*, they came to Monument Valley to recruit Navajos to play the Apache roles.

Following World War II, when prospectors were swarming over the red rock plateau of northern Arizona, southern Utah, western Colorado and New Mexico in quest of uranium ores, it was inevitable that interest should turn to the Navajo reservation where in many places the geology appeared favorable to U-ore production. Knowing that the Indians had once killed two white prospectors who came to develop a silver prospect said to have been located in Monument Valley, I was interested in learning their attitude toward the carnotite miners who in 1947 were working several claims on the reservation.

Harry told me the Indians not only had sanctioned the mining of uranium ores on their land, but had actually discovered and reported two deposits. Many of the Navajos, he explained, had brothers and sons in the armed forces, and when during the war days they were told this mineral was necessary to help win a victory and bring their kinsmen back, they accepted this explanation and gave sanction to mining on tribal lands. From other sources I learned that the Indians' confidence in Harry Goulding had much to do with their decision. Since then the Navajo Tribal Council has received many millions of dollars in royalties on ores mined in the reservation.

Goulding was once involved in a mining venture which revealed the religious prejudice among the older Indians against desecrating the earth by removing its mineral wealth. He had heard of the legendary Pish-la-ki mine somewhere in Monument Valley, where the original members of Hoskininni's band were said to have found a deposit of metal so pure they could work it into silver ornaments without milling it.

The secret of the mine's location was believed to have been lost when the last of the original discoverers died. But one day an old Navajo—whom Harry identified as Hosteen Yazzi, although this was not his name—came to the post and told the trader he knew the location of Pish-la-ki but was afraid to go there. Goulding knew his Navajos well enough not to press the matter, but in subsequent conversations with the old man he became convinced the Navajo was telling the truth—that he knew the secret.

The time came when Yazzi's large family was suffering from lack of food. It was then Harry suggested to the old man that he should bring out some of the silver so his wife and children and relatives would not go hungry. Hosteen Yazzi replied that he would not do that—the curse of the gods would be upon him.

Goulding did not insist, but as the plight of the Yazzi family grew worse he brought up the subject again. "Do not tell me the location of Pish-la-ki. I do not want any of the silver for my-self," he said. "But I will furnish pack animals and food for you to go alone and bring out enough silver to buy food for your family. A good father will not see his children go hungry. The gods will not be angry with a man who takes only what he needs to feed his family."

Hosteen Yazzi hesitated, but he knew the trader was his friend and was speaking words of wisdom. Finally he agreed to go. Within a few days Harry had gotten together a string of burros to bring out the ore, and Yazzi left with a three weeks' supply of food.

Several days elapsed. The weather turned cold and rainy, and Harry hoped the old man had found shelter to keep him dry and warm. Then in the afternoon of the sixth day Hosteen Yazzi staggered into the trading post, sick and frightened. He had neither pack animals nor food. His body was racked with coughing. The Gouldings gave him food and dry clothing, and then Yazzi told his story: The gods were displeased. They did not want the silver of Pish-la-ki disturbed. They had sent cold wind until his hands and feet had no feeling. They had drenched him with water. The arroyos were running full, and he could not cross. When Harry asked about the burros, he only pointed with his lips to the direction from which he had come. Maybe three four days, he could not be sure.

As soon as the weather would permit, Harry went out to find the pack animals and grubstake. After several days he rounded them up and returned the burros to their owners, and salvaged what he could from the packs.

Hosteen Yazzi did not recover quickly. His cough continued, and he was frightened. He had incurred the displeasure of the gods, and was very unhappy. Harry knew the answer. He called in the medicine man and arranged for a sing for his friend.

Goulding still believes the silver is out somewhere among the canyons. But after paying out over a hundred dollars to cover the cost of the sing, he decided to let the Navajo gods keep their secret.

For many years it has been the dream of Harry and Mike Goulding that the colorful buttes and spires and the golden sands of Monument Valley might some day be set aside and maintained as a national park for the benefit of all Americans. There were serious obstacles to such a plan, for the greater part of Monument Valley belongs to the Indians, and to insure them security in their ancestral homes it would be necessary to waive some of the rules which normally govern national park operation.

But the Gouldings' enthusiasm for the park idea has never dimmed. During one of my recent visits to the trading post Harry suggested that we spend a day exploring some sectors of the Valley seldom reached by white travelers. Since there were no improved roads in the area we would go in a jeep station wagon with four-wheel drive. During my many trips to Monument Valley I have in some measure learned to share the Gouldings' deep attachment for this peaceful land of primitive Americans and weird rock formations, and I was glad to accept the invitation.

Our destination was a great cove in the irregular rimrock cliffs which mark the boundaries of Monument Valley. Harry refers to this particular area as Mystery Valley because continued exploration constantly reveals new and spectacular rock formations and evidence of its occupation by prehistoric tribesmen.

A mile from the trading post we stopped briefly at the Seventh Day Adventist Mission and Hospital, where a staff of medical workers headed by Dr. J. Lloyd and Alice Mason are making a magnificent contribution to the health and education of the tribal families in this region. The mission was founded ten years ago by Rev. Marvin Walter and his wife Gwen, a registered nurse. The buildings were erected on a site donated by the

Gouldings. A fine new hospital is now nearing completion.

Their patients, mostly Indians, come from an area of 10,000 square miles, and the missionaries have so completely won the confidence and respect of the tribesmen that even the medicine men come to the clinic for treatment. They also have a school for Indian children. Last year the Navajo Tribal Council handed Dr. Mason an unsolicited check for $10,000 to help carry on the work of the institution.

Mystery Valley could well have been named Valley of the Arches, for in motoring along the floor of the desert the visitor is nearly always within view of one or more of the many stone windows which millions of years of erosion have carved in the cliff walls. There is Waterfall Arch, Stout Arch, Full Moon Arch, Double Arch—more than thirty of them, some vertical and others horizontal. The cliffs themselves are fantastically eroded. There are pinnacles, domes, turrets, castles—all the work of water and wind erosion in the De Chelly sandstone of the region.

Botanically, this is the zone of juniper and pinyon, and while the land is too arid for dense growth, these trees are sprinkled over the landscape in every direction. Growing on the sandy floor we saw hedgehog cactus, desert holly, lupine just coming into blossom and yellow bee clover in full bloom.

Once Harry pointed to a cliff rose which the Navajos call *Awai-itsa* or baby bush. The inner bark of this shrub is twisted and fluffed and used by Indian mothers to absorb the moisture in the baby's cradle board. It has a silky talcum feel and keeps the baby's skin from chafing.

As we drove along Harry stopped occasionally to pick up a discarded bottle or tin can which a thoughtless visitor had tossed to the sand. "The Indians do not litter the landscape," he said. "These discards were thrown here by motorists who do not share the reverence for the good earth which is part of the Navajo religion."

At long intervals we passed flocks of sheep, attended by children too young for school, or elders beyond school age. Harry always stopped to exchange a few words in their own language, and give them oranges from the crate he carried in the jeep. It was easy to understand the deep affection these people have for a white neighbor who has shared their problems for thirty-seven years.

My guide pointed out the crumbling ruins of ancient cliff dwellings—the former homes of an unidentified race of aborigines who found their way into this sheltered cove long before the embattled old warrior Hoskininni led his defiant little band of renegades here to outwit Kit Carson's soldiers.

While we ate our lunches at the base of one of the great stone arches, Harry expressed confidence that a national park which would encompass all this area seemed about to be realized—but not in just the way he had visualized it.

The Navajo Tribal Council had long been favorable to the proposal. As far back as 1934 they had passed a resolution providing " . . . that all areas of scenic beauty and scientific interest which require preservation be hereby reserved as Navajo Parks. Monuments or Ruins, to be managed by the Navajo themselves with the cooperation of the Indian Service, and other helpful agencies . . ."

The Council had sought the cooperation of the U. S. Park Service, and during the years when Miner R. Tillotson was regional director of Parks the negotiations for a joint project in Monument Valley were going smoothly. However, following Tillotson's death in January 1955, the men assigned to carry on for the NPS asked for concessions and restrictions which the Indians were unwilling to accept. Finally, the Tribal Council appointed its own Park Commission to carry out the program in its own way. The resolution establishing this Commission included the following paragraph: "The Navajo Tribal Park Commission shall not have authority to deprive any Navajo Indian or his heirs of the right to continue to use any area of Navajo Tribal land in the same manner he was using such area at the time a Navajo Tribal Park or Monument is established embracing such area."

One of the first acts of the new Commission was to designate Monument Valley as a Navajo Tribal Park. With substantial income now being derived from uranium, oil and gas royalties the Council already has completed an attractive administration headquarters and visitor center of native stone in the heart of the Valley, four miles from the main highway. The new Park has been enclosed with heavy wire fencing and Indian rangers now patrol the area. Roads have been graded, and regulations governing the use of the Park by the public have been issued.

The Navajos have a deep regard for the preservation of the natural landscape. They will tolerate no litterbugging or vandalism. In addition to its natural endowment of majestic scenery, the Navajo Park is unique in another important respect. The hogans and the family life of the hundred or more families who dwell and graze their sheep within the reserve are not to be disturbed. Thus the Park will have a human interest factor not to be found in any other national park area except Canyon de Chelly, where access is limited due to flood water and sand. If a national park is to be regarded as a great museum of natural history, the Navajo Park will have the added interest of a reserve in which the native tribesmen of the original American wilderness still pursue the customs and vocations of their ancestors. And if visitors will observe the simple rules suggested by Louisa Wetherill and quoted on a previous page, they will find the Park occupants delightful people.

Eight years ago the Utah highway department completed a blacktop road south from Monticello by way of Bluff and Mexican Hat to the state boundary in the heart of Monument Valley. Within the last two years the Arizona highway department, in cooperation with the Indian Bureau, has extended the paving of this route from the Utah line across Monument Valley to Kayenta, eliminating twenty-three miles of corrugated gravel which long had been a nightmare to motorists. More recently all but five miles of the seventy-four-mile span between Kayenta and Tuba City have been blacktopped, and a contract has been let for the completion of this road. Thus, before the end of 1961, if all goes according to schedule, the Navajo Tribal Park and the Goulding trading post will be accessible by paved roads both from Utah on the north and Arizona on the south. There are long spans of this road with neither service station nor overnight accommodations, but it is inevitable these improvements will come with increasing travel over this scenic desert route.

Late in the evening of our exploring trip into Mystery Valley, Harry and I wound our way back over the floor of the desert to the cliff house, which has been the home of the Gouldings for a generation. The mental cabinet where I keep pictures worth preserving was loaded to capacity with visions of golden sand dunes, fantastic natural arches, prehistoric Indian dwellings, and of dark-skinned and bright-eyed youngsters who perhaps will have a better opportunity to develop their latent talents if they have more contact with the best in the white man's civilization.

The Navajos do not seek charity from their white brothers. They are a courageous and highly intelligent people, and Americans may make their greatest contribution to the progress of these people by encouraging them to retain the virtues which have endeared them to Harry and Mike Goulding—their reverence for the Good Earth, which is the Mother of all the blessings which flow to mankind, the loyalty and gentleness of their hogan life, and the almost fierce determination they have inherited from Grandfather Hoskininni to preserve the dignity of independence.

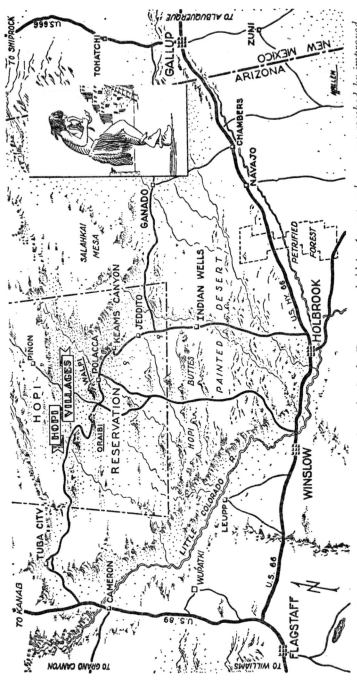

The Hopi Villages in northern Arizona where the Snake Dances are held in August each year are reached by improved —partly paved—roads from east, west and south. The Hopi reservation is entirely surrounded by the Navajo reservation. Visitors planning to make the journey to Hopiland should inquire as to prevailing road conditions on the reservations.

MEN WHO DANCE WITH SNAKES   XIV

One late afternoon in August 1939, I sat on the flat rooftop of a stone and adobe house in the pueblo of Walpi on the Hopi Indian reservation in northern Arizona and witnessed in the plaza below a spectacle so incredible as to lure me back to this place many times in subsequent years. This was the annual Snake Dance of the Hopi tribesmen—a religious ritual which is the traditional Indian prayer for rain.

There were many other uninvited guests perched on the perimeter of housetops surrounding the plaza: Hopis, Navajos,

Indian Bureau officials and Americans from near and distant places. Here also were medical men and anthropologists who had come to study the details of the religious ceremony or to seek new clues to the mysterious immunity these tribesmen have to the venom of rattlesnakes.

The Indians accept the intrusion of outsiders courteously, so long as they bring no cameras and maintain the same decorum they would observe in the religious sanctuaries of their own faith. Men in shorts and women in suntans are tolerated, but the reaction of the tribesmen is the same as would be that of any Protestant or Catholic if such costumes came down the aisle of the church or cathedral as the services were about to begin.

The pageant of costumed dancers we saw in the plaza that day was the climax of a ritualistic program which had been going on for eight days, most of the time in the underground kivas or ceremonial chambers of the Snake and Antelope Clans.

The Hopi Indians believe their ancestors emerged originally from the center of the earth, reaching the surface through a small vent at some secret place in the Grand Canyon, and identified in their legends as *Sipapu*. This belief in an under-world, where some of their gods dwell even today, gives significance to the snake ritual. The snakes, also living underground, are the Little Brothers who may be trusted to deliver to the gods the prayers of the tribesmen for rain and fertility.

Early in August each year the priests of the Snake and Antelope Clans determine the dates of the ceremonies to be held later in the month, based on a formula known only to them. The lay tribesmen know the dates have been set when they see a cluster of eagle feathers dangling from the top of the ladder which marks the entrance to the kiva. The word spreads through the pueblos and when the tribesmen have assembled, a snake priest emerges from the kiva and announces the times and places of the annual rituals. Traditionally, these dances are held at Shipolovi and Shongopovi on the Second Mesa and Hotevilla on the Third Mesa in even numbered years, and at Walpi on the

First Mesa and Mishongnovi on the Second Mesa in the odd years. In recent years there has been some variation in this schedule, but no two dances are ever held the same day. News of the dates soon reach Winslow, Holbrook and Flagstaff, Arizona, and goes out on the press wires for the benefit of those who wish to witness the ceremonies.

During the eight days preceding the public dance there are numerous details of the ritual to be performed by clansmen. There are the *bahos,* prayer sticks, to be made of slender willow branches tufted with feathers, a sand-painting altar to be created in the kiva, foot races to be held, and on the morning of the final day a *kisi,* built of cottonwood branches and shaped like a small tepee, to be erected on the plaza to house the reptiles preceding the dance. Then there is the washing of the snakes, which takes place in the kiva a few hours before the public ceremony.

In recent years no white person has been permitted to witness the washing ritual. However, nearly a half century ago when the late Godfrey Sykes was tending store for Tom Keams at the Keams Canyon trading post on the Navajo reservation, a Hopi snake priest invited him to take part in the cleansing detail. Sykes told me it was one of the most thrilling experiences in his life. His role was that of "snake herder." The ritual, he said, symbolized the purification process preparatory to the return of the snakes to their abode in the underworld where they would convey to the gods the prayers of the tribesmen for rain. Sykes described the ceremony:

"Each of us was handed a gourd rattle and a small 'snake whip' fashioned after the traditional prayer stick except that it had a larger tuft of feathers on the end. While the clansmen seated on stone benches around the wall of the kiva kept up a rhythmic chant to the accompaniment of the rattles, one of the snake priests reached into a big earthen olla on the floor, brought out a squirming snake and dipped it into another olla containing the sacred baptismal water. Then he tossed it on the sand floor in the center of the chamber. Soon other snake clansmen were doing the same, and snakes were crawling in all directions. We herders with our snake whips were expected to keep them corralled in the middle of the room. As the ceremony proceeded the tempo of the singers increased and an air of excitement prevailed. Snakes were being yanked out of the ollas, ducked in the water and tossed in all directions. The result was that not only the floor but the air around us seemed to be full of wiggling reptiles. Some of us who were taking part in this ceremony for the first time were almost as bewildered as the snakes and the last ten minutes of that orgy was an ordeal I would not want to repeat."

That was many years ago. The Snake Dances still follow the traditional pattern in most details. While the early visitors are finding seats on the housetops surrounding the plaza, the snake clansmen in the underground kiva are cleansing their Little Brothers for the roles they are to play in the public ceremonial.

On the occasion of my first visit to the snake ritual, I was seated next to a physician from the U. S. Public Health Service who wanted to ascertain if the dancers actually were bitten by the rattlesnakes, and to learn if he could what treatment, if any, was given the victims afterward.

The hour of four had passed and the sun was sinking toward the horizon when we saw emerging on the pole ladder which projected through the roof of the kiva at the far end of the plaza the first of the dancers. They were the Antelope clansmen, 22 of them, adorned in feather headdresses, silver necklaces, armlets, anklets and kilts, their faces and bodies grotesquely painted in white and ochre. They carried antelope-skin rattles which provided the rhythm as they advanced at a jog-trot and passed immediately in front of the *kisi* where the snakes already had been concealed. Four times they circled the plaza, each dancer stamping hard on the hinged stomp-board immediately in front of the *kisi* to notify the underground deities that the ritual was in progress. Then they formed a line in front of the snake shelter, continuing the rhythm with their rattles.

They were followed immediately by the Snake priests, also in single file but distinguishable by more elaborate costumes— foxtails dangling from their waists, white serpents painted on their blackened bodies, and tortoise-shell clackers strapped to their calves. Their hands would be too busy to carry rattles.

After circling the plaza four times they formed a line facing the Antelope clansmen and a low chant was begun, gradually increasing in volume until it reached a staccato climax. Then the snake clansmen broke up into teams of three: a carrier, a charmer and a gatherer, and as they passed in front of the *kisi* a snake priest handed to each carrier a serpent. He placed it in his mouth a few inches back of the head and began to circle the plaza. His charmer or hugger, his left arm around the dancer's shoulder, sought to distract the snake by brushing its head with his feather-tipped snake whip. As soon as the carrier had circled the plaza four times he dropped his snake in the center of the circle and returned to the plaza for another reptile. The cycle continued until the supply of snakes was exhausted. In the meantime it was the duty of the gatherers with their feathered sticks to keep the snakes on the ground herded into the center of the circle and away from the fringe of spectators around the plaza. As the dance continued Hopi maidens outside the circle sprinkled the reptiles as they passed with sacred cornmeal from their baskets. When the Little Brothers had all been four times around the plaza the dancers paused while a ring of cornmeal was drawn on the earth, and at a signal from the Snake Priest all the serpents were cast into the ring and showered with a final baptism of cornmeal. Then the snake clansmen all rushed in and gathered as many snakes as they could carry in their hands and ran down the rocky trail to the floor of the desert where the Little Brothers were re-leased to return to their underground abodes and deliver to the gods the supplication of the tribesmen for water that would pro-duce abundant food.

The dancers then returned to their kiva to remove their ceremonial gear. Each of them bathed and drank an emetic prepared from herbs gathered from the desert. This purification rite is an essential part of the ceremonial. Following the ritual the entire population took part in a gala program of fun-making and feasting.

The snakes gathered for this ceremonial are predominately rattlers of several species, including sidewinders, but there are always some gopher or bullsnakes, and occasionally a racer. The dancers handle them indiscriminately without fear or favor. I know some of the carriers are bitten. Standing just outside the dance circle I once saw a rattler strike the hand of a teen-age Hopi boy as he passed four feet in front of me with the reptile in his mouth. The lad did not wince.

Many theories have been suggested to explain the apparent immunity of the dancers to the venom of the rattlers. The most frequent questions asked: Have the fangs been removed? Have the snakes been "milked" of their poison, or the venom glands removed? An acquaintance of mine, a young biology student, once loitered at the foot of the mesa until the dancers had released their serpents, and captured one of them for a laboratory examination. He found the fangs intact, and the poison sacs normal. The venom of a rattler's strike goes into the blood stream of the victim, and cannot be affected by an emetic which empties the stomach. No white man, to my knowledge, knows the answer for sure, and the snake priests will not tell.

The details of the ritual I have described vary slightly in the different pueblos of the Three Mesas, and from year to year, but in general it follows the traditional pattern evolved by the priesthood of a prehistoric period. However, some of us who have returned to witness the ceremonial at intervals over a long period of years, have sensed a change more significant than the mere details of the ritual. Although the Hopi population is increasing, fewer dancers are taking part than a quarter of a century ago. I have heard youthful Indians predict that another generation will see the passing of this pagan rite. There is growing revolt on the Hopi Mesas against the ancient gods.

A few years ago when uranium prospectors wanted to explore the mineral possibilities of the Hopi reservation, as they are doing on the adjacent Navajo lands, there was a sharp clash in the tribal councils on the Three Mesas. The old men opposed the intrusion of the white miners. They were sure it would incur the wrath of the gods. The young men, many of whom had served in the armed forces in World War II could foresee many advantages to the tribe with additional income from mining royalties. The conflict is still unresolved. But there will be change. The Old Ones are passing.

Since the beginning of recorded history in North America, the Hopis have guarded jealously the traditional religion of their ancestors. When the intrepid Franciscan missionary-explorer Fray Francisco Garces in 1776 left Yuma alone and followed the Indian trails along the Colorado River north to the tribal lands of the Chemehuevi, Mojave, Hualpai and Havasupai people he received friendly hospitality everywhere. But when he turned eastward and arrived at the Hopi Mesas he was rebuffed. The Hopi feared the magic of his compass and cross. They would have none of his religion. He camped alone in the dusty streets of Oraibi for nearly a week, hoping the Indians would relent, and then departed from this "inhospitable band of savages."

The Hopis are essentially a people of peace. They prefer to live by toil, not plunder. They are believed to have migrated, at some prehistoric time, from more fertile lands elsewhere in the Southwest, to the sterile and almost impregnable mesa tops where they now dwell, to escape the looting of more warlike tribesmen. The springs and little fields where they now grow corn and beans and melons are at the base of the cliffs, and they preferred to scale the walls with ladders or narrow foot-trails every day to bring up water and tend their crops than to fight their enemies.

Later, when the marauding Apaches, Navajos and Utes found their way up the ladders and trails to the granaries where Hopi food supplies were stored, the tribesmen of Walpi brought in mercenaries to defend them. They offered generous concessions to a tribe of Tewas, then farming along the Rio Grande in New Mexico, to move to the First Mesa as guardians of the trail. The Tewas were given springs and lands to farm, and established the little colony known as Hano on the edge of the Mesa at the head of the trail to Walpi.

The tribesmen from the Rio Grande kept vigil day and night and as proof of their prowess as guardsmen they kept a scoreboard of the raiders they slaughtered on a great rock face near the top of the trail. Today a steep road leads to Walpi and the old scoreboard, known as Tally Rock, may be seen by motorists. Over a hundred years of erosion have dimmed the incised lines on the rock, but several years ago, an old Hopi told me the story and took me down the road to see Tally Rock. I counted 178 tallies—each representing the scalp of an enemy raider.

Strange people, the Hopi, according to the white man's sense of values. They will pick up a deadly serpent by the nape of the neck without batting an eye. But they recoil at the thought of going out and giving battle to savages who would rob and kill them. But they are smart traders. It is said that a Hopi will tuck a basket of peaches under his arm, leave for a day of barter among the Navajo, and return that night riding the Navajo's horse.

For many generations the Hopis have had a peaceful life based on agriculture and crafts work. Today the younger members of the tribe are going out into the white man's world and returning with ideas which would change the traditional Hopi way of life. It is not for those of us with a different culture to say which generation is right, the elders or the young people. Certainly there is much virtue in the customs and beliefs of the old people. They are honest, loyal to family and friends, faithful to their gods and diligent workers. They are good people, either by the white man's standard or their own.

Their tragedy is that they live in a world where change is one of the inescapable laws of the universe. It is easy for people to accept changes in the environment of things—new styles in clothing and housing and the gadgets of the machine age. But how difficult it is to change long established religious beliefs and the attitudes of life which determine conduct and manners.

Somehow, the Hopis will reconcile their differences. Those who know and like these fine people will hope that if the younger members of the tribe are to adopt the white man's ideas, they also will understand and accept his ideals—that before they discard the gods of their fathers they will acquire a reverence for the sacraments of another faith. For it generally is true—there are exceptions—that it is better to have faith in the wrong gods than to be without faith.

     ❁   ❁   ❁   ❁   ❁

There is another clan of snake dancers in the Southwest. They wear the costumes and paint of primitive tribesmen, but beneath their masks of colored pigments and feathery head-dresses are the fair skins of Anglo-Americans—doctors, lawyers, merchants, mechanics, rich men and poor, the everyday citizens of the mile-high community of Prescott in west central Arizona.

They are the Smoki People. Their annual ceremonial in August has no religious significance. Nevertheless it is presented with the solemnity of sincere people who strive faithfully to portray not only the Snake Dance of the Hopis but many of the other tribal rituals of the desert Indians. They enact the Devil Dance of the Apaches, the Fire Dance of the Navajos, the Zuni Weaving Dance, the Katchina, Shalako, Buffalo, Bear, Antelope, Eagle and a score of other dance ceremonials of the New Mexico and Arizona tribesmen.

The Smoki clan of Prescott was organized in 1921. Originally its dances were designed merely as an entertainment feature for a summer community festival. But among those who participated in the program were men and women whose long acquaintance with the tribal customs of desert Indians had convinced them the white man's civilization eventually would supplant much of the ancient Indian art and tradition.

"Let us study the rituals of the Southwestern Indians," they said, "and do what we can to preserve them, recording the chants and songs, re-enacting the dance rhythms and reproducing the art forms which many generations of tribesmen have evolved. Otherwise, these artifacts of native American culture will be lost forever."

The Smoki clan was formed to carry out this idea and has adhered faithfully to the original concept. However, during the forty years which have elapsed since the first make-believe Indian dances were held on the lawn of the Prescott courthouse square, the staging of the annual Ceremonial has become a major community project.

Membership in the Smoki People, the secret organization which underwrites and stages the annual spectacle, is limited to about 300 dedicated men and women. Soon after each year's performance the Smoki priests meet, select a new chief, and begin preparations for the following year's production. They employ no professional talent. Every detail in the month's preparation, from the research necessary to make these dances authentic replicas of the native American rituals, to the handiwork involved in costuming and stage construction, represents the voluntary services of the members. In the weeks immediately preceding the August presentation it becomes almost a full-time job for many of the People, with nightly rehearsals to perfect the rhythm of the various dance steps and the memorizing of the chants which have no accompaniment except tom toms and rattles.

Down through the years the town of Prescott has provided a fine amphitheater for the annual production and the Smoki People have built a museum which is a veritable treasure house of Indian artifacts. This is open to the public daily during the summer months. They also have erected a lodge hall, the Pueblo, which is the center of Smoki social and tribal life. In this stone building of pueblo architecture are the council chamber and library.

Research has played an important role in every year's production. Many years ago Barry Goldwater, now Senator Goldwater from Arizona, donated his personal library of Indian books and papers to the tribe, and on this foundation the Smoki People have assembled one of the most extensive sources of Indian ceremonial lore in the nation.

I have returned many times to witness the colorful Smoki ceremonials. The evening's program always starts with a Sand Painting and ends with the Snake Dance. The intervening rituals vary from year to year. In August 1960 I took my seat in the amphitheater just after dusk. As the overhead lighting was switched on, there was revealed a truly Indian setting—a composite of the dance plazas that may be seen in the pueblos of nearly every desert tribe.

In the background were the plastered walls with protruding vegas and the flat roofs of a typical pueblo, the only distinctive American architecture of a permanent nature in the United States. There were Indian children playing around the doorsteps, women bending over their stone metates grinding corn for the evening meal, a Navajo mother in velveteen jacket and flowing skirt at her weaving loom under a juniper tree, a potter working at her board, and on the bare dirt floor of the plaza in the foreground the medicine men kneeling to spread with thumb and finger the colored pigments of a great ceremonial altar—the sand painting.

As the design was completed the lights were dimmed and during a few minutes of darkness all traces of painting vanished, for among the tribesmen it is a religious imperative that sand paintings be destroyed at sundown.

Then followed the Hopi Home Dance or Niman Ceremony— one of the many Indian prayers for rain. In this the dancers were costumed in the elaborate masks and dress of the Katchinas which, like the snakes, are in communication with the spirit world of the gods to whom they will convey the tribal prayers for moisture to mature the crops.

In the next scene a Water Spirit in canoe emerges on a little estuary partly concealed in foliage, bringing a message from the Underworld that the tribesmen have won favor with the gods, assuring fruitful crops, good hunting and protection against enemies. This is the Canoe or Water Spirit Ceremonial.

The Ghost Dance of the plains Indians, the Sioux, is portrayed on a dimly lighted plaza by "skeletons," the effect being dramatized by flourescent outlines on dancers costumed in black tights and masks.

The Spider Woman of Hopi mythology plays the lead role in the next portrayal. She emerges, as did the ancestral Hopis, from the Underworld through the opening *Sipapu* somewhere in the Grand Canyon country, and transforms some of the snakes of her underground kingdom into beautiful dancing maidens.

The Lalakonti or Basket Dance which follows is a presentation of one of the rain ceremonials from the tribal pueblos in the Rio Grande Valley in New Mexico.

There was an air of expectancy among the spectators as the plaza was cleared for the grand finale—the Snake Dance of the Hopis. The detail followed very closely the pattern of the snake ceremonials on the Hopi Mesas, with one important exception. Among the Smoki People rattlesnakes are taboo. Their non-poisonous reptiles are gathered from the ranches in the surrounding area—generally brought in by school boys in exchange for tickets to the pageant. They accumulate in a pit at the Ceremonial grounds during the weeks preceding the program. Since ranchers value the non-poisonous species of snakes for rodent control, it generally is stipulated that after the Ceremonial the serpents are to be returned to the area from which they were captured.

A five-or-six-foot bullsnake is a more aggressive fighter than a rattler. Occasionally one of the big ones will rear up and hiss like a cobra. Although it has no rattles, its tail will quiver and the snake will lunge out at its tormentor. It is not uncommon for the Smoki dancers to be struck by these fighting bulls. But the wound is not serious for there is no venom. Just before the dance the snakes are all bathed in disinfectant.

Although the Smoki clan is an anonymous society, it is inevitable that the personnel engaged in the preparation and staging of such a spectacle will become known to their townsmen. There is a further identification: both men and women of the clan carry blue tattoo marks on the outside edge of the left hand, the dots and symbols indicating the number of dances in which they participated and their rank within the organization. The community of Prescott has a deep regard for its Smoki People, and there is always a waiting list of applications for membership.

Many years ago some of the leaders on the Hopi Mesas were quoted in the newspapers as being critical of the Smoki Snake Dance. They thought the people of Prescott were making a mockery of the Indian religion. The criticism was not justified, for the Smoki dances are in no sense a burlesque. Magnificently staged, in authentic native costumes, the players carry on the roles they have rehearsed for many weeks with all the solemnity of tribal priests. That the Hopis are now taking a more tolerant attitude toward the Smoki contemporaries was evidenced two years ago when a committee of Snake clansmen from the reservation came to Prescott to find out how the Smoki People contrived their long-haired wigs. It seems that some of the Hopi boys who were to participate in the dances were coming home from school with crew cuts. Actually, the wigs are made with ordinary yarn.

The Smoki People derive no personal profit from their participation in the annual Ceremonial. The amphitheater is always packed for the one-night performance, and all surplus gate receipts go into the fund for making next year's show better than the last one. They have accumulated a great wardrobe of costumes and ceremonial properties, and there are always the museum and the clan Pueblo to maintain.

Aside from the impressiveness of their pageant, the most amazing thing about these people is their modesty. Imagine, if you can, a troupe of actors shunning personal publicity. It is contrary to American custom. At Hollywood the second assistant costume girl must have her name flashed across the screen, and even the extra players hire press agents to keep them in the headlines. But in Prescott a stranger can sleuth around the town for a week without even learning the names of those who play lead roles in the Smoki Ceremonial. They are so good they do not have to resort to ballyhoo to hold their public.

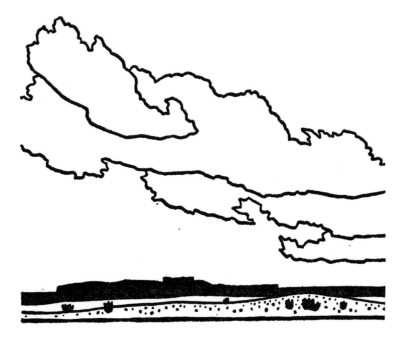

UTAH WILDERNESS TRAILS   XV

$\mathbb{S}$OME OF THE TRAILS we followed were first trod by cliff dwelling aborigines hundreds of years ago. Most of them had been blazed more recently by cowboys, and by rangers of the U. S. Forest Service. Some were so dim I wondered how Ross Musselman, our guide, was able to find his way. Others were deeply rutted by the hooves of thousands of head of cattle. At times they led through lovely vistas of quaking aspen, spruce and pine, while mariposa lilies and Indian paint brush blossoms peered at us from beneath the leafy undergrowth that bordered the path.

More often they followed the winding floors of steep-walled canyons, eroded by the abrasive power of silt-laden storm floods over countless millenniums of time.

For nineteen days we followed these trails on horseback, with an ever-changing panorama of red, tan and white sandstone palisades in the background. We rode 353 miles, and never went beyond the boundaries of San Juan County in southeastern Utah.

This is the Utah desert wilderness—the red rock country—one of the most spectacular regions in the United States, and the least known because of its inaccessibility. San Juan County has an area of 7,884 square miles, more than double that of Delaware and Rhode Island combined, and a population according to the 1960 census of 9,040 persons.

We started in mid-July from the 4-M Ranch near Monticello, then owned by the Musselman family. In addition to our guide and four packers there were nine riders in the party: Scott and Edyth Carpenter of Nutley, New Jersey; Clarence (Pete) and Faune Spang of Butler, Pennsylvania; Elsie Flaxon of Pittman, New Jersey; Leonard Martinson of San Francisco; Nancy Flack, 13-year-old of Pasadena, California; Gary Justice, 11-year-old of Berkeley, California; and the writer.

Our pack animals were seven horses and Kewpie, a little mule not much bigger than a burro, but the best pack animal in the train. Kewpie was the clown of the outfit.

Our trail led over the Abajo or Blue Mountains, an island like range rising to 11,357 feet above the plateau on which Monticello is located. The range is timbered with Gambel oak, Ponderosa pine, spruce and aspen, but its slopes are checkered with great splotches of granite talus where nothing will grow. For the first few miles we jogged along a well-beaten trail. The flowering season was at its best, and the dense underbrush which bordered our path was colored with sego lily, the state flower of Utah, mariposa lily, canterbury bells and wild roses. As we climbed, the oak trees gave way to spruce, and wild iris and columbine were added to the flower display.

We camped the first night at 7,600 feet, and filled our canteens from a trickle of water below a nearby snowbank. We were in La Sal National Forest, and we could look down on the checkerboard plateau where Utah farmers grow beans and wheat on land that until recent years was covered only by sage.

We spread our sleeping bags on a spongy mattress of spruce needles. Some of us had brought air mattresses, and in the nights ahead we made good use of them, but tonight nature had provided ample padding. Our bedtime lullaby was the swish of wind blowing through the foliage overhead. We had ridden eighteen miles the first day.

The next day our trail contoured the mountain at the 8,000-foot level and we often rode through dense forests of quaking aspen. The mountain people call these trees "quakies." The tall slender white-barked trunks grow so close together a rider must be on the alert constantly to avoid bruised legs. We passed a stream where fishermen were fly-casting for trout, and later we saw an ancient Indian metate along the trail. In the days ahead we passed many of these primitive grinding stones.

Mormon cattlemen run their herds on this range, and after riding sixteen miles we camped at Trough Spring in the shelter of oak, aspen and Ponderosa, with a great white cliff wall towering above on one side. The cowboys had improvised a water supply for their cattle by hollowing out six ten-foot logs like dugout canoes, and stringing them end to end on a slope below the spring. Each log overlapped the one below so that a constant trickle of water flowed the length of the series and kept them all filled.

Ross was chief cook of the expedition, and we all helped with the chores—gathering wood, peeling potatoes and bringing water. Generally wood was plentiful, but springs often had to be cleaned or dipping basins excavated. Pete Spang assumed the role of water engineer and generally was able to improvise easy access to the waterhole.

At mealtime, Ross followed the traditional routine of the range where fuel is plentiful. The method is to pile the fire high with wood, and when it is reduced to red embers, rake out little beds of them for the coffee pot, the skillets and stew pans. Thus the cooking is done around the fringes of the main fire, with each vessel on its own bed of coals. True, it smokes up the kitchenware, but it is easier on the packers and their stock. I can imagine the sarcastic remarks of a wrangler whose duty it would be to throw a squaw hitch over a portable camp stove every morning.

With the fire going, and the packs unloaded, each of us turned to the important task of selecting a smooth spot for the bedroll. At Trough Spring we had to choose between wet sand along the creek or a dry, steep hillside. Each solved the problem in his own way—and if we made a bad decision we would know it before morning.

There was little variation in the morning routine: Generally we were up between 5:30 and 6:00. Air mattresses were deflating while we did our toilettes. The horses must be given nosebags of oats and watered. Each rider tended his own horse, except that the wranglers saddled the women's mounts. The breakfast gong sounded soon after 7:00 and by 8:30 we were on our way. At Trough Spring one of the pack animals bolted as it was being loaded, and raced off through the timber, scattering bed-rolls and utensils as it went. It took two hours to capture the animal and recover the gear.

Today the trail climbed to the top of a ridge from which we looked on the Four Corners region, where the states of Utah, Colorado, New Mexico and Arizona meet at a common corner. To the southwest we could see the great monoliths in Monument Valley, and to the southeast the faint outline of New Mexico's well known landmark, Shiprock. Immediately below was a series of white sandstone cockscombs towering above the green of a Ponderosa forest.

Later in the afternoon we crossed a mountain meadow sprinkled with wildflowers, then through forests of pine and aspen, where ferns were growing as high as the horses' backs. We were riding in a verdant mountain oasis at an elevation of 7,000 feet. From an occasional promontory we could look down on a labyrinth of bare rock canyons where heat waves shimmered above the colorful sandstone.

At a lower level we entered a wide valley through endless fields of sage, where lupine and Indian paint brush were in blossom. I am sure lupine is the most adaptable flowering shrub in the Southwest. Its range covers four botanical zones, from sea level to 10,000 feet. As we rode down the valley turreted walls of red and white sandstone closed in to form a canyon where there was a little stream with deep pools.

While some of the riders bathed in the creek, I climbed a nearby butte, where the slope was sprinkled with broken Indian pottery and obsidian chips. On the summit were the ruins of a prehistoric Indian pueblo. In the days following we were to see many of these ancient Indian sites. There is nothing left today but the foundations, and these sometimes are covered with blow sand, but the sites generally can be identified by potsherds and flint chips on the surface. Many of these old ruins have not yet been excavated by archeologists, but the research is continuing under the direction of the department of anthropology at the University of Utah.

Several theories have been advanced as to why the prehistoric savages abandoned their stone and mud homes long before the white men came to Utah. They may have been forced to leave by prolonged drouth, by epidemic, or by the depredations of warring tribes. No one can say for certain. Ross Musselman suggests that these Indians may have been carried away as slave laborers by raiding Aztecs during the period when Montezuma was building his great temples in central Mexico. Doubtless many archeologists would dispute this idea.

We were to see other relics of the prehistoric Indian occupation of this land in the days ahead. Once when the canyon we were traversing circled in a great bend, we took a short-cut trail over a ridge at the neck of the loop. There was a natural arch through the sandstone dike at the top, and its walls were covered with Indian pictographs in white and red pigment. An unusual feature of these Indian paintings—something I have never seen before—was the presence of numerous handprints, as if the primitive artist had wearied of his tedious task, dipped his hand in his vessel of paint and then pressed it on the rock surface. He had well-shaped hands and the imprints were sharp and clear despite countless years of exposure.

On another occasion Ross led us a short distance off the trail to an overhanging sidewall where were painted four larger-than-life-size faces in brown and white. The figures had distinctly oriental features and were so well preserved I was reluctant at first to believe they had been placed there by primitive artists. Ross told us he had first seen them twenty years ago, and they had deteriorated little during that period.

At noon one day we stopped to fill our canteens from a spring which gushed from the sandy bank of a creek. Our guide said the spring had no name, as far as he knew. It has one now. To members of our party it will always be Yellow-Jacket Spring. We tied our horses in a thicket of oak while we went for water. A moment later the horses began pawing and snorting. We rushed back to the animals and found ourselves in a swarm of angry hornets. We had trespassed on their privacy. Several of us were stung before we could move the animals out of the danger zone. For the information of those who have never had the experience, the sting of one of these winged snipers is like being punctured with a red-hot darning needle. The swelling in my ear did not go down for three days.

Our average day in the saddle was from eight to ten hours. For the benefit of those of us who had done little riding in recent years, our guide would stop occasionally for a stretch. I often dismounted and led my horse down steep grades. It was easier for the horse and more comfortable for me. I did it partly because I like to walk, and more truthfully, because fifteen to twenty-five miles a day in the saddle in this rugged terrain requires callouses which I had never acquired sitting on an office chair in front of a typewriter.

One day I got my first glimpse of a western collared lizard, the prettiest member of the lizard family I am sure. Perhaps ten inches long, of which more than half is tail, the striking characteristic of this reptile is its coloring. The head is orange. Two black bands encircle the neck, and the body is a brilliant green, tapering off to a slate-gray tail. In the days ahead I was to see many of these brilliant-hued lizards, although not all of them were as brightly colored as that first one.

From the high elevations in the Abajo Mountains we gradually had been trekking westward toward the Colorado River and into the highly-eroded canyons of its immediate watershed. One day we climbed a slickrock trail to Salt Creek Mesa, where we could glimpse the sawtooth skyline of The Needles country. This is a flaming labyrinth of domes, spires and towers, a scenic fantasy which probably long ago would have become a national park were it more accessible.

The following day our guide led us up Squaw Creek into the heart of this gargantuan fairyland. Here millions of years of erosion have sculptured great cliffs of red, tan and cream sandstone into forms so fantastic as to make the term "The Needles" seem wholly inadequate. In the gigantic palisades which towered above us on both sides were many familiar images. The Sphinx was there, the Pyramids, battleships, pipe organs, toadstools, domed mosques—the range was limitless. Pinyon trees grow on ledges and in pockets, wherever they can find a roothold, and to add to the artistry of it all, the rock faces in many places are stained with tapestries in tan and brown, etched by the soluble desert varnish which the rains wash down from the capping at the top.

One day the trail led over a mesa and into Fable Valley, where the cattlemen bring their livestock for winter pasture. Forage is not as bountiful now as in previous years. Today the ground cover is mostly tumbleweeds, a plant that thrives on land which has been overgrazed. When the plant matures, its fragile root system gives way before strong winds and it rolls across the landscape, spreading seeds as it goes.

Here, as in many other valleys in this highly eroded region, storm floods have gouged deep gullies across the pasture lands. The soil is carried to the Colorado River and in ages past was an important contribution to the building of the fertile downstream valleys of Yuma in Arizona, Palo Verde and Imperial in California, and the great rich delta of the Colorado in Mexico. Since the completion of Hoover Dam in 1936, the silt is being deposited in Lake Mead. With the completion of Glen Canyon dam in two or three more years, it will find a new repository in the Lake Powell reservoir. Engineers have estimated that eventually—perhaps 200 or 300 years from now—these reservoirs will have become so clogged with silt they will become valueless for water storage purposes.

Among far-seeing conservationists there are some who are opposed to the further construction of giant dams in the Colorado. It is their contention that the hundreds of millions of dollars being invested in major dams more logically should be diverted to the construction of multiple small check dams and the maintenance of ground cover which will stop the erosion at its source. Ross told us these gullies in the Utah pastures have become noticeably wider and deeper during the twenty years he has been riding these trails. The rich soil which washed away during this period is now submerged in Lake Mead.

The twelfth day of our ride brought us to Dark Canyon, the daddy of all the gorges which drain this region and empty their storm waters into the Colorado. Our trail down the cliff walls was so precipitous we dismounted, hung the reins on the saddle pommels and let the horses pick their own way to the bottom.

This immense chasm is bordered by serrated ridges of cream, tan and red sandstone. When the later afternoon sun floods these sidewalls it reveals a hundred variations of exquisite shading. Against these bright-hued walls, the deep green of the pines which grow on the ledges provides a picture in kodachrome no words can describe.

From Dark Canyon, the trail made a long winding ascent to the top of Elk Ridge where at 8,000 feet we were again in a forest of pines and aspens, columbines and mariposa lilies. Deer are plentiful in this area and we passed hundreds of antlers along the trail, relics of the annual shedding period.

There is a forestry ranger station on Elk Ridge, with a good road leading to Blanding, and here Nancy Musselman, our guide's daughter, met us with a jeep loaded with food for the commissary and oats for the horses. We had been living out of our packtrain supplies for nine days. This was no hardship, for Ross is an old hand at dude wrangling and there had been no shortage of rations. But a couple of meals of fresh meat and vegetables were a welcome variation in the menu.

The next morning we left camp at nine o'clock and an hour later arrived at the Bear's Ears, two of the best known landmarks in the Four Corners region. Twin buttes, rising several hundred feet above the top of Elk Ridge, they are shaped like volcanic craters with one side of each cone broken down. Actually, they are sandstone pinnacles formed by some strange freak of erosion.

Here our trail connected with a well-maintained tourist road to Natural Bridges National Monument, our next destination. We jogged along this road through a forest of pinyon and juniper until late afternoon when we arrived at Monument headquarters. Across the arroyo from the park office is Owachomo natural bridge, much photographed by visitors because it is the only one of several natural bridges in the Monument which may be seen from a motor road. The others are reached only by foot trails.

We continued along one of these trails three miles to Katchina bridge, and camped on a sandbar beneath the massive arch. Katchina, like the other natural landmarks which give this Monument its name, was carved in sandstone by countless years of water erosion. It spans White Canyon, and wandering along the creek that evening I saw beautiful specimens of obsidian and petrified wood. Ross told me these fossil specimens probably had washed down from Woodenshoe Mountain where entire logs are weathering out on the slopes.

The next day we rode another three miles up White Canyon to Sipapu bridge, another of the gigantic arches spanning the streambed. We continued up the canyon to some ancient cliff dwellings in an erosion cavity high up in the cliff wall. There was a fifty-foot ladder, maintained by the park rangers, to enable visitors to reach the ruins. The Park Service has made no effort to restore the stone and mud dwellings. However, they are fairly well preserved, and especially the stick-in-the-mud granaries far back under the overhang.

That night we camped again under Katchina bridge and then returned to the forested summit of Elk Ridge. Our camp here was in a lush natural garden near a spring. It rained during the night but we were well water-proofed and merely had to pull the tarpaulin over our heads to keep dry. After living for many years on the desert it is a novel and pleasant experience to lie on the ground in a snug sleeping bag and listen to the patter of raindrops on the tarp that covers one.

Next day we stopped for a chat with one of the forest rangers. He pointed out the dire effects of overgrazing on this range. When cattlemen bring in stock in excess of the carrying capacity of the land a vicious cycle sets in. The animals not only strip the soil of its forage plants, but the destruction of the blossom prevents it from reseeding itself. When the plant cover is gone erosion of the soil begins and the fertility for reseeding is impaired. Certain species of weeds which thrive on sterile soil take over. For mile after mile we rode along a trail where the surviving vegetation was mainly sage and tumbleweeds. Range cattle shun these shrubs. In recent years the forestry service has been doing much of its reseeding with airplanes, but the aerial seeding is much more effective when livestock are kept off the range for two or three years.

With the exception of the three-day detour to the Natural Bridges, there was no backtracking in our schedule. Every day was an exciting new adventure in a strange and fascinating land. With our nineteen-day expedition nearing its end, we were heading back toward Abajo Mountain and Monticello. Our return route crossed the great canyon system of San Juan County at right angles. One hour we would be among the pines on top of a ridge, and a little later crossing a creek hundreds of feet below. In one of the canyons were many thickets of choke-cherries. The fruit was just ripening, and it looked luscious. But the flavor— well the name is quite descriptive.

Our last night was in a forestry campground at a lower level of the Abajos. The 4-H clubs of San Juan and Grant counties were having a weekend outing. The noise of many young voices was in strange contrast to the silence of the wilderness through which we had been riding. The only sounds heard along the trail were the calls of the canyon wren and pinyon jay, the soft swish of winds in the treetops, and the occasional jingle jangle of pots and pans on Kewpie's pack. Kewpie was such a little mule she had to trot to keep up with the long-legged horses, and we always knew when the packtrain was approaching by the rhythmic rattle of her load.

We were nearing the end of a rugged experience, but there had been many compensations. Ross Musselman is a hardy outdoorsman who regards the highest standards of living on earth as a dubious blessing. Americans, he believes, are paying a penalty for ease and luxury. His trips are planned to make the riders tough and fit. Our food was good, but there were only two meals a day. Generally, our breakfast was eaten before 7:30 in the morning, and we often ate dinner by lantern-light at night. We carried no lunches, and there were no snackbars along the way. All of us had lost weight, and perhaps that should be entered on the credit side of healthful living.

There were other compensations. Many of us carried cameras in our saddle-bags, and they were often used, but images on paper or projected on a screen have a missing dimension. The lens cannot record the subjective reaction to the majesty of creation. Being a purely mechanical device it cannot plumb the emotional response to the exquisite beauty of a cactus blossom shrouded in thorns, the call of a canyon wren echoing from the walls of a silent gorge, the tinkle of a tiny cascade in a land where water is more precious than gold, the camaraderie around an evening campfire among friends who have shared a hard day in the saddle.

As we rode along the lane to the 4-M Ranch one of the party summarized the adventure for all of us: "I wouldn't do it again for a thousand dollars, and I wouldn't take ten thousand for the experience."

A few months after our expedition returned, the 4-M Ranch was sold and Ross Musselman has now retired from dude ranch operation. Even in this scenic land of a thousand miniature grand canyons, motorized transportation gradually is replacing the horse and saddle. Kent Frost of Monticello and other dude wranglers are now running jeep excursions through many of the colorful canyon corridors where we rode.

San Juan county is comparatively poor in mineral and agricultural resources. But no region in the United States is richer in those intangible values of beauty and natural history. Its limited resources and sparse population, and its comparative inaccessibility, may become assets more desired than fertile soil and mineralized rock as increasing numbers of Americans seek relaxation in the silent places of the desert wilderness.

The scenic splendor of southern Utah is not limited to San Juan county. This area merely is one sector of a broad landscape of sculptured rock and fantastic color which extends from Mesa

Verde National Park in Southwestern Colorado across southern Utah and northern Arizona to Zion National Park.

That the American people and their governmental agencies recognize the scenic and recreational value of this region is evidenced by the fact that six national parks and ten national monuments already have been established here. The parks are Mesa Verde, Navajo Monument Valley, Petrified Forest, Grand Canyon, Bryce and Zion. The monuments: Hovenweep, Natural Bridges, Rainbow Natural Bridge, Navajo, Capitol Reef, Wupatki, Sunset Crater, Pipe Springs, Canyon de Chelly and Cedar Breaks.

In addition to these parks and monuments, the entire shoreline of Lake Mead has been reserved as a recreational area administered by the National Park Service, and a similar playground reservation is planned to surround Lake Powell after the completion of Glen Canyon dam. The State of Utah and the Navajo Tribal Council have plans for additional sites for state and tribal parks.

Utah not only is a land of magnificent landscape, much of it still virgin wilderness, but it also is the home of a deeply religious people who until recently have been reluctant to publicize the natural charm of their state. Less than a decade ago a western writer described them:

"The Mormons in their smaller communities have clung tenaciously to a way of life which prevailed in the small towns of the Middle West a half century ago. Nearly every family has a cow and a horse or two in the barn, chickens to supply eggs for the household and perhaps a few to sell, fruit trees around the house and a garden in the backyard.

"These people enjoy a measure of independence unknown to the more sophisticated younger generation today. Their comfort and security are determined very largely by the work they do with their own hands. Striking streetcar motormen, and pickets at the steel mills and coal mines in the distant industrial centers, disturb their way of life not at all.

"But they pay a price for the security and independence they enjoy. Cows have to be milked and chickens fed twice a day, seven days a week. There is no time for weekend motor trips.

"The smaller Mormon communities seldom go in for chamber of commerce ballyhoo. They have no night clubs or bingo palaces for entertainment. The church is the center of their social activity no less than their place of worship, and it fills both needs adequately.

"As an antidote for the distractions of a sophisticated society, these people have only peace and simplicity, and the majesty of great red sandstone cliffs fringed with juniper and pinyon. It is a grand place only for those who have learned to appreciate the artistry of natural things, and the companionship of a devout and frugal people."

CAMPFIRES IN SAGE AND SAND   XVI

MY FIRST GLIMPSE of a sixty-foot waterfall in upper Palm Canyon, eleven miles from the famed winter resort of Palm Springs, was many years ago. I had been following an old Indian trail which parallels the stream when I caught the faint boom of falling water. Making my way over a jumble of rocks to the edge of the cliff overlooking the floor of the canyon, I could see, far below, the spray of water dashing against rocks. The waterfall itself was concealed by a jutting promontory. It was late in the afternoon and there was not time for further exploration then, but I made a mental note that I must return to this place.

Later, when I asked old-timers in Palm Springs about the waterfall I got no information. They had never heard of it, and were rather incredulous. Not even the Cahuilla Indians, whose reservation includes every even-numbered section in this area, could throw any light on the subject. (The odd sections were part of a land-grant subsidy to the Southern Pacific Railroad before the reservation was established.)

It was three years before I again had the opportunity to make a trek into Palm Canyon. With a camera, a blanket, and a bag of dates and nuts in my backpack, I left the little trading post at the mouth of the canyon one Saturday morning. As I walked along the creek in the palm forest at the entrance to the gorge, where many Palm Springs visitors came for picnicking, an elderly couple stopped me. They were frankly curious to know what a lone hiker with a pack on his back would be doing in such a place. When I explained that I was carrying a blanket and planned to sleep that night in the upper canyon, the woman expressed a motherly concern for my welfare.

"But aren't you afraid?" she asked.

"Afraid of what?" I countered.

"Aren't there wild animals and snakes up there?"

It was a typical tenderfoot question, but she asked it in all sincerity. And so we sat on the rocks for a few minutes and I explained to her about the desert—the desert that is harsh and may be cruel to the imprudent, mysterious to the unknowing, fascinating to those who delve behind the mask of austerity, but never hostile to those who come with prudence and humility.

"You probably come from one of the cities," I suggested as I finished my impromptu lecture, "where hundreds of people are killed every year in motor accidents, and where the health of multitudes is impaired by raucous noises, and air that is poisoned by burning fuel. In truth, Palm Canyon is about the safest place on earth."

I left them seated on the rocks. Perhaps they thought I was crazy, possibly they envied me. It doesn't matter. The habits of a pampering civilization get a tragic grip on a majority of those who spend their lives in the cities. But nothing is gained by arguing with them about it.

That night I slept in my blanket on a sandbar formed by an eddy at the base of a giant Washingtonia palm. The packsack, stuffed with grass, made a comfortable pillow.

Early the next morning I continued up the creek, and found the sun just right for the pictures I wanted to take of the waterfall. It was easy to understand why this cataract was unknown to the hundreds of thousands of visitors who come to Palm Springs every winter season. There is no trail in the bottom of the canyon, and the water pouring over the sixty-foot precipice can be seen only by a hiker who has clambered over and around countless huge boulders strewn in the upstream approach.

Lower Palm Canyon is a well-shaded picnic area, but there is a wild rugged beauty in the upper canyon which holds an extra reward for those who follow the winding creekbed through occasional clumps of palms and cottonwoods to the point where they can see its tumbling waterfall through the misty spray which partially veils it.

While weekend hikes alone into the little known canyons are always a delight, my excursions into the desert hinterland more often are with companions. I have especially enjoyed my outings with those sturdy hikers of the Sierra Club of California, of which John Muir of the woods was one of the original organizers. The Los Angeles chapter of the club schedules many weekend and vacation safaris to scenic desert retreats.

My first view of Rainbow Natural Bridge in southern Utah, which Secretary Stewart Udall of the Interior Department has described as "the most awe-inspiring work of natural sculpture in the United States," was during an Easter week vacation with 77 Sierrans as companions. We hiked over a fourteen-mile trail from Rainbow Lodge, then operated by Bill and Catherine Wilson and owned in part by Barry Goldwater, now Senator from

Arizona. Flood storms have more recently destroyed much of this trail and the Rainbow Lodge was burned.

On the trails that day were many teachers, also lawyers, artisans, accountants, salesmen, engineers—a cross-section of American occupations. Some of them were parents, accompanied by teen-age children. Three members of the party were nearly 70, and several of the thirty women in the party were past 50 years of age. They are folks who like to spread their sleeping bags on the ground and explore remote places for rare flowers, strange birds, and unusual camera shots. Some go along just for the companionship they find in virgin forests and sheer-walled canyons. They are gallant campers and hikers.

On a well-established trail such as we were following, the Sierrans impose no regimentation. Each hiker is on his own. The seasoned walkers travel as fast as they wish. The short-rests-and-lots-of-them take their own time. The science students may botanize or study the geology as they go along. The photographers are free to detour off the trail as they wish, to obtain vantage points for their pictures.

During the morning tramp our view was always down, to gorgeous scenery in the landscape that spreads out below. Later in the day we walked between high cliff walls, looking up on either side to fantastic forms sculptured by time and erosion and decorated with water stain patterns draped like tapestries on the sidewalls.

Our trail crossed and re-crossed the creek many times. In places the water would disappear in the sands, only to reappear on the surface farther downstream. Water-cress grew on the fringes of tiny pools. Wildflowers were just beginning to blossom. Locoweed and wild onion were the most conspicuous. The names are unfair. Locoweed has a lovely purple bloom. This was my first acquaintance with wild onion, and I picked a couple of blossoms for their delicate fragrance. But that was a mistake. The broken stems also have a perfume—more accurately an odor. It was hours before I could get the smell of garlic off my hands. Wild onion belongs on the trailside where nature put it.

Rainbow Bridge, in the heart of a labyrinth of colorful sandstone canyons, has never been overrun with visitors. The first record of its existence was in 1909 when a Navajo Indian led Dr. Byron Cummings, archeologist, and John Wetherill, Indian trader and guide, to the spot. President Theodore Roosevelt established the 160-acre site as a national monument, and was one of the first visitors to sign the register beneath the arch in 1913. Zane Grey, the novelist, wrote his name there a few months later, and other early visitors were Irvin Cobb and J. B. Priestley. In April 1941, when I first visited Rainbow, I registered as No. 3,323. Seventeen years later, on my last visit to the Bridge in 1958, my number was 13,464.

Lounging in the shade of the arch, after the long hike, visitors invariably become interested in the inscriptions penciled in the National Park register. Some of the trekkers wrote poetry, others merely rhyme. There were uncomplimentary remarks about the pack mules which generally carried bedrolls and food. Some remarks were reverent, others humorous. I think the most expressive notation was that of the man who wrote: "I've hiked the 14 miles. I've been under the Bridge and on top of it and I've seen it from both sides and I still don't believe it."

A new and longer trail has been opened from Navajo Trading Post at the base of Navajo Mountain for those who prefer the overland approach to the Monument. In recent years a majority of the visitors have been walking in from a landing on the Colorado River. Boatmen operating passenger trips on the Glen Canyon sector of the river nearly always allow a day for the side-trip to Rainbow Bridge. Boats are moored at the mouth of Forbidden (Aztec) Canyon, a tributary of the Colorado. From there it is a six-mile walk up Forbidden and its fork, Bridge Canyon, to the great arch. Following the completion of Glen Canyon Dam within two or three years, backwater in the new Lake Powell reservoir will extend into Bridge Canyon, and at capacity level a narrow estuary of water will partially fill the creekbed beneath the Rainbow arch.

The Sierrans have perfected a cooperative plan which makes it possible for members to enjoy such outings as this at very moderate cost. Through the leaders appointed for each outing, transportation is arranged for those without cars, or preferring not to drive their own. The mileage of the round-trip is computed by the schedule committee and announced in advance, and car owners are paid two cents a mile by each rider. For meals, commissary groups are formed and the actual cost of the food is shared equally by those participating. Some groups carry portable camp stoves, others improvise fireplaces in the rocks. The trippers are advised in advance if it is to be a dry camp—if wood and water are to be brought along.

The Sierra Club is one of the most articulate conservation groups in the United States, and its members are meticulous campers. They not only leave clean camps, but the members often form work parties to gather up the litter left by less tidy picnickers. At one time it was the rule that waste packaging and garbage must be buried. When it was observed that coyotes often dig up old refuse pits and scatter the debris, it became the policy to burn everything possible and carry noncombustibles home for the garbage collector.

Camping with friends is a revealing experience. Primitive living divulges traits not exposed in normal association—the best in some people, the worst in others. Some campers spend hours preparing elaborate meals with soup, salad and all the frills of a full-course dinner. Others regard a camping trip as an escape from the chores of conventional living, and settle for a cheese sandwich and a handful of raisins.

I know a man and wife who cook hot camp dinners, and yet have reduced the chore to utter simplicity. They scoop a little cavity in the sand, build a fire in it, put the coffee pot and a couple of cans of food on the coals—a meat and a vegetable—and then eat their meal in paper plates and cups. When they are through they burn the plates, toss the cans in a litterbag to take home for the garbage collector. It takes thirty minutes and leaves them an extra hour or two for exploring the desert.

One of my own camp rules is that each member of the commissary be given the option of making his or her own flapjacks. Making hotcakes over a wood fire is a fine art. It takes much practice, and I have a chronic distrust of tenderfoot campers who volunteer to cook hotcakes for the crowd. Generally they do not know the first rule—the regulation of the wood fire. I do not like burned flapjacks, and so I reserve the right to make my own, and grant the same privilege to the others.

I have often camped with Boy Scouts, and after they have learned to cook their breakfast griddle cakes to a nice golden brown, the next lesson is flipping them over in the air. This takes courage, faith, good timing and perfect rhythm. Only cooks with a little music or poetry in their genes ever learn to flip pancakes gracefully. But one doesn't have to be a poet or musician to enjoy camping. It is good tonic for a jittery civilization—even if one has to eat burned flapjacks.

Residents of the arid Southwest, and those who dwell on its fringes, look forward to those occasional seasons when the floor of the desert becomes carpeted with the golds, reds, blues and whites of wildflower blossom. Nature's flower shows come only at long intervals, perhaps eight or ten years apart. They appear in March and April, and somewhat later at the higher elevations, after there have been heavy rains in December and January.

During long intervals of drouth billions of tiny seeds lie dormant in the sands awaiting the extra bit of moisture which will cause the seeds to germinate and begin the cycle which is essential to the perpetuation of the species. When the rain gods are generous, and the timing is just right, myriads of tiny sprouts appear on dune and *bajada,* and a few weeks later the ground literally is carpeted with purple verbena, white evening primrose, yellow poppies, desert sunflower, encelia, lupine, desert dandelion, coreopsis and a hundred less familiar species, including the

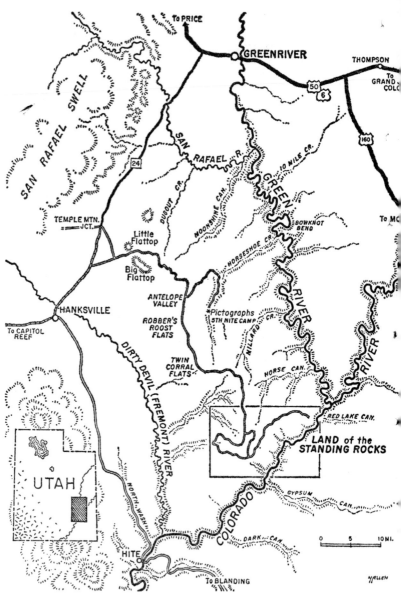

A paved road extends from Greenriver on Highway 50 to Temple Junction. From that point the Robber's Roost country, which includes the Land of the Standing Rocks, is accessible only in a four-wheel-drive vehicle. It is a wild and rugged terrain, with no habitations.

regal desert lily which grows from a bulb ten to twelve inches below the surface. The normally drab landscape is transformed to a panorama of color that brings delight to throngs of visiting motorists.

Since World War II uranium prospectors have opened up jeep trails into many desert wilderness areas which previously were accessible only by foot-trail. One of my most memorable camping trips was into such an area in 1957 in company with Kent and Fern Frost of Monticello, Utah, who conduct guided expeditions in their state.

We went into the Land of the Standing Rocks, which in the 1890s was one of the hideaways of Butch Cassidy and his notorious outlaws. Nine of us in three jeeps spent a week exploring a region of fantastic rock formations where prospectors and cowboys have labeled the landmarks with such place names as Robbers' Roost Flats, Stinking Spring Creek, Deadman's Hill, Moonshine Canyon and Wildcat Spring. Geographically, the area is between two tributaries of the Colorado River. To the east is the Green River and on the west is the Dirty Devil River, so named by John Wesley Powell in 1869 and now appearing on many maps as Fremont River.

In addition to the Frosts our party included: J. Frank Wright, fast water boatman on the Colorado; Drs. Melvin Hurley and W. L. Thompson, practicing physicians of Richmond, California; Joe Dudziak, shipping executive of San Francisco; Mary Beckwith, historian and explorer of Van Nuys, California; and J. Paul Wright, retired electrical engineer of Prescott, Arizona.

From our rendezvous at Green River, Utah, we followed a paved road 45 miles, then took off on a typical prospector's trail which became increasingly rough and rocky. Eventually it dipped off into the basin of the Standing Forks, down a newly bulldozed slip-and-skid trail which only a four-wheel-drive vehicle could traverse. We descended 1,200 feet in two miles.

We camped that night at Waterhole Canyon, and the next day got our first glimpse of some of the great sandstone spires and towers which the Ute Indians had described to early Mormon settlers in Utah as the Land of the Standing Rocks. The most conspicuous formations were of brilliant red Moenkopi sandstone. Moenkopi does not fracture and slab off as do Navajo, Kayenta and other sandstones of the region. Rather, it erodes away a grain at a time, forming delicately sculptured stone structures with vertical and horizontal fluting. Some of the formations have been given names: Lizard Rock, The Candlestick, Totem Pole, the Gong and Gavel, and there are scores of others. One slender tower is 150 feet high, perhaps 500 feet long, and not over 12 feet in thickness. Since it had no name of record I entered it in my notes as Tapestry Slab.

Botanically, we were in the Upper Sonoran Zone, with juniper and pinyon as the prevailing trees. While the vegetation was sparse, I recognized some old friends of the California desert— ephedra or squaw tea, evening primrose, Indian paintbrush and a species of yucca generally known as soapweed.

Our second night's camp was in a trackless little valley flanked on three sides by a gargantuan parade of sandstone gargoyles in orderly array, almost as if they were huge dolls on the shelves of a gigantic carnival booth.

Despite the fact that there are few springs and no flowing streams, the sand in many places was sprinkled with the chips of an ancient arrow industry, mostly chert, agate and jasper. More striking evidence of prehistoric Indian occupation was seen on the last day of the exploration when Kent Frost led us into Horseshoe Canyon where, in one place, the vertical sandstone wall is decorated with a display of Indian pictographs like nothing I had ever seen elsewhere in the Southwest. These were all robed figures, the kind of costuming one would associate with a Chinese mandarin. Of the 56 figures, 24 were life size, 31 smaller than the normal stature of a human being, and one a nine-foot figure with an intricate crown design on his head. There were also 24 small animal figures which appeared to have been sprinkled over the wall as an afterthought.

Presumably the ancients used brown hematite ore, ground in mortars, for the pigment, and then from some other natural source obtained a bonding fluid to give permanency to their artistry. Who painted the figures? When was it done, and what was the motivation? No living person knows the answers. But unquestionably this is prehistoric art. It simply bears out the conclusion that the impulse to create and to communicate are inherent endowments of the human species.

Another favorite camping retreat for those who like to spread their bedrolls in remote places is Havasupai Canyon in northern Arizona, where Cataract Creek tumbles over four magnificent waterfalls within a span of six miles.

At some prehistoric time a little band of Indians of Yuman lineage found their way to the floor of this secluded canyon. There was an ample supply of water, a few acres of fertile soil for cultivation, and I have no doubt they were impressed, as are the white visitors today, by the beauty and majesty of the 3,000-foot cliffs which enclose this valley.

The descendants of the original tribesmen are still there, living in a little one-street village where no automobile has ever been seen. It is eight miles by footpath to Hualapai Hilltop, the nearest motor terminal. Visitors either hike down the trail, or arrange in advance for Indian wranglers to meet them with pack and saddle animals at Hilltop.

The Indians are Supai. Havasu is the Indian word for bluegreen water—hence the name Havasupai Canyon. Springs which gush from the upper canyon are heavily charged with limestone, and this explains much of the bizarre beauty of this gorge. Limestone is highly soluble in water, and when the two come together it begins to dissolve. They flow together down the stream in a fickle sort of union. But water evidently does not fancy the partnership, for when the stream slows down it begins to redeposit its load of mineral. Thus the stone in Havasu Canyon is in constant process of creation and destruction. Limestone built the waterfalls and created lacy patterns of travertine which form

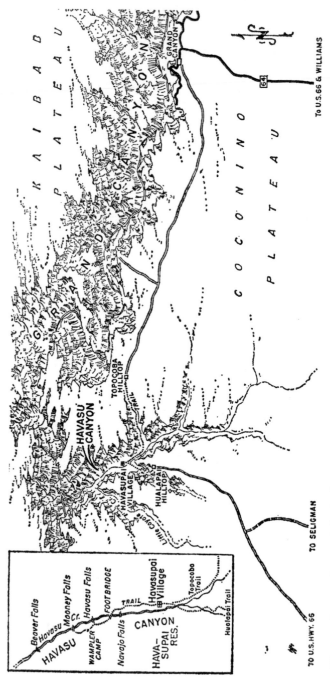

Havasu Canyon, home of the little tribe of Supai Indians, is a tributary of the Grand Canyon of the Colorado in northern Arizona. The nearest motor terminal is Hualapai Hilltop, eight miles from the Indian Village, but the tribesmen will provide riding and pack animals if arrangements are made in advance.

the backdrop of each cataract. It created caverns, and adorned them with stalactites and stalagmites.

Dr. Harold C. Bryant, former superintendent of Grand Canyon National Park, whom I accompanied on one trip to Supai village, told me there are two places in North America where the rock crust of the earth is in visible process of creation. One of these is the coral reefs in Florida and the other is Havasupai Canyon.

My first visit to the canyon was with 53 hikers from the Sierra Club during Easter week in 1942. Indian packers transported our gear, limited to 35 pounds of food, clothing and bedding for each member of the party. The trail took us first to the Indian village and then downstream a mile to Navajo Falls, where the stream drops 100 feet over a travertine-encrusted precipice. In another half mile we came to Havasu Falls, even higher and more spectacular than Navajo. A steep trail detours the waterfall, and downstream a short distance is a shady grove of ash and cottonwood trees which was our campground for the next four days.

Less than a mile below the campground is Mooney Falls, and in another three miles Beaver Falls, the fourth of the cataracts which give the creek its name. At Mooney Falls a stairway trail, partly in a tunnel, descends through the travertine face of the waterfall.

The blue-green water in the creek, its color due to the limestone in solution, becomes a lovely turquoise when churned by the tumbling water in the pools at the foot of each waterfall. Between the cataracts, wherever the current becomes sluggish, it begins depositing its mineral content, forming little dams resembling coral atolls in the Pacific. Water-cress thrives with its roots in the soft travertine. The result is myriad pools fringed with the luxuriant green of the water plant, like floating gardens in the stream. The red of the canyon walls, the blue of the turquoise water, the green of the marine vegetation, all add up to a photographer's dream. Mother Nature, somehow, is able to harmonize colors which would clash outrageously in a woman's dress or on an artist's canvas.

My most recent trip to Havasu was in 1958, with a small party arranged by Joseph Wampler. Joe is an archeologist who found classroom teaching too confining, and chose the hectic career of wrangling dudes in the High Sierras, and other out-of-the-way places, including Mexico.

During the sixteen years which had elapsed since I first became acquainted with the Supai and their Shangri-la, there had been a noticeable change in the economy of the tribesmen. The Indian Bureau has provided better tools for farming, but the gardens are not as well cultivated as formerly. The Supai are better horsemen than farmers. At least they prefer livestock husbandry to the toil of plowing, cultivating and irrigating. Increasing tourist travel now brings them a substantial income as packers and wranglers, and as the barometer of tourist revenue has risen the barometer of farm activity has fallen.

On my last trip down the Havasu trail I noted that one of the pack animals carried two panniers of fresh bakery bread. Perhaps that is symbolic of the change which has come to tribal life in Supai village, just as it is a symbol of change in the homes of Anglo-Americans. For the benefit of young readers perhaps I should explain that both white and Indian women once baked their own bread.

The Supai, like other tribesmen of the Colorado River basin, do not have the elaborate ceremonials of the Pueblo Indians further east. Among the Pueblans the kiva is the clubroom for men. Supai males use their sweathouse for the same purpose. Many of them gather at the mud-covered dugout in the afternoon to lounge and gossip. A few of the women weave fine baskets, which the visitors buy for souvenirs. But this is a vanishing craft industry. I will say in behalf of the Indians that the women did not spend as much of their time gambling as when I first became acquainted with them.

The lightweight sleeping bag which fits my backpack has given me comfort in many places, from the floor of Death Valley to the summit of Mt. Whitney, and from Brown's Hole in northern Utah to far down the Baja California peninsula. It is always in my car when I travel the desert roads and has been an adequate substitute many nights when the motels were all showing "No Vacancy" signs.

I think the strangest camping experience was a night on the Colorado River Indian Reservation in western Arizona. When twilight came I was following a dirt road that wound through the mesquite jungle of the river bottom. I parked my car in a little clearing and as I spread the bedroll on the ground a coyote sat on its haunches watching from the edge of the timber.

Sometime in the night I was awakened by the most eerie music I have ever heard—a coyote serenade. It sounded like hundreds of them—barking, howling, wailing, like so many howling dervishes, or a banshee glee club. For several minutes I lay there wondering what it was all about. Then, as if on signal, they stopped as suddenly as they had started.

I still do not know. But from other veteran campers I have learned that while this is an uncommon experience, it has happened before in other places in the desert wilderness. Just about anything can happen to a desert camper. And how I cherish the memory of that coyote serenade!

SAHARA INTERLUDE   XVII

"Y ou will proceed by military aircraft," my orders read, and the destination was the oasis of Atar in French Mauretania in North Africa, now an independent nation. I had asked for duty on the Sahara Desert, and this was it.

It came about this way: As a volunteer in World War I, I had completed my ground school training as a cadet at Ohio State University and qualified for pilot's rating at Kelly Field, Texas, where I was serving when the Armistice was signed. Then I was re-commissioned in the Air Corps Reserve with two weeks of active duty training each year.

Soon after Pearl Harbor in 1941, I was recalled to active service. My age disqualified me for pilot duty and I was assigned to ground operations in the Air Transport Command. After a brief tour of duty as Public Relations officer at Hobbs Field, New Mexico, I was ordered to report to the Commanding Officer at the Accra Air Transport Base in the African Gold Coast—now Ghana. There I asked for assignment to one of the maintenance and re-fueling stations maintained by the Air Corps on the Sahara Desert. It was several months before the request was granted, and in the meantime I served as Special Services Officer to Accra, and following the defeat of Rommel's army, was sent to Algiers as American ticket officer in the Allied Air Transport Command.

It was January 1944 when my long-awaited orders for the Sahara came through. I was to take charge of a detachment of five officers and 56 men responsible for re-fueling and servicing planes which crossed the south Atlantic and then continued north over the Sahara to the Mediterranean theater of war. The oasis of Atar was a midway station in the vast expanse of desert between Dakar and Casa Blanca. We also maintained a radio beam and furnished meteorological reports.

The military transport planes in World War II were built for service, not for sight-seeing. Two types of planes were in use for the transport of personnel, the plush seat jobs and the bucket seats—the C-47s. Generally the upholstered seats were reserved for high rank and special missions. My trip to the Sahara was in a C-47, with a row of seats on each side of the cabin, the passengers facing each other as in an old-fashioned streetcar. The seats were of aluminum and shaped like a tin washpan, and about as comfortable.

The small porthole-like windows back of every other seat were below shoulder level and it took much twisting and squirming to see the terrain below, and not much at that. But this was desert, my kind of country, and I wanted to see as much as possible. I turned and wiggled so much I had a sore neck, and the other passengers no doubt thought I was a victim of war jitters.

It was late in the afternoon when the bucket seats began to soften. I know of no better way to describe the manner in which one senses the long last easy glide toward the landing field. Combat planes lose altitude abruptly. They go down like an elevator. You feel it in the pit of your stomach, as if the elevator cable had broken at the twenty-third floor or higher. But when a transport plane goes into its normal glide toward a landing the feel is not in the pit of your stomach, but in the seat of your pants.

The oasis of Atar was a native settlement of 1,500 Arabs and Senegalese with a small French garrison. Our quarters were adobe barracks lend-leased from the French. Gasoline for the bombers and transport planes which stopped here every day was hauled 350 miles by truck from an Atlantic seaport. It was estimated the cost of 100 percent octane fuel delivered to our station in drums was $6.00 a gallon. It was a daily occurrence to pump $2,000 worth of gasoline into the wing tanks of a big bomber.

Through the village of adobe dwellings meandered a *wadi* lined with wild date palms. One of the French officers told me there were an estimated 30,000 of these palms extending along the dry watercourse in a span of forty miles. All of them were volunteer trees, seedlings which produced a hybrid miscellany of fruit. These were not marketable dates, but they were the staple item of food for the Arabs and blacks living in this sector of the Sahara. When the fruit began to ripen in mid-summer the nomad tribesmen moved in from all points of the compass, erected their black tents under the trees and remained until the fruit was picked. The surplus dates were packed in goatskin bags in reserve for the months between harvests.

There were no fences or visible markers to identify the ownership of the trees. When I asked the French *residente* about this he explained that the government kept hands off. "The Arabs know which trees belong to each family, and the ownership passes from generation to generation under an unwritten code which they know and respect." Barefoot Arab boys would climb the trees and shake the fruit stems until the ripe dates fell to the sand, where the women would gather them in home-woven baskets. At the end of the harvest the tribesmen would fold their tents, pack their camels and silently move out toward the distant horizon.

An Arab, in this part of the world, counts his wealth in camels, goats and palm trees. Concentration of wealth is a problem here just as it is in the U.S.A. A few rich sheiks—the "sixty families" of the Sahara—have acquired large numbers of trees which are "sold" to the poorer tribesmen during the harvest season at from 200 to 400 francs a tree. At the rate of exchange in 1944 this was from $4.00 to $6.00. When the fruit was all picked the tree reverted back to its original owner.

A palm must have its roots in moist sand. Beneath this oasis is a great underground reservoir that extends for miles along the *wadi*. Studying the geological history of the Sahara I learned that it was once a land of heavy rainfall, with rivers that flowed into great inland marshes. In digging for cesspools we encountered the cliffs of a prehistoric canyon. There was limestone only a few feet beneath the surface except along the *wadi*, which evidently follows the course of a canyon now buried beneath the sand. This submerged canyon was the reservoir from whence came our water supply.

Life on the Sahara, from the standpoint of one who has spent all his mature years on the American desert, was never dull. The culture of these primitive tribesmen—their economy, customs and religion—in daily association with strangers from overseas, is best revealed in the personal diary I kept during nearly a year of duty at this station. Much of the remainder of this chapter will be excerpts from my note book:

In the peaceful atmosphere of this African oasis it is hard to realize that in other parts of the world men are fighting a grim war for survival. Planes stop here every day. Men in uniform emerge from the cabins and stand by while the mechanics refill the fuel tanks. Then the motors roar and the huge crafts glide off the runway and disappear in the distant haze. They belong to a world that seems as remote as the planet Mars.

Twice a week the transport planes bring us fresh meat from Dakar. One evening when our meat ration was steaks, we went out among the sand dunes and broiled them over an open fire. It is an old desert custom in my home land. Many of the men in our outfit had never tasted campfire barbecue. Their verdict was: "good chop." By the time we got around to thirds the fresh meat was exhausted and we were finishing with canned sausage. There were a few pieces left on our improvised grill when the dinner was over. We invited the Arab mess boys to help themselves. They would have none of it. The prophet Mohammed put a taboo on pig meat.

Camel caravans arrive at the oasis every day, unload their packs of cotton yard goods, peanuts, tea, sugar, salt and kerosene and then go on their way, or the camels are hobbled and turned loose on the desert for such browse as they can find. Dates, goat meat and milk are the main items of food for these people, supplemented occasionally by the flesh of a camel that has gotten too old to work. A few of the villagers have little gardens of wheat and millet which they irrigate by drawing water in goatskin buckets by hand from shallow wells.

The camels seldom remain long in the oasis, for their food is the grass and shrubs which grow wild on the desert and they get nothing to eat while in the village. However, there are always a few of them staked at the market place when night comes and their raucous noise is our morning reveille. My vocabulary does not have a word that describes the vocal notes of a camel, but it is somewhere between the bawl of a cow and the roar of a lion. Recently a bomber pilot, who billeted overnight with us while his motors were being adjusted, asked if the noise that awakened him was made by lions. I assured him it was camels. He agreed with me that only a very tired old lion could sound off in such dismal tones.

Camels have not yet adapted to the age of air travel. We keep a vigilant eye on the runways, and it is necessary two or three times a day to drive out in the jeep and shoo off the beasts which have selected the smooth gravel floor of our landing field for a siesta.

We are learning about camels, but after all, the most interesting life of any land is the people who dwell there. My acquaintance with the native population at this oasis began with the houseboys on duty at our quarters—and Jello. Our most faithful servant is Jello, the Senegalese soldier assigned to us by the French *commandante*. He is on duty twenty-fours a day with instructions to keep other natives outside the adobe wall around our mud house. He is meek and obliging toward us Americans. But let an Arab peddler set foot inside the gate and he bristles into a domineering policeman who will take no back talk. I do not know where he got his name, for he understands not a word of English, but I suspect it was given to him by an American soldier who saw him wearing the red fez which is part of his uniform. He keeps it on day and night. All my efforts to find out what he was called before he became Jello have failed. He is proud of the name, and also likes to have his picture taken. When I start out with my camera he tags along, and grins with pleasure when I invite him to pose in the photograph.

The houseboys in the officers' quarters are Ahmed and Taleb, two bright Arab youngsters who make beds, shine shoes, do the laundry and run errands. They have reduced the effort of housekeeping to its lowest minimum. Some officers are more critical than others about such things as dirty floors and messy beds. These likable scoundrels know the minimum demands of each master, and they do just that and no more. Taleb has acquired the art of making up a cot that will stand perfect army inspection on the surface, with the bedding beneath in complete confusion.

Most of the plants which grow in this desert are complete strangers. But I have seen a few old friends—and enemies. The first shrub I recognized when I jeeped across the desert the day I arrived quite obviously is a first cousin to a milkweed. As a youngster I spent too many days hoeing this pesky weed out of the cornfield to have a kindly feeling toward it. But away off in this corner of the world it gives one a sort of warm feeling even to meet an old enemy. The Sahara species is a big hardy plant that grows in the most unexpected places.

I miss the creosote and burroweed. There is nothing that takes their place. Much of this area is as barren as Utah's Great Salt Desert. But the Sahara is not devoid of vegetation, and some of the plants are similar to those growing in my home desert. One resembles a locoweed, but has a yellow flower instead of purple. Another is a species of palo verde. I have seen desert gourds similar to those on the Colorado Desert, and a grass that resembles galleta. The camels feed on this.

Early in May, when the temperature reached 113 degrees at midday, I was ready to predict a long hot summer. But I have had to revise many of my school book notions about arid North Africa. I have learned that the Sahara is neither an unbroken expanse of shifting sand dunes, nor a region where unbearably hot days follow each other in monotonous succession.

Neither of these concepts is accurate. It is true there are endless plains of sand. I have flown over them for hours. But it is also true the sand wastes occasionally are broken by mountain ranges, gorges, escarpments, plateaus, buttes and in fact all the topographic features which give endless variety to our own American desert.

As for the weather in this western region of the Sahara, it is unpredictable—at least for a tenderfoot from the United States. One day in June the traffic crew loaded two big generators on a transport plane at noon. The metal was so hot the men had to use thick pads to protect their hands. Ordinary gloves were not adequate. And that night we slept under blankets. There are many days when a haze of yellow dust closes in around us until we cannot see the high escarpment four miles from the field. Occasionally, not even the end of the runway is visible. At the same time there is hardly enough breeze to fill the windsock which gives wind direction to incoming pilots.

The meteorological officer explains that this haze is due to sandstorms elsewhere on the Sahara. The fine dust is carried aloft at some distant point, and when these winds subside the fine particles descend in a yellow fog on the terrain below. By the same token, the sand that swirls aloft when we have a sandstorm at Atar may shower down many hours later on the black tents of Arabs hundreds of miles from our oasis. So we get the dust both coming up and coming down. When the wind blows we are blasted with our own sand, and when it stops we are enveloped in the sweepings from dunes far away. There is always a sandstorm blowing somewhere on the Sahara.

But I do not mean to imply that summer on the Sahara is a season of perpetual dust. The nights, with few exceptions, are delightful. The air generally clears after sundown. There are no malarial mosquitoes here and we sleep out under the stars. Toward morning a cool breeze nearly always makes it necessary to pull on a sheet or blanket. This refreshing breeze continues until eight or nine in the morning.

Anyway, we have lots of variety. For instance, at noon today while a plane circled overhead getting landing instructions from our operations tower the wind changed three times in eighteen minutes. The pilot finally decided we were all crazy down here on the ground, hung up his headphone, and picked his own runway. That was the smart thing to do under the circumstances.

Tomorrow we will start drawing water from a new well, dug by the French military for the exclusive use of our American camp. The well is in the bottom of the *wadi*. In the California desert a man would be foolish to locate a well in such a place. The first storm flood would fill it with sand, if it did not wash out entirely. But the French officers selected the site, and they know their Sahara much better than I do. Anyway, I hope they are right, for it required much time and red tape to get the necessary cement here by plane.

Native workers on the new well first dug down to water level—about six feet. Then they placed a flat metal disc, like a huge washer, on the damp sand at the bottom of the pit. Inside diameter of the disc was four feet. On this iron foundation they began laying a circular wall of stone and mortar. Two natives inside the ring began scooping out the sand, and as they undermined the wall from the inside it sank inch by inch under its own weight. Soon the diggers were in water up to their knees, then their waists, and finally their shoulders. At that point they would hold their breath and duck under the water to bring up another shovelful of sand. We wanted an ample supply of water so we brought in a portable pump to enable them to go deeper. When they reached nine feet the water was seeping into the well as fast as we could pump it out. We hoisted the men out on a rope and the job was finished.

This well caused me much embarrassment some time later. The General came down from Wing headquarters in Casa Blanca to inspect the station. As part of the jeep tour of the camp I took him down to the wadi to show him the new well, of which I was quite proud. A naked Arab was taking a bath in it. Fortunately for me, the General had a sense of humor. After that we put a lid and padlock on the well.

Every day the C-47s roll to a stop on the parking ramp in front of my office. The mechanics open the door and out pours a stream of passengers, most of them in uniform. They have been riding bucket seats for hours and want to walk around a bit while the plane is being serviced.

A blast of our 100-degree air greets them. They look around the drab horizon. They can see the shimmering mirage at the end of the runway, and the dust devils are dancing on the *bajada* at the far side of the valley. Sometimes they start wise-cracking: "What a helluva place to be fighting a war!"

I do not argue with them. If I told them I had asked for this assignment they would shrug me off as a crackpot. They have not yet learned that the grim aspect of the desert is merely a mask. And that for those who look behind and beyond the deception there is a world of infinite charm and inspiration. But one cannot tell these things to a stranger. I often think of the story about the woman who traveled across the American desert in mid-summer. She was hot and ill-tempered and wanted everyone to know that for her the desert was the door to hell. "This is an awful country," she exclaimed. "I don't understand how anybody can live in such a place." A quiet-spoken stranger who had gotten on the bus at the last stop turned to her with a look of pity. "Lady, don't you wish you could?"

Many of the air travelers who come this way now carry souvenirs away with them. I have given permits to two of the Arab metalsmiths to peddle their products to passengers at the parking ramp. Their best-sellers are paper knives and ingenious padlocks, crudely hammered out of brass and copper, and the salesmen are rather picturesque in their blue robes and turbans. They speak only a few words of English and when the customer is unable to understand their broken French, they squat down and draw figures in the sand. The prices are always quoted in francs, for that is the only kind of money we have here—ragged paper francs issued by various French colonial governments in many sizes and designs.

One of the smiths is an excellent craftsman, the other less skilled. They are very jealous of each other. The inferior craftsman complains that his competitor charges too much for his wares. I have been assured by each of them that the other is "no good." Every few days Hamed offers me a bribe to cancel the permit of Sidi, and vice versa. But I am against monopoly. We have some of it in America.

We want to extend the ramp, and a motley crew of Arabs and Senegalese is digging out rocks and filling the holes with clay. When I glanced out the door this morning one of the

workers appeared to be loafing on the job. He was squatting on
the ground apart from the others. I watched him a few moments.
He was not loafing. He was saying his prayers to Allah. When
he had bowed his forehead to the earth the proper number of
times he gathered up his pick and resumed work. Allah has not
showered these people with many material blessings. But they
have faith. And that is something—a very important something.

Our first summer shower came late one afternoon in June
when we were eating our evening chop. The sky clouded over and
a blast of wind filled the air with dust. I looked out the mess hall
window just in time to see the top blow off my jeep. Then the
rain came—rain on the desert! You have to spend months in a dry
parched land to appreciate the miracle of rain. There was a hum
of excitement around the mess tables. Some of the men rushed
out on the porch to see the shower. Others started a song. The
half-naked Arab mess boys went out to feel the cool drops of
water on their bodies. Two of them tackled the job of recovering
my jeep top—glad for an excuse to be out in the rain.

When it was over I went outside with the others. Everyone
was in high spirits, but there was something lacking. Then I knew
what it was—the scent of the creosote bush! Rain on my home
desert fills the air with the pungent odor of larrea. I like that
smell, perhaps because of its association with rain that is always
welcome. These two—rain and creosote—have been linked together in my life for so many years the Sahara shower did not
seem quite natural. There was no creosote here.

Taleb and Ahmed, our houseboys, continue to be a problem.
They are always courteous and apologetic, but the floors go
unswept, the laundry is always overdue and the tin washpans
never cleaned. When we scolded Taleb he became very indig-
nant—not toward us but Ahmed. Ahmed had failed in his duty.
When we reprimanded Ahmed he very sorrowfully told us,
"Taleb should have done that. Taleb go way, no work."

It was the old army game of passing the buck. Of course it is a very proper game when confined to the army. But when the army becomes the victim, that is something else.

The billeting officer solved the problem. He called the boys together and announced that for one month Ahmed would be the head houseboy. "Him boss, Taleb do what Ahmed say. Next, month Taleb is to be the head boy and Ahmed will be his helper." The wages were adjusted accordingly. It will add up the same as far as pay is concerned. But we are now getting better housekeeping in our four-room adobe.

It is big clumsy Jello who comes out second best in the native intrigues of our household. Jello has a heart as big as all outdoors, but he doesn't think as fast as Taleb and Ahmed. Consequently he does all the heavy work.

This evening just before sundown I heard singing so weird and familiar I rushed out of my quarters to see from whence it came. The music brought to my mind a picture of painted Indians—the Antelope clansmen coming out of their kiva and trotting along in single file toward the open court where they would participate with the Snake Priests in the annual Snake Dance on the Hopi mesas in northern Arizona.

At first there was no one in sight, but the chant grew louder. Then around the corner of a building a half block away came a motley gang of blacks—Senegalese. Two of them were pulling a two-wheel cart, others were pushing, and some were just straggling along. They were hauling adobe mud. Their song was not the high falsetto of the Navajo, but the guttural chant of the Hopi with a staccato emphasis at intervals. It was a chord one unconsciously identifies with primitive people. Such music stirs something deep within one—never to be forgotten.

The blacks, many of whom are on slave status, although under French law they could have their freedom if they wanted it, dance and sing in the oasis nearly every night. Their evening festivities are more like darky camp meetings than the ceremonial dances of aborigines. But somewhere out of the past the little group of mud-haulers had inherited an ancient chant from jungle or desert tribesmen.

Houmadi, chief of the oasis, is building a new business block in the market place. Rather, Houmadi sits by in a flowing white tunic while his Senegalese laborers haul mud and make the adobe bricks for the structure. It was one of his work gangs who sang the primitive chant I had heard.

In the remote areas of central and north Africa the mud for adobe blocks normally is carried on the heads of the workers. But Houmadi is progressive. He salvaged some old automobile wheels. They came from the junk yard, where lie the skeletons of vehicles once used on the long stage run from the seacoast to this oasis. With these wheels the Chief had carts made, also of salvaged material, to speed up the transport of rocks and mortar. One cart with a half dozen men can move as much material as would be done by a hundred head-carriers. This oasis is becoming civilized.

Native arts and crafts are not as far advanced here as among the desert tribesmen in the United States. I have found very little in the way of art that is worthy of the name, and yet I have a feeling these Sahara nomads have latent abilities which would be revealed if materials were made more accessible and there was a bit of guidance and encouragement.

Nearly every evening well-dressed Arabs come to our quarters offering rather crude but ingeniously designed articles of leather, brass, copper and silver. They make leather bags, jewel boxes, miniature scimitars to be used as paper knives, padlocks and other small items. Some of the craftsmen do slipshod work, others show considerable skill.

In a large adobe building, in the oasis, a score of Arab women are at work constantly weaving rugs and blankets. The equipment and methods are much the same as one sees on the Navajo reservation in Arizona and New Mexico. However, instead of dyed wool these women work almost entirely with camel's hair in natural color. Small embellishments of white goat's hair sometimes are woven into the pattern. These women do not attempt the intricate and colorful patterns one sees in Navajo blankets. The French government, through its local *residente,* sponsors the weaving industry and markets the product.

When I first visited the dark, crowded mud building where the weavers are working I came away with the feeling there was something wrong with this picture. Then I realized that my interest in Navajo rugs is partly due to the colorful setting in which they are made: a Navajo woman in bright-hued costume, her neck and arms and ears adorned with silver and turquoise, working in the shade of a juniper or mesquite tree while her sheep graze on the nearby sidehill.

These Arab women are turning out a very serviceable product, but the setting in which they work is without glamour. It is just a sweatshop, grimy and unlighted. But of course Atar is not a tourist town. If it were, I am sure the *residente* would soon recognize the value of setting the looms on sand dunes in the shade of palm trees, and perhaps adding a bit of color to the flowing black tunics of the weavers.

Most of the natives here wear giddy-giddys. I have never seen the term in print so I am not sure of the spelling, but that is the way the Arabs pronounce it. A giddy-giddy is a leather amulet on the end of a cord, worn as a necklace or around the arm or calf. I have seen Senegalese men and women draped with a dozen or more of them. They are good-luck charms. The most popular one protects the wearer against physical injury.

Taleb, one of the houseboys, assures us they are "veree good." To prove his point he told the experience of one of the black soldiers stationed at the French fort here. This soldier had bought a charm from one of the traveling magicians who work all the north African towns and settlements. The magician demonstrated the effectiveness of the amulet by hanging it around his neck and then having his stooge stab him with a dagger. The blade never made a scratch.

So the soldier bought one. That was good magic for a soldier going to war. It worked all right until the French army surgeon lined the company up for a periodic inoculation. When he came to the soldier with the giddy-giddy the needle broke. The next one broke. After three attempts to puncture the black man's skin, the problem was solved by having the Negro sell his giddy-giddy to a third party so the soldier could receive his shots. Taleb believed this story. "Giddy-giddy veree good."

One of the most popular men in our detachment is Sergeant Melvin Maloney. In addition to other duties he operated the camp post exchange. Selling soap, cigarets and candy to soldiers may be a drab sort of business to some folks, but for Maloney it was high adventure. He was a poet, artist and philosopher. Not one of those silent, heavy thinkers, but a quick-witted fellow with a glorious sense of humor and a line of patter that was sure cure for GI blues.

The walls of his tiny store were hung with his paintings of palm trees, mosques and Arab maidens, and while he passed out PX rations he entertained his customers by pointing out the crudities in his art work.

When orders came transferring Maloney to another station, his eight-year old helper Bopepe, was broken hearted. The little Arab boy practically lived at the post exchange. He made up the sergeant's cot every day, policed his quarters for the weekly inspection and stood by with admiring eyes while his big American pal painted Sahara landscapes. When Bopepe went out to the field to bid his friend goodbye he tried bravely to hold back the tears, and then hid his face in his arms when he could repress them no longer.

But Bopepe is still among friends. Every soldier on the post loves this bright-eyed little son of the desert. He doesn't speak English but he understands nearly everything that is said to him. He is just one of several Arab youngsters we would like to take home with us if it were possible.

Wadou is another of our favorites. He is a handsome lad of fourteen, with a sturdy pair of shoulders. He works with the native maintenance crew and despite his youth and small stature does a man's work. One day I sent him out with three adult Arabs to put a fresh coat of white paint on the stone markers along the runways. It was not a highly skilled job, but painting rocks was something new in the experience of the tribesmen. I indicated what was to be done and then stood by to see if they understood. The older men were rather awkward at first, but not Wadou. He immediately became the self-appointed foreman of the detail and soon had the job well organized. He has a pair of sparkling black eyes that would melt the heart of a stone man.

Then there is eleven-year-old Braheme, my personal "aide-de-camp." The ages I quote are not accurate. None of these sons of the desert tribesmen know how old they are by the Christian standard. Braheme's father owns several camels and a hundred palm trees, which means he is well-to-do according to Arab standards. Braheme not only does my laundry and house-keeping duties well, but he is a sort of liaison for the American officers in our dealings with the local population. In addition to his native language and French he has mastered enough English to serve as interpreter in our ordinary communication with the villagers.

Braheme has had only one year of school. His home is a bleak tent of camelskin surrounded by a high mud wall. His playmates have been the unwashed and unclothed urchins of the dusty oasis. And yet he has wisdom beyond his years, and traits which we identify with culture: Modesty, gentleness, honesty, industry, diplomacy and a fine appraisal of human nature. He is a devout Moslem and when I expressed an interest in his religion he told me his creed: "Good Arab no steal; no drink cognac; give plenty chop to poor neighbors; always tell truth. Then when he die Mohammed take him up . . ." At that point his English vocabulary ran out, and he gave a sweep of his hand toward the sky.

We had to part with Jello, our Senegalese soldier guard. The French major changed guards—at our request. Now we have Gabriel, another black soldier recruited from Senegal. Jello was the victim of too much kindness. He was big and likeable and we became rather lax with our discipline. Jello also become lax. And now his days of ease are gone. He is carrying mud on his head to build adobe walls at the French fort.

After my association here, I will never regard the Arabs as an inferior race. Give them the dignity of free men, schools for their children and ample wages for their industry, and they may teach the white-skinned races some virtues which the capitalist and communist worlds have neglected or forgotten.

Bopepe, Wadou and Braheme typify the best traits to be found among our neighbors of this oasis. But my picture would not be an accurate cross-section of the primitive life of this desert without a glimpse of the ignorance also to be found here.

This evening just before dusk there was much chattering outside our quarters. I went out to see what was going on. A crowd of Arabs and Negroes was in the yard. The center of interest was a sullen-looking black in custody of a native policeman. The houseboys explained that the prisoner had stolen some clothing from an American officer formerly stationed here, and had just been captured. While the palaver was going on, Gabriel rushed out of the little room where he sleeps in the officers' quarters and started lashing the naked back of the prisoner with a heavy belt.

Of course we stopped that. Since the affair was being explained in three languages, and the natives were in a high state of excitement, it was rather confusing at first. The theft had occurred long before any of the present personnel had been assigned to this station. When the story became clear we instructed the policeman to turn the prisoner over to the French authorities.

Later we learned that the Negro in custody had been a slave owned by Houmadi, the local chieftan. We also learned the reason for the excitement among the Arabs. Houmadi had sent the prisoner over to us to be executed. "He no good; shoot him!" was the terse message.

I think Gabriel was quite surprised when we made him quit lashing the man. And I suspect the crowd was disappointed when we ordered the thief taken to jail instead of standing him up before a firing squad. But we Americans should not judge too harshly the inhumanity of these untutored tribesmen. Less than 100 years have elapsed since human chattels were beaten and killed in our own civilized U.S.A.

Like all humans everywhere, the Arabs have an inherent capacity for both love and hate, honesty and dishonesty, courage and cowardice, generosity and selfishness, for tolerance and haughty bigotry. Americans have these same potentials, just as do the English and Germans, the Russians, Chinese and Eskimos. None of us is altogether good, nor hopelessly bad. These genetic potentials plus environment, and the decisions we make and the will with which we carry them out are the factors which shape our lives. The color of the skin, the geography of the birthplace, are secondary.

During July and August we had many days when the thermometer passed the 118-degree mark. Of course there were no air-cooling installations here, but we had refrigeration for the storage of food and to provide iced drinks. The transport planes brought in Servels operated with the flame of coal-oil lamps. As long as the lamps were kept filled with kerosene and the wicks trimmed, there were ice cubes for our tea and water.

Because of the rugged conditions under which we were living, it was the policy of the Air Command to rotate the personnel here every three months, and in most instances the men looked forward to these transfers. But I found the assignment intensely interesting and asked for a continuing tour of duty here. A few days later the Personnel Officer from Wing Headquarters flew out to the station to see if I was in my right mind.

"Oh, I am just an old desert rat who doesn't know any better," I explained to him.

The summer temperatures were especially trying to men from the northern zone of the United States. A corporal from Minnesota who found it almost unbearable, put a little sign beside the parking ramp:

◀ *North Pole 4837 Miles*

South Pole 7773 Miles ▶

Hell 22 Feet

▼

I overheard some of the men arguing about the distance to hell. The soldier who put up the sign was defending his figures by explaining it happened to be a cool day when he took his measurement.

Lieut. Paul Thomasset, of the French garrison, has been telling us about some lakes of fresh water where we can catch fish— somewhere out among the rocky hills to the west of our oasis. From his description, our guess is catfish. But who would expect to find catfish in the middle of the Sahara Desert? Fishermen's tales are one of the great indoor sports in America, we assured Paul, but no one ever believes them. When it was evident we doubted his story he offered to take us on a fishing trip.

We accepted the invitation. Our party consisted of Lieut. Thomasset and his native houseboy Query, Lieut. Bruce Cabot of Hollywood, and myself. The distance was eleven miles and we were to travel by jeep to the next oasis eight miles away, and the rest of the way on camels. The last three miles, we were told, were too rough for a jeep.

Paul sent word ahead to have the camels ready, and we left one Saturday afternoon. There was no road. We alternately mushed along through fine sand and across flats covered with big cobblestones. The going finally became too rough for our sturdy little war-wagon. A mile and a half from the oasis it gave a final gasp and quit.

Our French guide solved the dilemma by sending Query ahead on foot to get the camels. While we waited, Paul hailed a couple of passing Arabs and asked them to come and make tea for us. Until now I thought the British were the champion tea drinkers of the world. But my tour of duty on the Sahara convinced me that the British learned the tea habit from the Arabs, and are still novices at the art of brewing and serving the beverage.

Tea is a ritual among those turbaned desert dwellers. No caravan would ever start across the Sahara without its teapots, glasses, loaf sugar and mint leaves. On the caravan treks they stop four or five times a day for tea. Always it is prepared and served according to the time-honored tradition.

The properties for our tea party were two small teapots, one for water and the other for tea, a long cotton "stocking" with tea, brick sugar and mint leaves, the ingredients being separated by knots to keep them from becoming mixed, and several small glasses. The tea and sugar and mint may be carried in small goatskin pouches. The drink is never served in cups.

The desert may be as barren of vegetation as the Devil's Golf Course in Death Valley, but an Arab can always find a few twigs and roots with which to build a tiny fire. While the water is heating, the tea leaves are carefully measured according to the number of persons to be served. It is known in advance how much each will drink and never a leaf is wasted. The tea goes into the other pot. Then sugar loaf is broken with a little hammer especially made for that purpose. Tea and sugar just about fill the teapot. The Arabs like it sweet. Finally a pinch of mint leaves is sprinkled over the top and the hot water added.

Both indoors and out, the tea is prepared by a master of ceremonies sitting cross-legged on the ground with the glasses in an orderly row in front of him. The syrupy tea is mixed by pouring it into one of the glasses and back into the pot repeatedly. After the proper amount of mixing, the MC pours a few drops in a glass for sampling. He has made tea in this manner a thousand times and knows to the last tea leaf and grain of sugar whether it is properly prepared. Nevertheless it must be tasted, and if a distinguished guest is present he also is invited to taste it.

Then the tea is poured, with a dexterity that would make the ace soda jerk in a drug store look like an awkward clown. There is a graceful flourish, and from the spout two or three feet in the air a tiny stream of tea emerges and scores a perfect bullseye in the center of the glass on the ground, with never a drop lost. Men and women, boys and girls, all are masters of the art of making tea. The Arab whom Paul had drafted for our tea party beside the crippled jeep was a villainous-looking fellow with matted hair and dirty rags and tatters on his back. But when he started to make tea he became an artist.

Three glasses are served to each guest—always. It is discourteous to drink less. It would be rude to drink more. And when the Arab had finished serving, he washed the glasses with the few drops of water left in the kettle, then threw his carbine over his shoulder and with his companion continued the journey to the next oasis.

The sun was sinking behind the distant brown hills when the camels and their driver arrived. Our food and canteens and blankets were packed in the saddlebags, and the camels brought to their knees with a soft-voiced "sh-sh-sh-sh" and a gentle tug at the leather rein attached to rings in their noses.

Cabot and I were each given a baton, with instructions for guiding the animals by tapping them on the neck, the left side for a right turn and vice versa. We climbed into the pocket saddles and gripped the leather rim while the beasts got to their feet. This is a ticklish moment for a novice. There are neither stirrups nor saddle horn. Starting with his belly resting on the sand, the camel first rises on his front knees, giving the rider a sudden pitch backward. Then his rump comes up as he straightens out those long hind legs, and the rider lurches forward. Finally, the camel's shoulders come up as he straightens out his front legs. And there you are, perched on the peak of a one-hump camel with nothing to cling to—wondering where you would land if the beast starts to buck.

But camels do not buck. They have a more docile way of expressing their dislike for humans in general and the rider in particular. From the time the driver starts putting on the saddle, they groan and grumble. I was quite sympathetic at first. I thought the cameleer was cinching them up too tightly. But later I concluded their moans were mostly bluff—or habit.

It was one of those perfect moonlight nights on the desert. A cool breeze was blowing and there was no sound except the impact of padded feet on the sand. We rode single file, through an oasis and then over drifted sand dunes. Once we stopped by thatched huts, and the nomads who lived there brought us each a bowl of goat's milk.

We crossed a wide sandy valley and started up a rocky arroyo that soon became a cliff-walled canyon as the mountain closed in on both sides. When the boulders became too big and numerous we dismounted and led the animals. While I am not sure Nature designed a camel's back for riding purposes, I would award this beast all the medals in the world for its sure-footedness in traveling over and among rocks. No one would think of taking a shod horse or mule over the boulders along that route, and a low-slung burro would have become hopelessly wedged between the huge rocks on both sides. But the camels with long legs and pad-like feet marched along without a slip or stumble.

Despite the awkward contour of a dromedary's back, the Arabs have designed a pack saddle that for simplicity and utility beats anything I have ever seen on an American mule. Perhaps that is because these desert tribesmen had been working at it for several centuries before dude ranchers were discovered.

It was ten o'clock when we reached the first of the "lakes" described by the French lieutenant. I was not disappointed to find they simply were natural tanks in the floor of the desert— the *tinajas* of the American desert. Knowing the aridity of this country and the hundreds of miles of comparatively level sandy terrain between this oasis and the snow-capped peaks of the Atlas Mountains to the north, it was inconceivable that there would be fresh water lakes other than from the storage of storm water.

Here was a lovely pool of cool sweet water, captured and stored in a great erosion basin in solid limestone, protected against evaporation by the vertical walls all around. While I was barbecuing some steaks which had arrived by plane before we left Atar, the camel driver unpacked the animals and brought out the teapots. There was a fringe of wild palms around the pool, and dry fronds provided the necessary firewood.

When we had sipped our three glasses of tea and consumed our steaks, we stretched out on the goatskins which were our beds for the night. The Arabs had spread them on the sand, with saddle and kit-bag at the head of each skin, just as a Camel Corps trooper would bed down for the night. The moon passed behind a towering cliff, a gentle breeze came down the canyon, and I lay there under the Sahara stars with the same feeling of relaxation and peace with the world I have experienced many times on that desert across the sea, which is my home.

We were up at sunrise, and Query already was brewing our early morning tea. Then I got my first sight of fish on the Sahara desert, and they truly resembled catfish. Scores of them, eight to twelve inches long, were swimming in the clear water of the pool, making ripples on the surface as they came up for air—or whatever it is that causes a catfish to stick its nose out of the water.

There was a series of these *tinajas* along the ascending floor of the canyon, and by noon we had caught enough fish for a meal, with several intermissions for swimming. While we were fishing, the camels were given their weekly drink of nearly a half barrel of water each. Then they browsed in the canyon, passing by a little patch of grass to chew the twigs from the thorniest Acacia tree I have ever seen. The thorns were an inch long. Those beasts must have shoe leather in their mouths.

Query served a delicious fish dinner to us at noon, and we loafed in the shade of the palm trees. Then we had tea again, and at mid-afternoon started the trek back to the home oasis. The camels went through their usual groaning and bellowing. But by now I had little sympathy for them. A beast that will pass up a luscious patch of grass to browse on a thorn tree should not be irritated by the mere tightening of a saddle girth.

This fishing excursion on the Sahara was such a delightful experience I told the men in the outfit about it, and Lieut. Cabot, our Special Services officer, arranged with a local camel owner to take a caravan of GIs out to the fishing pond every weekend. But I will never suggest to the dude ranchers in my home desert that camels be substituted for saddle horses or jeeps. Three hours in one of those pocket saddles on the summit of a swaying camel is about all a tenderfoot can take at one sitting.

In this untutored community it does not appear difficult for men to dwell together in peace. French, Arabs, Senegalese and Americans all are neighbors. We greet each other with a friendly salute, sometimes French and sometimes American. It makes no difference. We draw our water from the same wells. We have no common language except that universal symbol of goodwill—the smile. It is good to live among people who can laugh, and do. I do not mean the artificial laughter of the drinking party, or the polite grimace of courtesy. I mean the smile that springs spontaneously from humans who have goodwill in their hearts.

For more than a year I have been living close to the primitive tribesmen of Africa—dark-skinned, unschooled, uncivilized according to our standards. But in the jungle and on the desert I have found them responsive to friendliness. And I have asked myself these questions: Why have we allowed the grim business of getting ahead in the world to crowd out so much of the warmth in our natures? Why do wealth and power tend to make men haughty and cynical? Are we paying too high a price for the luxuries and speed of our civilization when these things are acquired at the expense of good wholesome neighborliness?

I do not know the answers, but I am sure they will be found neither in the concept of service to a mechanistic state, nor in a capitalism that sanctions unrestricted competition and puts a premium on selfishness.

The essence of neighborliness is cooperation. Not the cooperation imposed by a Marxist dictatorship nor the mutual aid which has for its goal monetary gain for its participants as in trade associations, chambers of commerce and labor unions. I am thinking rather of that cooperation which springs spontaneously from the hearts of men who trust and like each other. I will always treasure the opportunity I had to discover the beauty of these dark-skinned primitives of the African desert and jungle.

Today, 16-17 years after my sojourn among these people, they are torn and confused by the infiltration of ideas and values which are inexplicably strange to them. Unwittingly perhaps, we of the white race have brought this to pass. It is our responsibility to resolve the problem we have created. It is a dilemma that will require infinite patience and understanding for its solution. It is a task for men with soft hearts and hard heads—and our prayer should be for leadership in which these often contradictory human traits have been fully reconciled.

Do not look down on these African savages because their skins are dark and most of them can neither read nor write. I have found they respond to friendship with friendship.

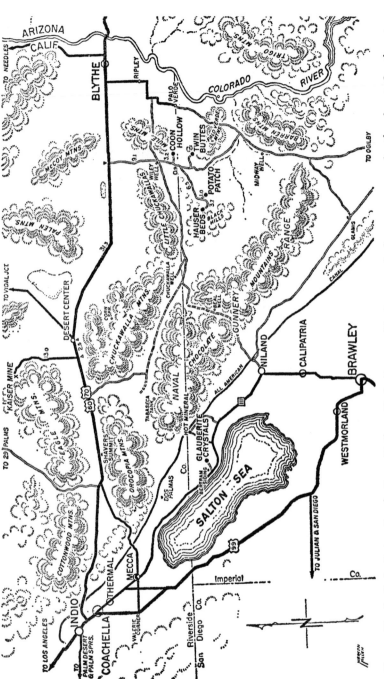

Hauser Geode Beds, Potato Patch, Coon Hollow, Twin Butte—this is one of the many areas in the desert Southwest where rock and gem collectors tramp the hills or dig beneath the surface for semi-precious gem stones. This is one of the most *totuly collecting fields in Southern California*

THERE'S GEMS IN THE HILLS **XVIII**

ONE FEBRUARY morning in 1872 two roughly dressed miners appeared at the window of a San Francisco bank. They carried a heavy canvas bag, which they wanted to leave in the bank vault for safe-keeping. When they were asked about the contents of the bag they untied the cord and dumped on the counter a dazzling cascade of uncut diamonds, rubies, emeralds and sapphires, and referred vaguely to a mine they had found "up in the hills." They gave their names as Philip Arnold and John Slack.

The display of so much sparkling wealth, by two men who obviously were prospectors from the back country, caused a flurry of excitement among employees in the bank. A report of the incident was soon passed along to William C. Ralston, head of the banking firm, and one of the best known financiers in California. He asked to talk with the men.

There were several conferences in the days following. The men admitted they needed capital to develop their jewel mine, but they were cagey with their information. Quite by accident, they said, they had found what they believed to be an extensive area of placer ground containing precious stones, but they were unwilling to give the exact location, and they did not want to relinquish control of the property without ample safeguards as to their personal equity.

Finally it was agreed they would accompany Ralston's personal representatives to investigate the discovery, with the stipulation that the men would be blindfolded before approaching the field.

The two men selected by the banker to accompany the discoverers carried out their mission, and returned with glowing reports of the richness of the field, and another bag of diamonds to confirm their findings. Ralston was delighted. Perhaps this was a fabulous new diamond field which would rival the fame and fortune of the great South African gem deposits discovered five years previously and widely known as the Kimberley diamond field.

News of the diamond strike spread rapidly, and Ralston's associates in other financial ventures were eager to invest with him in what might prove to be the world's greatest producer of precious gem stones. As an extra precaution samples of the uncut diamonds were sent to Tiffany of New York for expert appraisal. A mining engineer of high standing was sent into the field to make a full report as to the extent of the deposits. To all these arrangements the discoverers gave ready assent. They asked only that an advance payment of $100,000 be deposited in escrow as evidence of good faith on the part of the men who were to invest in the property.

Tiffany confirmed the genuineness of the diamonds, and the mining engineer returned with an enthusiastic report. "Twenty laborers could wash out a million dollars' worth of gems in a month," he said.

Ralston and his associates then organized the San Francisco and New York Mining and Commercial Company, with a capitalization of $10,000,000. They paid Arnold and Slack a total of $660,000 for all their rights to the claims, giving the money to Arnold, who had a power of attorney from his partner.

In the meantime, Clarence King, an engineer who had long been in the employ of the federal government, and had done much surveying along the 40th parallel, became suspicious. Piecing together what information he could gather, he became certain the reported diamond field was located in the mountainous area of northeastern Utah, west of what recently became the Dinosaur National Park. He knew the mineralogy of this region, and was unwilling to believe it contained gem stones of any value. Unknown to any of the interested parties, he found his way into the field to make a personal appraisal.

A few days later the president of the newly formed mining syndicate received a telegram from King stating flatly that the deposits were a fake—that the gem stones had been planted there for fraudulent purposes, and the investors had been duped. He had found diamonds in the soil, but some of them bore the marks of lapidary tools.

Investors in the property were stunned. They again sent a mining engineer into the field. He confirmed King's report, that the area had been "salted" and the alleged discovery was a gigantic swindle.

Then the story unfolded. Arnold and Slack had acquired $50,000 through the sale of some mining property. Arnold had made two trips to various lapidary establishments in England and Europe and invested $35,000 in uncut stones, many of them culls known in the trade as "niggerheads." With an iron rod the partners had planted the stones over an area of 30 or 40 acres, where the first rainstorm would wash away all evidence of their chicanery.

The diamond episode had a tragic sequel for some of those who played leading roles in the hoax. Slack disappeared and was never heard from again. Arnold, who had retained most of the money, was located in Kentucky. The wounds of the Civil War had not begun to heal, and the state refused to extradite a man who had outwitted the Yankees. Arnold agreed, however, to surrender $150,000 of his loot for immunity from further prosecution. Later he opened a bank and the following year was killed in a gun fight with one of his competitors.

Ralston personally made good the losses of his associates in the diamond venture. But this and other ventures so depleted his resources that his bank closed its doors three years later. Two days after the bank closing, his body was found floating in the bay at San Francisco. The verdict of an autopsy was that he had died from natural causes.

The great diamond hoax was a rather ignominious fore-runner of what has become one of the most popular and healthful hobbies in the Southwest—the collecting, cutting and polishing of semi-precious stones which occur in widespread areas of Arizona, Utah, Nevada, New Mexico and California.

Nearly every weekend during the months of favorable weather, motor caravans of a clan known as rockhounds trek out of the cities and towns in and adjacent to the desert and comb the hills and mesas, and with their prospector's handpicks pry into rock formations and old mining dumps in quest of stones which the polishing wheel will reveal as gems of sparkling color. These trophies may be fire-agate, turquoise, any of the many species of colored quartz, hematite, topaz crystals, petrified wood, fossilized bone, rhyolite—there are innumerable varieties of rock hard enough for cutting on a diamond saw and requiring only shaping and buffing on the lap wheel to bring out their hidden beauty. In 1960 it was estimated that in this region there are between 50,000 and 60,000 rock collectors, many of them members of the scores of gem and lapidary societies which arrange periodic field trips to areas where semi-precious gem stones are found.

While there are gem and mineral societies in all parts of the United States, the desert is regarded as the prime collecting area, partly because much of the arid Southwest is still in the public domain, and partly because the mineral wealth of this region, while not always on the surface, is never concealed beneath a cover of plant life. Except in the higher elevations, nearly every day from October through April is hunting weather for the gem stone collectors.

One of the most common semi-precious gems found in the Southwest is garnet, occurring in both metamorphic and igneous rock, but only infrequently of gem quality. More often garnets are seen as brown intrusions in the process of disintegration. However, they do occur in hard crystalline form in some places.

My prospector friend, Guy Hazen, once took me into such a location in the Aquarius Mountains of western Arizona. Guy was engaged near the little settlement of Wikieup with paleontologists from one of the universities, excavating prehistoric birds and animal bones in a clay and limestone pit. Walking up a nearby arroyo one evening he discovered rhyolite float carrying garnets. Continuing up the wash he found the source of the gems. They were weathering out of a lava butte near the head of the water course. He wrote, inviting me to join him in further exploration of the area.

Accepting Guy's invitation, my route was a winding dirt road (now paved U. S. Highway 93) through a magnificent forest of silver leaf Joshua trees. This is one of the few places in the Southwest where the Joshua tree and the giant Saguaro cactus, the Arizona state flower, are intermingled. These fantastic members of the plant world, surmounting a dense undergrowth of palo verde, catsclaw, agave, creosote and echinocactus, have created here a lovely natural park which might almost be termed a desert jungle.

That night I spread my bedroll on the sand, and next morning we hiked up the arroyo to the hill of the garnets. Generally the gems occurred in vugs or small cavities, beautifully faceted on the exposed side, their deep red color in sharp contrast to the light colored rhyolite of their matrix. They ranged up to a half inch in diameter. The technique for recovering them is to use a small chisel or screw-driver and a handpick with a hammer-head, being careful not to place the edge of the cutting tool too close to the stone. The matrix material which comes out with the stone can be ground off later.

We ranged over the butte, selecting only a nice specimen here and there. The volcanic structure in which they occur extends over a wide area, but it is rugged terrain and the gem collector will feel he has done a day's work when he hikes up the arroyo and gathers a few specimens in a small area. It is this factor no doubt which has discouraged commercial dealers from going into these mountains to mine the stones.

One of the most rewarding field trips I have taken with the gem collectors—rewarding in values of camaraderie even more than in the trophies we gathered—was to Coon Hollow on the Southern California desert, with the Coachella Valley Mineral Society. Coon Hollow is a fire-agate field—one sector of a wider area near the Chuckawalla Mountains, which for many years has been one of the most popular hunting grounds.

We camped at Wiley's Well, a watering place which has been a rendezvous for prospectors and rock collectors for nearly half a century. Much of the surface material in that area has been recovered, but beneath the sand and gravel there remain unknown quantities of the kind of stones which delight the rock hobbyist. In one small sector of the field, known as the Hauser geode beds, the rockhounds have done so much excavating the hillside and ravine look like an old California gold placer field. The geodes—sometimes called thunder-eggs—which come from this bed generally are from two to six inches in diameter, and are hollow, with a beautiful crystalline interior which is exposed when the stone is halved with a lapidary saw.

When I arrived at the camp late in the afternoon, Glenn Vargas, president of the society, had been lowered into the open well with a rope to be sure no varmints had fallen in and polluted the water. Charlene Carney, the camping chairman, and some of the women, were gathering up litter left by untidy campers. Others were gathering deadwood for a campfire program.

Dinner that evening was served buffet style at the society's chuckwagon. This cooperative commissary, equipped with stove, icebox, collapsible tables, cupboards for utensils, and a generator for night-lighting, seemed to be about the last word in efficiency for group camping. There was even a clothes line, towel rack and a dinner gong.

The Coachella members also have perfected the detail of assigning camp chores. Previous to a field trip, a committee plans the menus and prepares the "blacklist," which is a duty roster of those appointed for commissary work. All members of the field party have definite duties and when their turns come they don chef's hats and white aprons and wise-crack as they work. Mealtime becomes a hilarious occasion.

The next day our party ranged over the hills around Coon Hollow, picking up attractive pieces of agate and chalcedony. Gradually we worked our way to a hilltop which was reported to have fire or opalized agate. Here, just a few inches beneath the surface in many places we uncovered choice specimens having opalescent colors in red, yellow and green. These were the prime trophies of the day, and it was certain that sooner or later the choicest of them would be exhibited in one of the annual gem shows sponsored by the society.

For the most part, gem collecting is a hobby of amateurs. Occasionally one of them turns professional, and sets up a shop as a dealer in raw material and polished stones. But the societies are composed of teachers, mechanics, tradesmen, clerks and professional people, students and adults in all walks of life who look forward to the weekend and vacation opportunities to go out and roam the hills in quest of hidden jewels.

Generally the gem rock found is rough and begrimed. It requires an experienced eye to detect the radiance beneath the coarse exterior, and even the experts guess wrong sometimes. Only the lapidary tools will bring out the color and luster of a cabachon. Sooner or later the confirmed rockhound aspires to have his own diamond saw and grinding and polishing wheels—and large numbers of them do acquire these accessories.

Anglo-Americans were not the first to gather gem material on the desert. In Nevada and New Mexico old turquoise workings have been found, along with primitive mining tools, bearing evidence of a prehistoric quest for the blue stones. Turquoise was highly prized by the ancients of North America, and even today is preferred to all other gems by Navajo and pueblo tribesmen. The Indians also gathered flint, agate, chalcedony, obsidian and jasper for their arrow and spear points, and also for beads.

Fossilized wood is found widely scattered in all the western states, the best known being the Petrified Forest National Park in northeastern Arizona. The Park, of course, is off-limits to collectors, but some of the wood found elsewhere in Utah, Nevada and Arizona has beautiful coloring even before it is polished. One prospector found petrified logs in northern Arizona which, under the Geiger counter test, showed such high values in uranium, they were mined for military use.

Nevada is the source of much of the best opal mined in the United States. From the Thomas Mountains in Utah, in a location known as Topaz Cove, come topaz crystals which the eminent authority, George Frederick Kunz, once appraised as the finest in the United States. Collectors have been going to this area for many years.

The rock collectors do not limit their hobby entirely to stones which can be cut and polished. They gather non-crystalline forms of silky white quartz known as chalcedony roses. They seek out deposits of marine fossils, relics of a period when much of the Southwestern desert was submerged in inland seas. High in the Fish Creek Mountains of Southern California is an uplifted sea bed known as Coral Reef, where many forms of fossilized marine material are found. Another collector's item is obsidian nodules, volcanic pebbles known as Apache tears because of an Indian legend associated with an escarpment near Superior, Arizona, where great quantities of them have been weathering out of a lava formation for years.

Near Taos, New Mexico, a Spanish-American boy herding sheep for his father many years ago, picked up pieces of mica schist, in which were embedded twin crystals, the two bars crossed at right angles. With the matrix material removed they are mounted and worn as necklaces or charms. They are composed of hematite, aluminum and silicate and are known to mineralogists as staurolite. They occur east of the Allegheny Mountains, and especially in Patrick County, Virginia, where they are known as Fairy stones. They have been found only in two or three small areas west of the Rocky Mountains.

Petrified palm root is found on the Southern California desert, and in western Colorado and eastern Utah fossilized dinosaur bones have been uncovered. Calcite and gypsum crystals, although not hard enough to be regarded as gem material, are sought for their attractive forms of crystallization. Pumice stone is picked up for the novelty of having a rock which will not sink in water.

The prize trophy sought by every collector is a fragment of meteorite from the sky. There are two general types of material from outer space. The stony meteorite would seldom be recognized as such because it looks so much like common rock, although it generally contains small grains of nickel-iron. Metallic meteorites are composed mainly of nickel and iron, and are three times as heavy as ordinary rock. Dr. H. H. Nininger, a foremost authority on celestial material which has found its way to this planet, suggests a simple test for identifying meteoritic material. Ground on an emery wheel, the metallic content beneath the crust will be exposed as bright specks of steel-white metal.

Although meteorites have been pelting the earth for millions of years, comparatively few of them have been found, either by the prospectors who roam the hills or the rock collecting fraternity.

Harold O. Weight, writer and desert explorer of Twentynine Palms, California, probably is the best informed contemporary authority on the location of semi-precious gem fields in the Southwest. Writing for the gem and mineral periodicals, of which there are four with a national circulation, Weight has reported the discovery of geodes near Searchlight, Nevada, and scores of other places; petrified wood near Kanab and in the White Canyon country of Utah; carnelian, agate and opalite in ancient river terraces in the lower Colorado River basin; fossilized palm root and a score of other gem quality minerals on the Mojave desert of California; fossilized dinosaur bones near Fruita, Colorado; chalcedony around the Turtle Mountains of California and in the Papago country of southern Arizona. These are just a few of literally hundreds of locations in which gem material and cabinet rock specimens may be found.

They seldom occur in concentration which will justify commercial exploitation—and that of course is the good fortune of the amateur collectors. Rather, they are scattered over and beneath the surface, where they are available to those hobbyists who tramp the arid landscape, not alone for the trophies to be acquired, but for the sheer pleasure of exploration in a virgin desert land.

THE TRUTH-SEEKERS   XIX

ONE SUNNY MORNING in February 1958 I followed a sandy road that wound among the palo verde and smoke trees of a desert arroyo and came eventually to an isolated cove at the base of California's Santa Rosa Mountains. Parked in a little clearing at the end of the road was a huge house trailer and the heavy-duty truck which evidently had towed it to this out-of-the-way place.

The detail in this scene which immediately caught my interest was a transparent plastic box about the size of a small bird cage perched on a tripod which straddled a pygmy cedar bush. Enclosed in the box I could see a small branch of the shrub. Attached to the floor of the cage were flexible plastic tubes leading to a portable table on which was mounted a panel of dials in an instrument box, something like a portable radio.

Seated at the table was a middle-aged man in sport shirt, a stop-watch in one hand and a pencil in the other, his attention focused on the dials in front of him as he jotted figures on the papers spread out before him.

This was my introduction to Dr. Fritz Went and the Mobile Desert Laboratory, then maintained by the California Institute of Technology of Pasadena. It is a gypsy outfit that moves from place to place to gather basic scientific data, which at some future time may have an important bearing on the food supply of a world already becoming overcrowded with human beings.

Since that first visit, the Mobile Laboratory has been transferred to the science department of the University of California and Dr. Went has become director of the Missouri Botanical Gardens near St. Louis. But the work of the mobile unit goes on. One month it may be stationed in the Joshua tree forest of the Mojave Desert, and the next six weeks on a desert mesa where the ground is honeycombed with rodent burrows.

Botanists, zoologists, ecologists—teachers and research students in all the natural sciences, and from many schools, come here for field observation on the particular subject in which each is interested. On one of my subsequent visits to the laboratory I met two biologists from Sweden, and Dr. Jane Philpott, professor of botany at Duke University. On another occasion two guest scientists from Australia were working on projects of their special interest.

On the truck is mounted a 4,000-watt generator and air-compressor, the power plant of the laboratory. It carries a 500-gallon water tank, and the trailer has both refrigerative and evaporative air-conditioning equipment. The interior space is occupied by all the essential facilities of a science laboratory—a battery of microscopes, photo equipment, burners, test tubes, running hot and cold water, the walls lined with cupboards and shelves. Also, there is a tiny kitchen. There are no sleeping accommodations. Members of the staff and visitors spread their bedrolls on the sandy floor of the desert, which is no hardship in this climate, either summer or winter.

The special project on which Dr. Went was engaged at the time of my first visit was the chemical process which takes place in the foliage of plants. In addition to pygmy cedar, he also had plastic boxes enclosing small branches of creosote and catsclaw. On another occasion his dials were recording the photosynthesis and transpiration of ocotillo, jojoba and Canterbury bells, a species of phacelia.

Most people are aware that every living plant is a miniature factory, using radiant energy from the sun, taking in carbon dioxide and moisture from the air and converting them to sugar and other compounds which have food value for the animal world, and giving off water vapor and oxygen which help maintain an atmosphere conducive to life on this planet. It is only in recent years that scientists and technicians have perfected tools which make possible an intensive study of the role of plants in the ecology of life in general. Dr. Went perfected some of the instruments himself, and he is doing important pioneering in this field of study.

While the botanist carried on his study of photosynthesis in plants, Lloyd Tevis, Jr., a zoologist who is director of the Mobile Laboratory, was devoting his research to desert animal life. His current study was ants and mites. His method was to stake out typical colonies of these tiny insects and study their work and social habits through their complete life cycles, keeping detailed records of his findings.

And if the reader wonders what importance attaches to the study of the lowly ant, I can only cite the conclusion of Dr. G. Murray McKinley, zoologist at the University of Pittsburgh who, in *Evolution: The Ages and Tomorrow*, wrote, "Except for humans, ants are the most successful organisms on earth, and like human beings, have no serious enemy except their own kind." They have farmers and nurses, policemen and baby-sitters, each functioning in the role to which it was born.

It has long been known that one of the main contributions of the ant world to other forms of life is in the pulverization of leaves and deadwood. They supplement the work of sun and water in adding organic matter to the soil. In other words, they help fertilize the earth. A single ant colony would not make an important contribution, but when it is realized there are billions and billions of colonies of many species scattered over the face of the earth, all working industriously at their hereditary tasks, it will be recognized that they play no small part in converting organic matter to food for other forms of life, including man.

Dr. Went and Lloyd Tevis are two members of a great fraternity of men and women all around the world whose lives are being devoted to an intensive study of the basic problems of origin, evolution and survival on a planet of which the average layman has only a superficial knowledge. They are the students of pure science as differentiated from the men of applied science who devote their study and effort mainly to the application of basic knowledge to the immediate benefit of the human race. Without basic science there could be no applied science. In many of the great industrial laboratories basic and applied science are being carried on simultaneously, for knowledge and its utilization go hand in hand.

The virgin desert is a great outdoor laboratory, favored by the men and women of science because here the basic ingredients of the physical world lie bare and exposed. The book of geological time lies open for all to read. Here the impact of the forces of uplift and erosion and long-range climatic change is plainly evident. The dry air is a preservative. The organic structures which would decay and disintegrate in a land of greater moisture, are more likely to mummify and thus retain some of their original form and substance. Even the low desert has a season of seven or eight months when field work can be carried on without discomfort.

Science, in its quest for rational answers to a million questions which may be asked as to the origin and continuity of life in this universe, has come a long way in the last 150 years. In his book *In Search of Adam,* Herbert Wendt tells us that as recently as the early 19th century, scholarly men in Europe were engaged in a spirited controversy concerning the origin of fossil bones and imprints found in continental limestones. One faction was clinging stubbornly to the theory that the fossilized vertebrae they had collected were the bones of victims of Noah's flood, as recorded in the book of Genesis. How else, they were asking, could fossils of marine origin have found their way to the interior of a land mass far above sea level? They had little understanding then of the eons of time and the convulsive forces of creation which preceded the advent of man on this planet. In that period, the sciences of dynamic geology and paleontology were having their birth pangs.

I have mentioned the role of pure science, and the technologists of applied science. There is also a third category which more or less encompasses both basic knowledge and its utilization in the service of mankind. I am referring now to the men and women of the teaching profession. They are the instructors in classroom, laboratory and field who are making certain that the accumulated storehouse of fact and theory will be communicated to the future.

Dr. Edmund C. Jaeger is one of these. His interest in the desert dates back to 1915 when as a young man earning money for a college education he lived in a tent and taught a one-room school in Palm Springs, California. Later, with a degree in science, he became head of the zoology department in Riverside City College, where he taught for twenty-eight years. Since that first contact at Palm Springs he has spent practically all his weekends and vacation time tramping and camping on the desert and expanding his knowledge not only of wildlife, but of botany, zoology, geology and the artifacts of prehistoric tribal life in this arid region.

His first book, *Denizens of the Desert*, was published in 1920, and he has added four more desert titles since then, the last published in 1957 being *Deserts of North America*. In the classroom and through his published work, which includes many papers and magazine articles, Dr. Jaeger has contributed more perhaps than any other scientist to the layman's knowledge of the Southwestern desert and the many complex forms of life which have adapted to this region of little rainfall. More recently he has retired from teaching and is now curator of the Riverside Municipal Museum, with much free time to spend in the field. His current interest is the desert of northwestern Mexico, in Baja California and Sonora, and it is likely that sooner or later there will be a new book on this subject.

During the years when Dr. Jaeger was teaching natural science courses in Riverside College, it was his custom to invite young men in his classes to accompany him on his weekend camping trips. Those former students are now successful professional and business men, many of them still residing in Southern California. To keep touch with them he holds an annual campfire reunion—the Jaeger Palaver—at some remote desert spot of special interest.

It has been my privilege to be present as a guest at many of these Palavers. The informal campfire talks always reveal the deep respect these men have for their former teacher, and their appreciation for the acquaintance he had given them with the world of nature.

I recall one such outing on the Mojave Desert at a location Dr. Jaeger had given the name Jelly-Roll Rocks because of the unusual stratification of the huge granite boulders in this place. We spread our sleeping bags on the sand that night and the next morning accompanied our leader on a revealing hike across the desert. He told us about the brawny little workers, the harvester ants, which add humus to the soil, and pointed out the match-weed which has so much resin in its stems it can be used to start a campfire even when green. When we came to a vertical crevice in the granite he called attention to the carpet of pebbles just outside the opening—evidence that somewhere in the depths was the nest of a rock wren. Every stone and shrub had a story, and even the holes in the ground have significance to one who knows the answers.

Another companion on many of my desert jaunts was Dr. Maris Harvey, plant pathologist then serving the U. S. Department of Agriculture. His hobby was desert taxonomy—the names and classifications of all forms of plant life. From him I learned about the built-in time clock mechanisms of botanical species, especially the faculty for delayed germination characteristic of nearly all desert shrubs.

We had paused to rest along the desert trail one day when he pointed to a lowly cocklebur, a nuisance weed to farmers, despised even by the coyotes because of the tenacity with which it clings to their bushy tails. "Generally the pod of the cocklebur carries two seeds," he explained. "One of them will germinate the first year if moisture conditions are favorable. The smaller of the seeds is equipped with a thick hull impervious to moisture and oxygen until two or three years later when the wear and tear of the elements have broken down its air and waterproofing. Eventually, when the outer husk has disintegrated and moisture and temperature conditions are right, it will sprout and grow. Nearly all the seeds of desert species are endowed with the potential for postponed germination. They may lie dormant during long periods of drouth until conditions are right for them to resume their life's cycle. It is thus that the perpetuation of the species is assured."

One of the most versatile scientists of my acquaintance was Jerry Laudermilk. Jerry never attained a doctorate in his profession, nor even a high role in scholastic circles. But in the laboratory of basic science he was thorough and highly competent. He not only had a fine knowledge of geology and botany, but he acquired a faculty rare among highly skilled technicians—the art of writing understandable and even sparkling copy for the lay reader. For many years he was a contributor to the *Desert Magazine*. He was an entertaining companion, and I spent many delightful hours in his company.

In 1937 he was selected by the Carnegie Institution in Washington to take charge of a research expedition to Rampart Cave, discovered by an Indian, Willis Evans, near the shoreline when the waters of the Colorado River were filling the Lake Mead reservoir behind the newly constructed Hoover Dam. The Carnegie Institution was interested because the cave contained the remains of the extinct giant sloth which prowled this desert region an estimated 20,000 years ago.

Skeletons and mummified carcasses were found beneath the dust of the cave floor, but the most revealing material was sloth dung which was six feet deep in some places. The dung would disclose the diet of these herbiferous animals in that period of long ago, and a microscopic study of the plant remains in comparison with the vegetable life of the region today would reveal climatic changes. Back at the laboratory at Pomona College where he was associated until his death in 1955, Laudermilk identified many of the same plants found in the area today—desert tea, maidenhair fern, nolina, wild hollyhock, beavertail cactus, ground cherry and desert holly. The conclusion was that there had been little change in climate in 20,000 years. But the mystery remains as to why those sluggish beasts became extinct.

Jerry's research probably brought to light little that is new in the world of natural science. His main contribution was his skill in translating the vernacular of high-level science to understandable images for the lay reader. For desert people, he told how the common "desert varnish" was formed on the rocks, the origin and composition of ordinary sand, the mystery of desert mirages, the evolution of flowering plants, and nature's varied composition and affinity of the lichens for shady stone walls, the methods of seed dispersal as a factor in the perpetuation of species. One of his last projects, and one he never lived to complete was the identification of the petrified wood widely distributed over the basin of the lower Colorado River.

My old prospector friend Guy Hazen had no more than a high school education, but for many years he was a valued contributor to scientific research on the desert. Guy's assets were a couple of keen eyes and an uncanny faculty for discovering fossil deposits for the paleontologists. For many years he was on the payroll of the American Museum of Natural History as a field prospector. To him, the desert was just a great prehistoric graveyard, with the bones of long extinct birds and beasts close to the surface in a thousand different places, if one knows how to look for them.

I camped with Guy one evening at a site near Wikieup, Arizona, where a clay and limestone deposit was yielding a wealth of fossil material. I arrived in the camp that afternoon, and he took me out to the pit where his scientific associates were excavating the bones of prehistoric horses and other mammals from an ancient pliocene shoreline now high in the mountains. I do not know much about paleontology, but for a layman it was a fascinating experience to stand on the rim of the pit watching experts with picks, trowels and camel's hair brushes expose and carefully extract from its stone matrix the jawbone of a carniverous animal which roamed the face of the earth countless ages ago.

One summer I spent a month with Arthur Woodward, then curator of history in the Los Angeles County Museum, logging and photographing the Indian picture writings to be seen on rock faces and boulders widely scattered over the desert Southwest. Woodward also is a student of archeology and anthropology, and his project on this occasion was to gather field data for a laboratory study of these mysterious relics of an earlier culture.

There are two general types of ancient Indian art work—if it is art work. The more common symbols are petroglyphs, incised in the rock with crude stone chisels. In caves and sheltered places, especially in the canyon country of southern Utah, also are numerous pictographs—painted on the walls with colored pigments. Some of the latter are amazingly well preserved, considering the hundreds of years which have elapsed since they were placed there.

Archeologists have been puzzling over the significance of these markings since they first were observed by white settlers in this region over a hundred years ago. Some of the figures are easily recognizable. Mountain sheep and snakes appear frequently. The sun and rain symbols also have been identified by comparison with more recent Indian art. The figures of human beings also are common, sometimes with bow and arrow or war club. But for the most part the dating and motivation of these ancient scrolls are unsolved mysteries.

Arthur wanted to obtain data in widely separated areas where different tribal groups are known to have lived, to determine by comparison if there were any key factors which might throw light on an avocation widely characteristic of the primitives of that period. We followed the by-ways in the Four Corners region where the states of Utah, Arizona, Colorado and New Mexico meet at a common point, and then continued westerly across Ute and Navajo country to Tuba City, Arizona.

At an old Indian campground at Willow Springs near Tuba City, we were able for the first time to piece together a plausible explanation of the glyphs which cover many of the rocks at that place. This was possible because these petroglyphs were made by the ancestors of living Hopi tribesmen, and the story has been handed down from generation to generation.

Willow Springs is one of the camps used by the Hopis of long ago when a party of their young men made an annual trek from their mesa pueblos to a ledge in the canyon of the Little Colorado River to obtain their tribal supply of salt. The route is known as the old Salt Trail. As they camped overnight at the Springs, each clansman added the symbol of his own fraternity to an orderly row on one of the rock faces. Thus there is a row of corn stalks representing the corn clan, each stalk representing an interval of one year. The aging of erosion is quite evident in the older symbols. We were able to identify the emblems of the corn, sun, spider, katchina, eagle, lizard, coyote and a score of other clans, some of them no longer extant.

With the exception of this ancient Hopi art gallery, there was no obvious significance to the rather disorderly array of figures found in scores of other places. Many months after this expedition, I asked Woodward if his home work had yielded any clue to the origin or meaning of the Indian scrolls.

"I've been studying the enlargements of those pictures for months," he said, "and I do not know yet whether they express the wisdom of the tribal medicine men, or the doodlings of primitive morons."

The branch of natural science which has always held the greatest fascination for me is ecology—the study of the vast complex of natural balance. It involves the relationship of one form of life to all the other forms, for it has become increasingly evident since the days of Charles Darwin that there is an interdependence not often apparent to the casual observer. Although considerable study has been given to this field, scientists are just beginning to penetrate the darkness of this vast sphere of knowledge.

One of the scientists who has done important work in this field in the semi-arid intermountain region of the Southwest is Dr. Angus M. Woodbury, for many years a professor in the division of biological sciences at the University of Utah. He also has made a notable contribution to the continuing study of the Darwinian theory of evolution.

Darwin in his *Origin of Species* and *The Descent of Man* developed the idea of an orderly process in nature wherein the strongest and most adaptable members of each species would be most likely to survive, and competition would tend to weed out the unfit. He did not preclude the element of mutual aid in the progression of life, but he placed the greater emphasis on survival by competitive struggle.

In 1902 a Russian scientist, Peter Kropotkin, after no less exhaustive research than Darwin had done, wrote *Mutual Aid* in which he emphasized the major role which cooperation plays in the perpetuation of individuals and generic groups and even ecological units.

There is no conflict between the theories of Darwin and Kropotkin. Rather they are offered as complementary factors in the broad pattern of both physical and social progress on this earth. They are quite generally understood, and in principle at least, widely accepted by the natural scientists of today.

Dr. Woodbury made a further contribution to this study of the evolutionary process. In his book *Comfort for Survival*, he presents the conclusion that "Those young animals that can find a comfortable environment with congenial surroundings are much more likely to survive their intense competition than those that find uncomfortable environments which require more energy to obtain the necessities of life."

His conclusions are based almost entirely on field and experimental research in the desert region where all forms of life are subject to extremes of temperature, and where some forms of life, like the sidewinder, can withstand less exposure to the summer sun than can human beings.

The quest for comfort as a factor in survival is not offered as a major premise in evolutionary biology, and Dr. Woodbury—like all true scientists—is never a dogmatist. Rather, he is a studious and competent member of a worthy fraternity of men and women all around the world who are dedicating their lives to an earnest quest for greater understanding of the natural laws which govern all life on this planet.

For thirty-two years, beginning in 1906, the Carnegie Institution of Washington maintained a Desert Laboratory near Tucson, Arizona, where under the direction of Dr. D. T. Mac-Dougal and later, Dr. Forrest Shreve, basic studies in the adaptation of plant life and wildlife to an arid environment were carried on. The Laboratory was discontinued following a fire in 1938 which burned the main building.

Today this basic research in desert biology is being fostered in scores of schools and museums in the Southwest and beyond. At the Arizona-Sonora Desert Museum near Tucson, and at the California Institute of Technology, intensive studies are being made of desert life in relation to climate, soil, rainfall and its ecological association.

The Arizona-Sonora Desert Museum, founded by William E. Carr, and depending on private endowment and a modest income from a nominal admission charge, combines the features of zoo, museum, botanical gardens and research center. Here are exhibited living specimens of the flora and fauna native to the Sonoran desert which extends into southern Arizona.

Under the direction of William H. Woodin and his assistant, Lewis W. Walker, there has been created here a revealing exposition of that mysterious desert which lies beyond the ken of the lay American.

Insofar as is feasible, the wildlife specimens here are housed and displayed in the terrain, dens and burrows of their natural environment. Devices of communication to visitors are designed for maximum educational value. For instance, there is an underground tunnel cross-sectioned with glass so that the denizens of the underworld may be seen as they live in their natural habitat.

One of the exhibits is Water Street—where no one lives but thousands come every month and gain a new understanding of the utilization of America's indispensable but dwindling resource, water. Visitors are delighted with the do-it-yourself devices—flashing lights, animated electronic instruments, buttons to push, switches to operate, telescopes to look through and even cages containing living creatures.

As funds become available it is the goal of the Museum administration to devote increasing attention to basic research. Current studies are being carried on by Dr. Keith Justice, mammalogist, in the field of ecology and genetics. More extensive research in pure science has been made possible by the newly established Roy Chapman Andrews Research Fund. Dr. Andrews was one of the original trustees of the institution, and is an enthusiastic backer.

Future plans include housing facilities where visiting scientists may come and carry on their work in residence.

I recall a report made by Dr. James Bonner of Cal-Tech, in which he told of experiments indicating that nature had evolved methods of birth control long before this question became pertinent to mankind. He had noted that desert brittle or incense bush (*Encelia farinos*) seldom grew in close proximity to other plant life. Seeking the explanation he gathered leaves of the shrub and spread them around the stems of potted tomato plants, then sprinkled them with water. In three or four days the tomatoes were dead. Then he made a brew of the leaves and found it killed many species of plants, including corn and peppers. The extract, it developed, acted to prevent the roots of many other species from absorbing water and thus reduced the rate of germination in the immediate vicinity.

I have mentioned some of the men of science with whom I have had the privilege of personal acquaintance. The list of scholars past and present who have come to the desert to carry on research in natural science could be extended indefinitely. They include such widely known men as Lyman Benson, Philip Munz, John J. Thornber, Ira A. Wiggins, E. A. Goldman, W. A. Cannon, F. W. Colville, S. B. Parish, V. M. Spaulding and Marcus E. Jones, botanists; Joseph Grinnel, Walter P. Taylor, and E. W. Nelson, zoologists; David G. Thompson, W. C. Mendenhall, Herbert Gregory and Thomas E. Clements, geologists; H. French Gilman, T. S. Palmer and Alden H. Miller, ornithologists; C. H. Orcutt and Natt M. Dodge, naturalists; Percival Lowell and Earl Slipher, astronomers; Edgar A. Means, mammalogist; Laurence M. Klauber, Herbert Stahnke and Charles Bogert, herpetologists, and Charles Camp, paleontologist.

While the versatile Joseph Wood Krutch would make no claim to distinction as a scientist, he came to the desert in comparatively recent years after distinguished careers as a dramatic critic, biographer and nature philosopher, and in his books *The Desert Year, Voice of the Desert, Grand Canyon, The Great Chain of Life,* and *The Forgotten Peninsula,* has created delightful and informative media of communication betweeen the ivory towerism of the scientific world and the perceptive faculties of the thoughtful lay reader.

These men of the natural sciences and their associates in every land are the great truth-seekers of mankind. On land, in the sea and skies, their quest is always for a better understanding of the elusive laws of the physical universe.

While we are certain that the attainment of man's highest destiny depends on the maturity and zeal with which he pursues moral and spiritual ideals, it is also certain that his physical environment plays an essential role in his progress. Man cannot live by bread alone—but it also is true that he cannot live without bread.

SURVIVAL ON THE DESERT   XX

L ATE ONE APRIL afternoon I was motoring down a seven-mile sandy arroyo which leads to one of the scenic palm canyons in Baja California, a few miles south of the California border. I had driven up the wash early in the morning for a day of exploring in a wild area which had once been the habitat of desert Indian tribesmen.

There was no road. It was one of those winding arroyos where the art of driving is to keep to the main channel of the dry stream bed and dodge the smoke trees. They grow thickly in the waterways in this area, and the driver must think fast for it is folly to slow down when driving in heavy sand. This was in the pre-jeep days, and my car was a Model A Ford coupe, with 7½-inch tires.

Rounding a bend I came upon a scene which would have been funny if it had not been for the tragic expression on the face of a man whose head projected above the rim of a huge pit in the middle of the arroyo just ahead. The pit had a second occupant—a heavy four-door sedan of a current model. The top of the car was just about level with the great mounds of sand piled on each side.

Evidently the driver had tried to follow my tracks up the wash soon after I passed that way in the early morning. He had become stuck. He had no shovel or axe, no tool or gadget of any kind suitable for extricating the car from its sandy berth. His hands were blistered and bleeding from pulling the harsh brush to give traction to the wheels. His clothes were dripping with perspiration and his water supply was nearly gone. But he was game. He had been excavating for seven hours with a tin drinking cup.

It was a simple chore for my outfit, with a shovel, tow-rope and a pair of old Model T running boards for traction under my wheels to pull in on the downstream side and yank him out of his dilemma.

I have met many tenderfoot drivers during my years on the desert, but that experience made a more lasting impression on my mind than the others because I would not have believed that a man could move so much sand in a day with a tin cup. I had too much admiration for his guts to criticize his folly.

Fortunately, a man cannot be sent to jail for getting stuck in the sand. If it were a penal offense I would be serving life as an habitual criminal. I not only have been mired in the sand so many times my friends have accused me of doing it on purpose, but at various times I have been bogged down in marshy quick-sand, snow, cienagas, mountain streams, on mesas honeycombed

with rodent holes, and in dry lakes that were dry only on the surface. Once as a reporter, I drove across the delta of the Colorado
River, and nearly lost my car in an earthquake crevasse I was
trying to straddle—on a perfectly hard road. As I proceeded, the
crack became too wide for my running gear, and when I tried
to back up the earth gave way and I had to send for a towcar
with a crane. And up in Monument Valley, in Utah, Harry
Goulding and I once hung up our car on a drift of tumbleweeds.

Some of the experiences were unpleasant at times, but I do
not regret them now. Out of them I acquired a technique, and
a philosophy.

Philosophy for getting stuck in the sand? Laugh if you wish,
but let me tell the rest of my story. It not only is no disgrace
to have to dig the car out, but if the driver is cheerful about it,
it may even be good for his health, like a game of golf or an invigorating hike. It is an adventure, not a catastrophe.

It is characteristic of humans to want life to go along smoothly, with nothing to disrupt the normal way of doing and thinking. That is true of most of us. We are seeking constantly to create
a rut for ourselves—a nice, comfortable sort of rut that will pay
the maximum reward for the minimum of effort. To the extent
that we succeed we bring about our own decay. I am not quot-
ing my own wisdom, but passing along the conclusions of Dr.
Alexis Carrel in his book *Man the Unknown*.

Getting stuck in the sand may be somewhat disconcerting to
one's peace of mind, but it may react as an excellent tonic for his
mental and physical health if he will accept the situation gracefully. Now I am not suggesting that the reader rush out to the
nearest dune and deliberately bury the wheels in the sand. But
if one drives these desert roads long enough, sooner or later he
will arrive in that kind of a situation. And if he is one of those cau-
tious drivers who approaches the soft places with careful deliberation he is more likely to get into trouble than if he hits them with
a firm hand on the wheel, a bold heart, and a heavy foot on the
throttle. I am quite sure the old adage, "he who hesitates is lost,"

was inspired by the experience of a hesitant driver on a sandy road. The moral of this is to keep up the momentum when driving in the sand.

But I try not to be foolish. If in doubt, I park the car on a hard spot and scout ahead on foot to see what pitfalls there may be. If the decision is to go ahead, I shift to low gear and give'er the works. It is fatal to slow down in the middle of a sand patch to shift gears.

I learned these lessons the hard way. For instance, there is that experience many years ago when the sand was deeper than I thought, and I failed to shift gears soon enough. Being quite ignorant of the ways of sand driving I pressed down hard on the accelerator. That merely dug the car in deeper.

What am I going to do about it? Well, let us take a hypothetical case. Here I am, out on a lonely roadless desert with two passengers in the car, the wheels mired down to the hub and the nearest tow car twelve miles away.

My first problem is one of morale. It is too late to correct my error. But I can still prove to my companions that while I may be a very dumb driver, I am a cheerful sort of dumbbell. So I switch off the ignition, swallow my embarrassment, turn to the passengers on the seat beside me—and grin. I pulled a boner, and the quickest way to make peace with myself and my party is a full confession of guilt. That will be good for my soul, and it will put the others in a better frame of mind for the shoveling and pushing I may call on them to do later.

They are innocent parties to this dilemma, and if they want to make a few sarcastic remarks about the bozo at the wheel, that is their privilege. And it is part of the price of my stupidity to accept all comment and suggestions as becomes a graceful loser. But the car is still mired in the sand while all this psychological byplay goes on.

I climb out and inspect the compartment where the shovel and axe and jack are kept. Then I take a couple of tours of inspection around the car, observing the landscape to determine the available supply of greasewood, rocks and other properties which may be needed. Having completed my engineering survey I walk over and sit down on a rock or sandbank—whatever is available. This is important, because undue haste, ill-temper or that panicky feeling are about the poorest tools in the world for getting a mired car out of trouble.

Of course if the shovel is missing I really am in the doghouse. And deserve to be. Among desert folks, getting stuck in the sand is a pardonable offense. But getting stuck without a shovel— well that is the lowest form of stupidity.

Now I don't want all this patter to be misleading. I merely am telling how I would go about solving my problem if I were one of those supermen who are never perturbed by anything— which I am not. I have been caught without a shovel—but not for many years. I never go anywhere now without the needed tools, and I am still toting an old pair of Model T running boards in the back of my car. They are just as necessary a part of my equipment as the steering wheel, and they make good substitutes for shovels.

And now, having completed my meditation, I will go to work. First I let some of the air out of the tires. It is easier to pump them up again later than do a lot of unnecessary shoveling. With one of those motor pumps which plug into a sparkplug socket on the engine, pumping up a tire no longer is a serious chore.

My engineering survey has told me whether I should try to go ahead, or back out of my predicament. Also, whether to jack up the car and put brush or rocks under the rear wheels, or try making it without the jack.

Once, before I learned better, I tried roping the wheels, like skid chains. I was up in Barrett Canyon in the Fish Creek Mountains of Southern California looking for a coral reef I had heard about, a relic of that period of long ago when these mountains were submerged in water. When the car mired down I cut the rope in two and carefully wrapped the rear wheels with it. When I started the motor those roped wheels immediately began digging a new short cut route to Hong Kong. That night on the twelve-mile hike out to Plaster City, where the nearest tow car was located, I had plenty of time to meditate the folly of trying to get out of soft sand with skid chains or any of their substitutes.

In my present predicament I have decided to try pulling out without resorting to the jack. We shovel away the sand in front of all four wheels and gather what brush we can for traction. I start the motor and try to ease out—heavy on the gas, light on the clutch. If the wheels start spinning again it is time to resort to the jack. The bumper type simplifies the problem, and I learned long ago to carry a 2x6x8 block of wood on which to base the tool.

With the rear wheels hefted well above the sand trap, we stuff brush or preferably rocks, under the wheels. Then we build a brush runway, the longer the better. And with my cooperative companions adding a bit of manpower to the horsepower in the motor, we make it out to hard ground.

It is only a modest exaggeration to say I have been stuck in the sand a hundred times, and each time it was a somewhat different problem. I mentioned the old model running boards, but they are hard to find today. Some motorists carry strips of canvas, but they are not very satisfactory. Strips of wide, heavy belting are better, or heavy mesh wire or chain-link fencing cut in suitable strips to roll up.

Of course the four-wheel drive cars of today make much of this sand technique unnecessary. But even a jeep can get stuck. I learned that on the Sahara Desert during the last war, when I started across the desert to the next oasis in an army jeep, and finished the trip several hours later riding a camel.

One doesn't have to be a master mechanic to drive the desert byways. Today there few places even in remote parts of the American desert where one is not within walking distance of help. But on long trips it is well to travel in two-car parties, and of course it goes without saying that it is important to have plenty of fuel, water, food and bedrolls. Thus fortified, the motorist has nothing to fear during the months from October to April. Summer travel on unimproved roads is another matter. Inexperienced or poorly equipped motorists should keep to the improved roads during the hot season.

After all, if you or I have to spend a few hours digging out, or waiting for help, the world probably will struggle along somehow in our absence. Such an experience adds variety to life, and helps keep down the waistline. But I cannot recommend a tincup as an excavating tool. It will be more fun if there is a shovel in the back of the car.

Being bogged down in the sand merely is one of several contingencies which involve not only comfort but the actual survival of desert travelers. I do not wish to exaggerate these dangers, for motor travel across the Great American Desert today probably is less hazardous even in 110-degree temperatures than driving the streets of a metropolitan area. For the reason that the traffic is less congested.

The death toll from thirst and heat prostration today is just a tiny fraction of the mortality of that period when ox teams, horses and burros furnished the motive power for emigrants and prospectors following the unpaved trails across the arid region. The problem of desert travel today is less a matter of survival than of comfort. Air-conditioning in automobiles has provided some measure of relief in high temperatures, but only a small fraction of the cars on the road have that equipment. Such equipment is useless in a car with a dead motor, and old-timers on the desert scorn such pampering devices.

There are some common sense rules it is well for every motorist who travels the desert from May through September to know about.

The late Godfrey Sykes, during the years he was associated with the Carnegie Desert Laboratory at Tucson, made a scientific study of the reaction of the human anatomy to high temperatures under various circumstances. Once on an August day he purposely let his car become mired in the sand along the old

Camino del Diablo between Yuma and Sonoyta, in southern Arizona. This is a long-abandoned road used by Mexican emigrants to the California gold fields in 1849 and the years following. There were few waterholes and no habitants in a span of over 100 miles.

Using himself as a guinea pig, Sykes methodically recorded his own pulse and temperature at intervals as he undertook to extricate his car. When the exertion brought him to the danger point he would lie in the shade of a bush until his body functions returned to normal. He wanted to determine how much heat and exertion his anatomy would take, short of heat prostration. Dehydration also was a factor. The intake of water was a measure of his hydration. He later wrote a paper on this experience.

Probably the most exhaustive study of human reaction to extreme heat was made during 1942-43 when General Patton's army, in training in Southern California near Desert Center, provided both motive and opportunity for intensive research as to man's adaptation to life on a hot desert. The army was being trained on the desert because it seemed inevitable that American troops would become involved in the north African campaign.

Not only were the American soldiers trained in desert tactics, but the U. S. Office of Scientific Research and Development contracted with the University of Rochester School of Medicine to send scientists to the Patton camp to study factors of health, food, water, clothing and morale involved in effective desert warfare.

The Rochester Desert Unit was composed of eleven scientists headed by Dr. Edward F. Adolph, associate professor of physiology. Their findings were available not only to the high command in all branches of the armed forces, but were briefed as a handbook for all men in uniform stationed on or flying over desert terrain. The book, *Afoot on the Desert,* was written by Alonzo W. Pond, chief of the Arctic, Desert, Tropical Information Center, and was available only for the military, but the complete report of the Rochester Desert Unit was published later for public distribution under the title *Physiology of Man on the Desert.*

From the research of the Rochester Unit, a monograph written by Godfrey Sykes and other similar studies, plus a half century of personal experience in desert exploration and reportting, I have summarized data and conclusions which I believe will be interesting and informative to motorists who travel the desert no less than to its permanent residents.

Some people can adapt to high temperatures better than others. The adjustment is not merely a matter of psychology. Some individuals have more sweat glands to the square inch of skin than others. Those with the greater number of glands—who perspire easily—will acclimate more readily than those with fewer glands. There are also other involved physical factors which make it easier for one person to adapt to high temperatures than another.

Clothes are important. Shorts and suntans may be adequate clothing for a tenderfoot visitor lolling around the pool of a swanky desert resort during the winter season. But direct exposure of the skin to the sun in the months of summer heat accelerates dehydration and reduces personal efficiency. Under these circumstances the body should be kept covered with clothing, and a helmet or other covering for the head is especially important. I knew an American railroad construction foreman who had spent most of his mature life bossing a track-laying crew in Mexico. On a similar job in one of the hottest sectors of the California desert he wore a coat all summer, and defended this practice.

Any healthy human body may become acclimated to high temperatures, but it is never possible to become conditioned to reduced water rations. Alonzo W. Pond reports the experience of a general on desert maneuvers who thought his troops could be toughened to lack of water. A colonel in his command knew better, and took his superior on a jeep ride with only two quarts of water for each member of the party. The general's water ration was exhausted in less than three hours. Long before the ride was finished he was convinced there should be no limitation on the water supply. Under hard working conditions in daytime summer heat on the desert, soldiers consumed as much as three gallons of water a day.

Dehydration is the cause of many summer discomforts and even ailments, and water is the simple remedy in most instances. Medical men have told me that heat prostrations on the desert more often are due to dehydration of the body than any other cause. Thirst is not always a dependable gauge of the body's need for water. As water is lost through perspiration, the blood stream becomes thicker and its circulation more sluggish. The symptoms of a water shortage are easily recognized. First there is drowsiness and lack of appetite, and when dehydration reaches five percent of the body weight there may be nausea. Beyond this point the symptoms may be dizziness, headache, difficulty in breathing, tingling in legs and arms. When the mouth becomes dry speech is difficult and indistinct.

I experienced most of these symptoms on a memorable August day many years ago when, as a young reporter, I accompanied a constable and his deputy to a remote sector of the Chuckawalla Valley in Southern California to rescue a couple of burros. A prospector had been brought in seriously ill, and when he regained consciousness at the local hospital he began worrying about his burros which, according to his recollection, had been tied to an ironwood tree not far from his mining claim. His partner, who had brought him to town in an old jalopy, could not be found, and the officer volunteered to go out and release the animals and bring in his camp outfit which included a flask of gold dust and nuggets.

We found the camp, but the burros already had broken free. We salvaged everything worth saving, including the gold. There were no roads, the terrain was rocky, and soon after leaving the camp something went wrong with the transmission in our car. We were stranded at mid-day six miles from the nearest well. With only a quart of water each, we started across the sand in the direction of the well.

I will not go into the unpleasant details, but at sundown that evening I staggered to the well with just enough energy left to work the pump handle. An hour later I had so far recovered that I could backtrack with three canteens of water to where my much-older companions had stopped, completely exhausted, in the shade of a palo verde tree.

Today I would know better. If we had waited in the shade of the car until the sun went down we could have made it to the well without serious hardship. The Rochester Desert Unit learned that a soldier on desert duty can march twenty miles at night on a gallon of water without serious dehydration. In the heat of the summer sun the same distance requires three or more gallons.

The normal temperature of the body is 98.6 degrees, and the evaporation of sweat on the skin operates as a cooling system to maintain that temperature. But the higher the air temperature, the more water is required to keep the cooling system operating effectively. There is no substitute for water. Chewing gum or a pebble in the mouth may stimulate the flow of saliva but they add nothing to the water supply. They will do no harm, but will be of no value in keeping the body temperature at normal. Alcohol, salt water or any liquid containing waste materials which must be eliminated through the kidneys do not take the place of water. They merely increase the rate of dehydration.

For many years the scientists and veteran denizens of the desert have been feuding over the value of barrel or bisnaga cactus as a thirst-quencher for desert travelers in distress. Several years ago Ladislau Cutak, in charge of succulents at the Missouri Botanical Gardens near St. Louis, published two papers supporting the conclusion "that barrel cactus juice can be drunk to allay thirst and save a life."

W. Taylor Marshall of the Desert Botanical Garden near Phoenix, took an opposite view. In a newspaper interview published early in 1950 he was quoted as saying that the legend of the life-saving value of bisnaga is pure myth—that the juice actually is "acrid to the taste and thirst-producing."

My own experience will throw some further light on these contradictory reports. Many years ago I tried extracting the juice of bisnaga—not because I was in distress, but to make my own evaluation of the thirst-quenching value of the sap. My only tool was a Scout knife. I got a dozen bloody punctures in my hands while spending forty minutes trying to scalp one of the bisnagas, and finally decided that if a thirsty traveler had enough energy to cut through the armor of long wire-like spines which cover the barrel of the cactus, he probably could have made it to the next waterhole with much less pain.

More recently, after reading the Marshall and Cutak reports, I tried it again. On a trip into Baja California with three companions I selected a 3½-foot bisnaga, *Echinocactus acandhodes*, which is common to the area, for the experiment. There are no laws protecting cactus in this part of Mexico and, since this was a remote region where billions of desert shrubs mature and die without ever being seen by human beings, I felt no qualms about destroying one of them in the interest of a truthful report on the subject.

We had a machete in the car, and one of my companions took a vicious swing at the crown of the cactus. The blade bounced off the thick spines as if they were made of indestructible rubber. After two more efforts to scalp the cactus by the strong-arm method, we went into a huddle to plan new tactics. We finally solved the problem by slicing the spines from one side of the barrel and then cutting through from that side.

The pith inside the cactus is similar but somewhat whiter than that of cucumber, without the seeds. With the handle of a pick we pounded the pulp into a soggy mass. We got our drinks by sucking the juice from handfuls of the sponge-like pulp, and also by chewing it.

The flavor was bitter. It reminded me of the taste when I take an aspirin without water. But in 30 minutes the unpleasant taste had disappeared. We all drank heartily of the juice and felt no ill-effects later. My conclusion was that the juice is thirst-quenching—if one has the energy, tools and patience to penetrate the spiny armor which no doubt has evolved down through the ages to protect the plant against the depredations of thirsty animals.

Regardless of its source, large quantities of water are necessary for comfort if not survival when the direct and reflected heat from the desert sun exceeds the normal temperature of the body. Even when no physical exercise is involved, the dehydrating process goes on. Motorists driving the desert in summertime, even on paved roads, may prevent the drowsiness of dehydration by keeping a thermos bottle on the seat and taking a drink every fifteen minutes.

It is well to keep in mind that it is the water in the stomach—not the canteen—that compensates for dehydration. Nothing is gained by trying to hoard the water supply. This is one of the conclusions of the Rochester Desert Unit. An inactive person may need a gallon of water a day when the temperatures are high. If walking or exercising, the need is at least three times that amount.

Various studies have been made as to the value of salt tablets, or extra salt on the food at mealtime, when sojourning in regions of high summer temperatures. The results of these tests are inconclusive. Extra salt causes distress to some people. On the Sahara Desert during World War II we were required to keep salt tablets on the mess hall tables at all meals. Some of the men could take them, others could not. Unless plenty of water is available the salt may do positive harm. My own experience was that the salt stimulated thirst for more water, and to that extent was beneficial. It was the water, not the salt, that kept my body functioning actively.

While the members of the Rochester Desert Unit were employed primarily to appraise and deal with the harsh aspects of life and occupation on the desert at its worst, they were professional men who had the vision to see beyond the sordid details of their assignment to that other desert—the desert which holds a poetic fascination for those who come with courage and understanding. Summarizing their report, they wrote:

"Once the desert environment is understood, it loses its mystery. The great open desert soon grows to be a friendly place with an ever-changing beauty of shifting color and shadow. It becomes a joy to view its vast distances to bordering mountains, painted in sunrise and sunset colors; its landmarks of wells, trails, habitations, and salt lakes; its hills emerging from the desert plain as from a sea. The scurrying lizards and hardy plants belie the conception of the desert as a barren waste. And, once or twice a year for a few weeks after a rain, brilliant red, orange, and white flower colors outdo the brown and yellow of rock and sand. Then the desert is a garden spot with hovering insects and the scent of blossoms. Especially at night is the desert serene and friendly; the stars stud the sky, or the landscape is flooded with moonlight. We hope that the precise definition of man's limitations will enable many persons to sojourn in the open desert in safety and enjoyment."

FAR HORIZONS   **XXI**

I<small>N THE PREFACE</small> to this book I wrote: "A mature lifetime of close association with the things and people of the desert, and particularly the natural environment of this arid land, has had a profound impact on my habits, education, religion and my response to life in general."

And now, in the closing chapter of this reporter's journal, I want to reveal more specifically some of the more or less unrelated personal responses which down through the years have been recorded in my note books and, in part, quoted in my editor-

ial contributions to the *Desert Magazine* and the newspapers
with which I have been associated.

I would like to believe that my observations have been quite
objective, and yet that isn't possible. This world would be a drab
and dreary place without human emotions which color and
often distort our sense of values.

If some of my conclusions are tinged with idealism, I make
no apology for that. The space and solitude of this land of far
horizons are conducive to dreaming. Out on the desert trails, or
by the campfire, alone or with a kindred soul or two, one feels
a deep sense of detachment. In an environment where the
immediate interest is the unfolding of the gorgeous blossom of
the night-blooming cereus or the efforts of a kit fox to raid the
grub box without detection, the world of men and their affairs
seems remote, and even unimportant.

And yet it is never possible completely to escape the impact
of that complex of man and machines beyond the horizon, to
which one must return sooner or later. Nor would we want to,
for after all, the most intriguing species on this planet is *homo
sapiens*. He may be stupid and selfish and vain, but he also has
an infinite capacity for love and courage and faith.

One of the characters in a book I have been reading was
described as having no imagination. "He was quick and alert in
the things of life, but only in the things, not in the significances."

Probably that explains why some folks love the desert land,
and others find it repellent. Those who see only the things find
no beauty in the often drab colors and forms of the desert
landscape. Perhaps appreciation of nature's artistry is limited
to those with the vision to see behind and beyond the superficial
aspect of things—those with the gift of understanding significances.

To these the desert is fascinating because they recognize in
this strange land of paradoxes the opportunity to gain new understanding of the miracle of Creation and of the continuity of life.
It is inconceivable to me that one could live for long years in

close association with the natural world as revealed in the incessant struggle for survival in a hard and fruitless land without acquiring a deep reverence for the Creator of all this. The editorial vignettes which follow are less concerned with the things of the desert than with their significances as interpreted by one whose roots have grown deep in this seemingly sterile land.

During a brief interval in my early life on the desert I was employed as an axeman on a U. S. Land Office surveying crew engaged in establishing boundary lines and section corners in the Colorado River Indian reservation at Parker, Arizona. It was during those days spent in hewing section lines through the mesquite and arrowweed jungles of a valley along the Colorado River that I gained my first knowledge of the fine balance, undisturbed by the tools of man, which prevails in the complex world of God's creation.

In this primitive environment the parasitic mistletoe drew its vitality from, and was the most destructive enemy of its host plant, the mesquite. But the mistletoe was kept in check by great flocks of quail which during much of the year depended on its berry-like seeds for sustenance. The quail in turn were the main source of food for the coyotes, of which there were great numbers. If coyotes became too numerous, disease and starvation removed the excess. Thus did natural law operate in a virgin desert wilderness.

If the world is in turmoil today and human beings have in some degree lost their sense of security, perhaps it is because man is less adept than the Creator in maintaining the balance necessary for survival. Where the lower species killed only for food and the protection of their young—in other words, for the perpetuation of their species—the superior animal, man, has sought to justify the destruction of life for sport, for the satisfaction of personal vanity, or for monetary profit.

While we Christians are inclined to regard the religion of the Hopi and Navajo Indians as mere superstition, I have found in their faith an element of virtue which we self-styled civilized humans have in large measure lost. These tribesmen have a reverent affection for the Good Earth which is the source of all life, and for the creatures which share the planet with man. They are hunters, yes, but they kill only for their own sustenance—not for sport or profit. I am referring of course to the tribesmen as they lived when the white man first invaded this continent. While the missionaries have been teaching them some of the white man's virtues, they also have acquired some of his vices.

When we humans toss our garbage along the highways, when we contaminate the atmosphere and pollute the streams with poison, when we mine the soil and pay taxes for the storage of great surpluses of food we cannot consume, and mine the rocks for metals with which to slaughter both wild life and other human beings, then it is certain we have drifted far away from the concept of beauty and natural law which the Creator designed for this universe.

* * * * *

After many failures, there has been introduced again in the 87th Congress a bill to establish a national wilderness preservation system. This measure is of special interest to desert people because in this region there are still a hundred thousand remote canyons and isolated mountains where the elemental processes of creation and evolution are still unaltered by man's acquisitive enterprise.

It is not intended that these areas should be closed to Americans, but rather that they be off-limit for commercial exploitation—closed to any enterprise which would disturb the natural balance. As the National Wildlife Federation has pointed out, they would not be recreational areas, but rather sanctuaries where members of the human family would go in reverent quest for the intangible values of beauty in solitude. Surely we need places where youth may go or be taken to get acquainted and commune with the earth and its creatures as God created them. To such a place went Jesus Christ in preparation for his ministry.

Somehow, the idea seems to have gained prevalence that the earth and all that is on it were created for the sole benefit of the human species—to deface, to destroy, to kill if it seems to serve the useful purposes of a particular individual or group. Anything that does not serve the immediate physical needs of mankind is regarded as worthless.

All of which would not be so tragic if man were always an enlightened creature. But we humans have come such a few rounds up the ladder of evolution; our vision is still so obscure, our emotions so undisciplined. Because the coyote kills a few chickens, the state makes war on the coyote, and the rodent population increases to the point where it does tenfold more damage to the human food supply than did the coyotes. We have so much to learn.

The bright side of the picture is that the scientists today are finding answers which will enable us to discard many of the ancient myths and superstitions and prejudices which today keep our world in a state of turmoil. Somehow, our religion and our science must be reconciled. I believe it can be done. In the meantime we need natural sanctuaries to which earnest, thoughtful people may retreat, for it is only in such an environment that we may best seek the answers in truth and beauty and humility.

＊　　＊　　＊　　＊　　＊

It has been my privilege to spend many hours at various times in the villages, pueblos and hogans of Southwestern Indians—the Mojaves, Yumas, Apaches, Navajos, Hopis, Supai and Zuni. I always come away from such visits impressed by the gentleness of these people in their home-life.

I found the same thing true among the black tribesmen of Africa and the untamed Arabs of the Sahara. We call them heathen, and it is true some of them have barbarous religious rites, and vicious methods of warfare. But among themselves, in the security of their own homes and settlements, they are almost always soft-spoken and kindly.

It is a characteristic, I believe, which becomes habitual among people who live in close association with the natural world— people dependent directly on the earth for their food and shelter.

Our civilization has brought many artificial comforts, and advantages which we value highly. But it has also brought an appalling variety of raucous noises which, according to medical authorities are harmful to our nervous systems whether we are conscious of it or not.

Perhaps after we have solved the problems of the litterbug and restored beauty to the roadside landscape, it will be time to see what can be done about tooting auto horns, badly muffled exhausts, blatant radios, sonic blasts, and the prattle of garrulous and ill-tempered humans.

❋   ❋   ❋   ❋   ❋

In theory, we Americans defend the good old-fashioned idea of free enterprise. In practice, we are moving constantly toward an economy of federal paternalism which is closely related to socialism.

Perhaps it is possible to observe these trends more clearly out here in the unclouded atmosphere of the desert than in the artificial environment of the densely populated areas. The desert has a way of exposing the bare reality of things.

These thoughts were in my mind recently when I visited one of the dams being built in the Colorado River by the Bureau of Reclamation. There I had the opportunity to observe the comparative operation of a planned economy and the free enterprise system as applied to community building.

On a site overlooking the construction job is a pretty little town with painted houses, orderly streets and well-kept lawns and flower gardens. The houses were built and the lawns are mowed with funds from the federal treasury. This community was founded to house the several hundred Bureau of Reclamation employees engaged in the construction of the dam. Uncle Sam has plenty of money. He planned well and built well.

Down the river three miles below the Reclamation Service community—just outside the federal reserve—is another town, promoted and financed by private capital. It has few sidewalks and fewer lawns. Apparently there was little planning and there are no building restrictions. It is just a typical frontier town with lots of weeds and not much order.

It would not be correct to say the Reclamation Bureau town is a socialistic community. Yet it was constructed with public funds under the same bureaucratic regimentation that prevails under socialism. Uncle Sam built the town and owns it. It is a nationalistic enterprise.

The down-river community is a free enterprise town. It was built for private profit. Beauty and order and cleanliness are secondary to return on the investment.

These are stark extremes. I am not advocating either of them. Rather, I am presenting these pictures for the consideration of thoughtful people. I believe there is an attainable middle ground between the ugliness which free enterprise seems to sanction, and the stifling regimentation of the totalitarian state.

I can visualize a society in which the little people—you and me—through cooperative enterprise, on a voluntary basis, would make the rules which govern the bigs—big capital and big labor. I am thinking of organized consumer cooperatives which involve nothing more nor less than the application of the democratic theory to the national economy. What a power the consumers of this nation would be if in voluntary association they would use the pressure of their buying power to thwart such corruptions of the free enterprise system as planned obsolescence, price-fixing conspiracy and the monopolistic greed of both capital and organized labor.

Today we look to political government to police the malpractices in the economy, and that makes for centralized power in Washington. I would like to believe that eventually the organized consumers, through their privately-formed cooperatives, will assume this power. Then we will have 100 percent democracy.

❀   ❀   ❀   ❀   ❀

Recently a good friend gave me four seedlings of his new hybrid mesquite tree to plant in my garden. When I told the workman whom I had employed for some maintenance chores where to plant the trees he gave me a puzzled look. Then I learned something that amazed me. Here was a 35-year-old man who did not know how to plant a tree—had never in his life planted one. So I helped him do the job. When I mentioned this experience to friends, some of them confessed that they too had never planted a tree.

To me this is a tragic thing. Perhaps my years on the desert have given me an exaggerated idea of the value and importance of trees, but I still think every youngster should have the experience of planting a tree, and then watching it grow to maturity.

What a drab and unhealthy place this world would be without its trees! For every leaf is a tiny factory engaged much of the time in taking radiant energy from the sun and giving off water vapor and oxygen which purify the atmosphere and make this planet a habitable place for human beings.

But I am thinking not so much of the overall benefit of trees to mankind, but rather the values which accrue to the individual who plants the seed or cutting or sapling, tends it through the years, and observes for himself the miracle of growth and the beauty of its maturity, for in the life cycle of a tree is revealed much of the story of God's creation.

One is never too old to plant a tree, and for those who have not had the experience I would recommend it—even if they have to play hooky from church some Sunday to do it. For in the growth and maturity of a tree a thoughtful person will derive more understanding of, and faith in the works of the Creator than is possible from any 45-minute sermon.

❀   ❀   ❀   ❀   ❀

On a recent trip through the Indian country of northern Arizona I spent a delightful evening with Shine Smith.

Good ol' Shine! He came to the Navajo reservation forty-five years ago as a young Protestant missionary. According to his creed the dogma of heaven for the saints and hell for the sinners was less important than the immediate need for food and clothing, medicine for the ill, courage for the down-hearted, and love expressed in terms of service to all, regardless of the gods they worshipped.

In 1921 the Navajos had a bad winter. Frigid weather and much snow and ice brought sickness and death to many of these ill-clad and badly housed tribesmen. Hugh Dickson Smith, the missionary, kept a string of saddle ponies at Tuba City, and rode day and night on errands of mercy to the Indians. Friends marveled at his endurance.

Due to his unorthodox ministry, the church long ago withdrew its support, but he continued to carry on with faith that from some source the funds for his meager personal needs and those of the Indians would be forthcoming, and they always have.

To the Indians he became known as the friend "who brings hope and life like the sun shining on Mother Earth." Gradually he became known as Sunshine Smith. Today he is plain Shine Smith, loved by everyone who has the privilege of knowing him.

＊　　＊　　＊　　＊　　＊

A scientist was quoted in today's newspaper: "By 1968 man will be able to control the world's weather."

I hope he is wrong. Human beings are not ready for that yet. The suggestion brings to mind some terrifying questions: Who is to control the weather? And for whose benefit? If the Russians do not like the Americans are they to have the power to scourge our land with drouth? Or destroy us with floods? And vice versa? Weather, as a weapon of warfare, could become more catastrophic than hydrogen bombs or biological invasions.

Human beings have not yet progressed far enough in the evolution of their species to be given so much power.

I am for science, for the scientists are the great truth-seekers of this earth. But perhaps too much emphasis has been given to the physical sciences. A greater need at this stage in our evolution is a better understanding of human nature—the humanities. Surely it is more important just now to learn how to control human greed, selfishness, intolerance and vanity than that we learn how to control the weather.

*   *   *   *   *

Speaking of foreign policy, I am ready to go half way with Nikita K. of Moscow. I am in favor of moving the United Nations headquarters—but not to Austria or Switzerland or Russia. I would locate the offices and assembly rooms on an isolated bluff on the North Rim of Grand Canyon. The delegates—black, white, and yellow—would eat together in a big mess hall and sleep in bunkhouses with huge picture windows where every morning and evening and throughout the day they would be confronted with the harmony and majesty of God's creation, or Allah's creation, or Jehovah's—it doesn't matter. In such a setting, petty human struggles for power and selfish advantage become very insignificant indeed. That is a place to learn humility.

*   *   *   *   *

The New Mexico State University, near Las Cruces, is working on a project which will be of interest to motor travelers. The plan is to install, not far from the campus, on the main highway leading to El Paso, what will be known as the "Model Mile."

With the help of experts in agriculture, horticulture, architecture and landscaping, it is planned to make the roadside along this mile of highway a showcase for the orderly display of the state's resources, wherein will be combined beauty, interest and educational values. Included in the plan are two roadside parks to serve as information centers for visiting motorists.

As far as I am concerned this is much more signifiicant than sending a man to the moon. For the moon is far away, and all of us have to live with the ugliness which clutters so many of the roadsides on this sector of the planet. It is to be hoped the faculty and students at NMSU will establish a pattern so pleasing and informative it will become a model for American roadside planning.

This New Mexico project brings to mind a conversation I had with a landscape engineer not long ago. He was discussing the problem of billboards which more and more are fouling the landscape along most of the well-traveled roads. He suggested what I regard as a sensible answer to the problem:

"When the human race has advanced a little further along the road toward civilization," he said, "it will not tolerate this unsightly device for huckstering its wares and services. Billboards, like the blatant commercials which come over the air waves, merely are the trademarks of an age which gives a higher priority to profits than to esthetic and moral values.

"These things will pass. I think I can foresee the day when the billboard industry will have gone the way of the dinosaurs, when with only a fraction of the large sums spent in disfiguring the landscape, attractive information centers will be erected along the main highway entrances to every town of any importance. These centers will be neat little parks with rest room facilities and complete directories of the merchandise and services available in the town and a courteous information clerk always on duty."

Perhaps the planners at New Mexico State University are pioneering a more important project than they realize.

✸   ✸   ✸   ✸   ✸

One weekend recently I took my twelve-year-old grandson into the mountains on a camping trip, and gave him his first lesson in the art of cooking flapjacks over an open fire. There will be many more lessons before he becomes a proficient camp cook—

even in the making of griddle cakes. It requires a two track mind to make good camp flapjacks—one to watch the batter as it acquires a nice golden brown, and the other to watch the fire under the frying pan.

Of course the modern way is to take along a portable stove. Then one does not have to worry about the fire. But I am teaching my grandson to do his camp cooking the hard way, as I am going to teach him to do many other things the hard way. As a student of history I am sometimes frightened by what I see going on around me—people using their high wages and big incomes to buy ease and luxury.

Not only have I learned from Arnold J. Toynbee's *A Study of History* what has happened to a society when it became too rich and powerful and addicted to ease and luxury, but I have learned from Dr. Alexis Carrel in *Man the Unknown* the role of the individual in maintaining the virility of a society. Dr. Carrel wrote a revealing chapter on functions of the human body which are seldom mentioned in the school, or home. Discussing the adaptive faculties, he wrote:

"Man attains his highest development when he is exposed to the rigors of the seasons, when he sometimes goes without sleep and sometimes sleeps for long hours, when his meals are sometimes abundant and sometimes scanty, when he conquers food and shelter at the price of strenuous efforts. He has also to train his muscles, to tire himself and rest, to fight, suffer, and be happy, to love and to hate. His will needs alternatively to strain and relax. He must strive against his environment or against himself. He is made for such existence just as the stomach is made for digesting food. When his adaptive functions work most intensely, he develops his virility to the fullest extent. It is a primary datum of observation that hardships make for nervous resistance and health. We know how strong physically and morally are those who, since childhood, have been subjected to intelligent discipline, who have endured privations, and adapted themselves to adverse conditions."

I am sure that if all parents, and those who have the responsibility for the training and disciplining of children, would learn and live that important lesson there would be less juvenile delinquency in the land. In my dictionary, personal ease and boredom are synonymous terms, and I suspect that much of the youth revolt of this period is the product of boredom.

✿   ✿   ✿   ✿   ✿

During the years before World War II, in which my son later was one of the casualties, he and I did much camping and mountain-climbing together. Our campfire chats in the evening when he and I were alone and relaxed, generally were on the serious side, for he was an eager student. Out of those campfire talks I came to have a better understanding of the confusion of youth in a period when the world was torn by the conflicting ideologies of fascism, communism and capitalism.

One evening he confronted me with the problem of reconciling the story of creation as narrated in the Book of Genesis with the evolutionary theories of creation and biological progress.

In many discussions which followed, we solved the problem to his satisfaction and mine, but our solution was one which would be regarded as heresy by those theologians who regard the Bible story as a literal revelation from God.

We came to the conclusion that we should look to science for enlightenment as to the physical facts and processes of this earth, and to our religion for understanding and guidance as to moral and spiritual values. We discarded the concept of a God who leads victorious armies, who grants special favors to chosen people, who tortures men and women in hell for their sins, or who speaks to men out of a burning bush.

The God we visualized for ourselves is the great Lawmaker, not the policeman of the universe. It is for men to study and try to understand Natural Law—and to the extent they succeed or fail they create their own rewards and punishments. Our faith is in the ultimate triumph of Truth and Justice and Beauty. The scientists are God's most active allies on this earth, for they are the most avid truth-seekers among us.

Thus we reconciled—for ourselves at least—any seeming conflict between religion and science. Another conclusion: That the clergy probably would double their effectiveness if they would study the Works of God as revealed in the natural world, no less than the Word as reported by the ancient medicine men who have been given the more dignified term of prophets. Every clergyman should be a naturalist.

❂   ❂   ❂   ❂   ❂

Many years ago my friend, the late Marshal South, convinced me that it is possible even on the desert—for a person to live off the country as did the prehistoric Indians in the Southwest.

I thought of Marshal and his experiment in primitive living recently when a radio reporter told of plans by the Civil Defense Administration whereby natural caves and mine tunnels would be used as shelters in the event of an atomic attack.

I am sure the danger of such an attack is very remote, but if the time ever comes when it is necessary for me to seek protection in a bomb shelter I am going to quit pretending I am a civilized man in a civilized world.

My immediate destination will be a remote desert spring, where, with my family and a few kindred souls, I will try to make a new start. And as I go prowling around in a G-string looking for edible seeds and some tender roots on which to make a meal, I am going to become a crusader for one idea. I am going to try to convince the other surviving savages that in starting to rebuild the bomb-shattered world we not only will outlaw fascism and communism, but also the selfish aspects of competitive capitalism —meaning competition for dollars and land and world trade and beans.

We will pattern our new civilization after the natural world and make cooperation, not competition, the basis of the economy.

Oh yes, we will have competition, but it will not be the frenzied game of trying to accumulate more rabbit skins than any one person can possibly use while some other poor devil shivers in the cold. We will argue among ourselves over the election of a chief, and we will try to raise more maize on the patch of ground below the spring than our dumb neighbor can raise on his. But after we've proved we are smarter than he is we will take our surplus corn over to him so he and his family will not go hungry. And if any member of our tribe ever tries to corner the supply of mesquite beans or make a profit on an improved way of making earthen pots, we will banish him from the clan.

We won't be able to build our new world as fast as has been going on over the last hundred years but it will be a very secure place for unselfish men and women. And there will be a lot of beauty in it. We may not have as many and such effective weapons with which to slaughter each other, but there will be plenty of food and shelter, and more real freedom than we had known in the pre-bomb days. There will be only one law—the Golden Rule.

INDEX

JACKET AND CHAPTER ILLUSTRATIONS
BY DON LOUIS PERCEVAL

MAPS BY NORTON ALLEN

DESIGNED AND PRINTED BY PAUL BAILEY
AT HIS WESTERNLORE PRESS

TYPOGRAPHY IN LINOTYPE CALEDONIA
AND HAND-TOOLED HADRIANO

PRINTED ON MEAD'S SUEDE BOOK, LAID FINISH

F
786
H49

Henderson, Randall.
On desert trails, today and yesterday. Designs by Don Louis Perceval. Desert maps by
Norton Allen. Los Angeles, Westernlore Press
₍1961₎
357p. illus. 22cm.

252286

1.Deserts-Southwest, New. 2.Southwest, New-Descr. &
trav. 3.Southwest, New-Hist. I.Title.